The Perfect Cruise

HOW TO FIND, PLAN AND ENJOY THE PERFECT CRUISE VACATION

By Chris B Dikmen

THE PERFECT CRUISE. Copyright ©2004 by Chris B. Dikmen. All rights reserved. No part of this book may be used or reproduced in any manner whatsoever without written permission except in the case of brief quotations embodied in critical articles or reviews. For information: R-Squared Publishing, 4464 Young Dr #200, Carrollton, TX 75010.

ISBN 0-9760517-0-2

Printed in the United States of America

FIRST EDITION

Cover design by Choreographics, Inc.

R-Squared paperback edition/August 2004

R-Squared Publishing, 4464 Young Dr #200, Carrollton TX 75010

To the thousands of dedicated
professional travel agents who make
dreams come true every day

www.PerfectCruiseBook.com

Acknowledgements

Writing a book is like any other business venture. It requires time, commitment and dedication. Most of all, it requires the cooperation and contribution of people without whom the book would never become a reality. I am very fortunate to be surrounded by some of the most talented and supportive individuals I have every met. Included in this group are:

My good friends Michael and Sharon Czarnecki who were a great help as my travel agent consultants on this book.

My brother, John, President of Choreographics, Inc. who designed the book cover and worked on all of the graphic elements and photos used throughout the book.

Steve Cosgrove and Kay Orr without whom Online Agency would have never been possible, and who have been constant sources of inspiration.

Vincent & Mary Finelli for their contribution on Cruising with Special Needs.

Jim Orr and Michael Heygood, the best attorneys in the world.

My best friend of 35 years, Jess Dullnig, who has always been there for me.

And last, but certainly not least, this book was edited by my girlfriend, Rickee, who works countless hours proofing and correcting my numerous grammatical errors and misspelled words. Rickee also accompanies me on most of the cruises reviewed at CruiseReport.com.

A special thank you to the public relations departments of: Carnival Cruise Line, Crystal Cruises, Cunard Line, Holland America Line, Oceania Cruises, Radisson Seven Seas Cruises, Royal Caribbean International, SeaDream Yacht Club, The Yachts of Seabourn, Silversea Cruises, Viking River Cruises and Windstar Cruises.

Table of Contents

About the Author 8

Introduction 10

1. The Perfect Vacation 15

2. 5 Mistakes That Can Ruin a Perfect Cruise 21

3. Planning the Perfect Cruise 26

4. Things to Know Before You Go 83

5. Enjoying Your Cruise 90

6. Cruise Lines 162

7. Our Favorite Cruises 223

8. The Best Cruise Lines in the World 285

9. Extras 287

Index 293

About the Author

Chris B. Dikmen is the President of The Professional Internet Travel Alliance (PITA), President and Managing Editor of CruiseReport.com, a popular cruise information web site and President of Dikmen Investments, LLC.

Mr. Dikmen began a career as a computer software developer in 1985, after teaching himself a variety of programming languages. In spite of having no formal education or training in computers or software, Dikmen's small software company, Diamante Software, Inc., published Control Classic™ in 1991, the first sales automation software available for the Apple Macintosh. The program was selected as the Editor's Choice by MacUser Magazine in the February 1992 issue when it was awarded 4 ½ stars (out of a possible 5).

Mr. Dikmen continued to develop and support Control Classic until 1996, when he diverted his database and application development skills toward Internet-based solutions. In 1996, he worked as a consultant to help develop one of the first major Internet shopping web sites for Ziff-Davis, a major magazine publisher at that time. In 1997, he began development of OnlineAgency.com, a service which would allow travel agents to build and maintain their own web sites using a revolutionary template system. OnlineAgency.com was the first commercial web site template system to incorporate dynamic content. The service allowed a travel agent to fill out a form online, pay with a credit card, and have a turn-key web site complete with every cruise line's content in less than 10 minutes.

OnlineAgency.com also provided cruise lines with a special web site giving them the ability to enter and maintain their current cruise promotions which instantly appeared on the travel agent subscribers' web sites. OnlineAgency.com became the fastest growing network of travel agents between 1998 and 2001 averaging 150 new members each month. Mr. Dikmen resigned as President and CEO and sold his interest in OnlineAgency.com in April of 2001.

In 2002, Mr. Dikmen developed and released CruiseReport.com, a consumer-friendly cruise research web site. CruiseReport.com is designed as a 'one-stop shopping' place where consumers can shop and compare, side-by-side, up to 26 different cruise lines. Travel agents can subscribe to CruiseReport.com content and have it appear on their web sites for their customers. CruiseReport.com contains every itinerary and sailing date for over 220 cruise ships complete with itinerary maps, ship deck plans, port information and consumer reviews of cruise ships. The most popular content on CruiseReport.com is the editorial review section written by Chris Dikmen with the assistance of Senior Editor, Rickee Richardson. Together, Mr. Dikmen and Ms. Richardson have experienced over 30 different cruises in less than 36 months. Their editorial reviews appear exclusively on the CruiseReport.com web site. Today, CruiseReport.com is one of the leading cruise web sites on the Internet with over 1 million unique visitors in 2003.

In addition to his duties as President of PITA, LLC, and Dikmen Investments, Mr. Dikmen has been a regular speaker to groups of travel agents ranging in size from 75 to 800 people. Mr. Dikmen teaches agents how they can utilize the Internet more effectively as a business marketing tool. He has a background in public speaking going back as far as 1980 when he spoke to civic groups and organizations on such topics as motivation and business ethics.

Introduction

We love to cruise! In the past two years we have averaged one cruise per month. Of course, as cruise editors of a major web site, that is part of the job. Who says you can't mix business and pleasure? When I say "we", I am referring to myself and my girlfriend, Rickee.

Long before Rickee and I met and fell in love, I fell in love with cruising. The year was 1979 and I was only 23 years old and living in Midland, Texas. My close friends, Steve and Beverly Wallach, had been encouraging me to go on a cruise for over a year. After seeing pictures from their cruises and hearing their stories, I was ready to go. At that time I believed bigger was better so I decided to sail on the SS Norway, the largest cruise ship afloat at just over 70,000 tons[1]. That almost seems small compared to today's mega-liners.

I went to the first travel agent I could find in Midland and booked the cruise as a "single" male. My travel agent booked me under a "single guarantee" with NCL[2]. This meant that the cruise line would find a roommate to share the cost of the two-person cabin. Even though I was hoping for a shapely blonde female roommate, the cruise line only would agree to match me up with another male.

---

[1] The term "tons" does not actually refer to the dry weight of a ship. It is a marine term used to describe the amount of interior space available aboard a vessel. You can impress your friends and cruise mates with this little tidbit.

[2] NCL are the initials of Norwegian Cruise Line, the cruise line which operated the SS Norway.

Nevertheless, my roommate, Dave, and I had a great time. We were both in our 20's and we met and spent time with about 30 other singles traveling on the same cruise.

I can still remember the feeling of excitement I had as our airport shuttle approached the Port of Miami and I first saw the Norway. There she was, this long and lean, gigantic, regal-looking ship with a dark blue hull and white upper decks.

It may seem odd, but even after 40+ cruises I still get that same feeling of anticipation when preparing to board a ship. To make a long story a little shorter, the cruise on the Norway was incredible. I had a great time and was totally hooked on cruising. I had no way of knowing how this new love for cruising would eventually become an integral part of my vocation.

Rickee's first cruise experience was a little different. In 1975, she was working as a flight attendant for Eastern Airlines and decided to go on a cruise with a co-worker. Coincidentally, they were also booked to sail on the Norway. However, a week before Rickee's scheduled cruise, the Norway caught fire and had to have extensive repairs. The travel agency with whom she had booked offered her and her friend passage on another ship, the SS Victoria.

The SS Victoria was one of the oldest, if not the oldest, ships afloat at the time and was operated by the Chandris line. Rickee has no fond memories of her first cruise. Lack of entertainment, poor food quality and cramped quarters left her with little desire to take another cruise anytime soon (this is a classic example of choosing the wrong cruise line and ship).

Rickee and I met in 1994 and it took me three years to convince her to give cruising another try. Our first cruise together was in May of 1997, aboard Royal Caribbean's Grandeur of the Seas. Even though we had the cheapest and smallest inside stateroom, we had the time of our lives! We made some great new friends at our dinner table and spent most of the cruise hanging out with them. The shows were great, the activities were great, and the food was great… you get the idea. We were both now hooked on cruising and Rickee could not wait until the next cruise. A lot has happened since that cruise in 1997. In 1998, I decided to start a new company that would combine my love for cruising with my background in technology. At that time, the Internet was the hottest thing going. So I started OnlineAgency.com, a service that enabled travel agents to have their own inexpensive, easy-to-maintain web site for under $300 a year. The business was a huge success. Within 18 months we had close to 2,000 travel agencies using our service and we had contracts with every major cruise line to advertise on our network. A misunderstanding between me and my business partners on how the business should be operated resulted in my departure from OnlineAgency.com in 2001.

During my tenure at OnlineAgency.com I recognized the marketing value of cruise reviews. Consumers considering a cruise, myself included, loved reading about the actual experiences of other passengers. We did an informal survey in 2001 and found that 65% of cruise passengers surveyed were using the Internet to read reviews of cruises. Amazingly, 75% of those said that their decision to book a particular cruise was influenced by reading one or more reviews. In 2002, CruiseReport.com was created to accumulate and deliver the most comprehensive database of cruise reviews on the Internet. Today, CruiseReport.com is one of the most popular cruise informational web sites on the Internet. Nearly 1 million[1] consumers visited CruiseReport.com in 2003 to shop for their cruise vacations.

I think it is safe to say that, since 1998, between OnlineAgency.com and CruiseReport.com, more consumers have used these two web sites to research cruise vacations than any other web sites in the world. I only point this out to let you know that we know a little bit about the cruise industry. First and foremost, Rickee and I are cruise *consumers*. While we have worked closely with hundreds *of travel agents* and have had close business dealings with most of the major *cruise lines,* neither of us has ever been a travel agent. I believe

---

[1] Based on unique IP address sessions from our web server.

that this gives us a very unique perspective on the industry and on cruise travel in general.

This book is different from other cruise travel guides. While other books include directories of cruise lines and ships accompanied by lots of statistics, deck plans, and company information, we wanted this book to reflect our actual experiences and the experiences of those whom we trust. Part of the reason we decided not to include reams of information about ships, deck plans and itineraries is that the information changes almost daily. The Internet, and more specifically our web site, CruiseReport.com, is a much better resource for that kind of information than a printed book.

This book is a "quick read" for people who are interested in a cruise vacation, or those who already love to cruise and want to learn more about other exciting cruise options. The Perfect Cruise is small enough to pack in your carry-on bag so that you will have it available on your cruise for reference purposes.

We want to hear from you. We look forward to hearing your comments about this book and about your personal cruise experiences. You can email Rickee or me at the addresses below and you can post your cruise reviews on the PerfectCruiseBook.com. Reviews posted here will appear on CruiseReport.com.

To email me – cdikmen@perfectcruisebook.com

To email Rickee – rickee@perfectcruisebook.com

You can check out the web site for this book at:

www.PerfectCruiseBook.com

CruiseReport.com

I make frequent references to CruiseReport.com throughout this book. This is the web site that Rickee and I operate as Managing

Editor and Senior Editor. CruiseReport.com is a leading cruise research and information web site and is free to consumers. Feel free visit the web site as often as you like and use the research tools, examples of which are listed, to help you plan your next cruise vacation.

- Thousands of cruise itineraries, sailing dates and maps.
- Professionally written editorial reviews of cruise ships and destinations.
- Consumer reviews and ratings of cruise ships.
- Ship information and photos of 140 popular cruise ships from 30 cruise lines.
- Port information on more than 1,800 ports-of-call around the world.
- A powerful search engine allowing you to locate cruises based on a destination, an individual port-of-call, month/year of travel, or special interest.
- A cruise specialist locator to assist you in finding a qualified travel agent.

What distinguishes CruiseReport.com is that it is not owned or in any way affiliated with a travel agency or seller of travel. Most cruise oriented web sites on the Internet are actually owned and operated by a travel agency or a consortium of agencies. While this is not necessarily a bad thing, it can have an impact on the content that you are presented. CruiseReport.com's editorial reviews are fair and balanced because we have no hidden agenda of trying to sell you a cruise.

As a consumer, there is no cost to you for using CruiseReport.com

> Over 1 million people used CruiseReport.com in 2003 to research their cruise vacations. Approximately 110,000 consumers visit CruiseReport.com each month!

The Perfect Vacation

It was the trip of a lifetime, the kind of vacation that most people can only dream of. Our days were spent soaking up the sun by the pool, reading a good book on our private balcony, or exploring an exotic new port. Evenings found us enjoying cocktails with new friends, taking in an amazing show, and dancing until midnight under the stars.

And then there was the food. On some mornings we indulged in the lavish breakfast buffet; on others, we went to the dining room for a full-service breakfast. One day we even decided to have breakfast delivered to our room. For lunch there were buffets with fresh pasta and carving stations, four-course luncheons in the dining room, or bar-b-ques by the pool. Dinnertime was an amazing display of culinary artistry and delight. Each night we enjoyed a 5-course dinner with a choice of appetizers, soups, salads, pastas, main courses and desserts. After the first night, our waiter knew us by name and remembered our favorite drink. He and his assistant bent over backwards to make each meal special.

When we returned to our stateroom, we found that our cabin attendant had turned down our bed, placed delicious chocolates on our pillows and left a schedule of events for the next day on our bed. We went to bed each night more relaxed and refreshed than the night before. This was *the perfect cruise*.

My wish for you is that you will experience this type of vacation, a *perfect cruise* that will live in your memories forever. Rickee and I have been so fortunate to have experienced many such cruises over the past few years. At last count, we have sailed with 18 different cruise lines. Because we have cruised so many times on so many different cruise lines, we have a unique perspective on the cruise industry and how cruise lines and ships compare to one another.

Every cruise is a perfect cruise for someone. Regardless of the ship, the destination, the time of year or the circumstances, there will be people who will walk off the ship claiming to have had the time of their lives. By the same token, there are some people who, regardless of the ship and the conditions, will never have a good thing to say about their experience. I think most people fall somewhere in between and those are the people for whom this book is written.

When we meet other passengers on a cruise and they learn about our experiences, we are often asked the same question, "So what is your favorite cruise line?" Or, "What is the best cruise line?" I'd venture that we have been asked those questions at least 500 times over the past three years. These are very difficult questions to answer because we have had so many great cruises. It is hard to pick a "best". On our web site, (www.cruisereport.com), we do give an award for BEST cruise line each year, but it is a very difficult award to bestow. What we have found is that most cruise lines do a good job in all areas, a very good job in most areas, and an *exceptional* job in a few areas. Therefore, we instituted a series of BEST AT SEA awards in several service categories. The winners of this award are much easier to determine than an overall BEST cruise line. It also allows consumers to examine our award ratings and determine what areas are most important to them.

The fact is, every cruise line has a *following*, a group of loyal passengers who believe that *their* cruise line is the best. Often, this turns out to be the first and only cruise line these folks have experienced. Since their first cruise was so memorable, why take a risk and try a different cruise line? This is why I have always questioned the credibility of travel magazines' 'Reader Survey' awards. Some cruise lines seem to win the same awards year after year. But how many of the people responding to these surveys have ever sailed on more than one cruise line? In the survey, they say that *their* cruise line is the best, but how many other lines have they experienced? Surveys can also be very unfair to a small cruise line that may only serve a few hundred people each week as opposed to large cruise lines that carry thousands of passengers a week. Depending on the magazine, it is also possible that the demographics of their readers closely match the demographics of a particular cruise line's market, giving that cruise line a huge advantage in the award's outcome.

Rather than trying to identify the *best* cruise line, it is more important to find the best cruise line *for you*. Every cruise line has a distinct personality. From the design and décor of the ships, to the level of service, to the planned activities and entertainment, each cruise line is unique. Sometimes these differences are very subtle and, other times, they are quite dramatic.

If you have never taken a cruise vacation before, you may ask yourself *why not*? The same may be true if your last cruise was 20 or more years ago. A lot has changed in the cruise industry over the past 20 years. There are more compelling reasons today than ever before to take a cruise vacation.

Reason One: A Cruise Is an Unbeatable Inclusive Value

By far, a cruise offers the best vacation value going. You can spend a week aboard a 4 or 5-star cruise ship for much less than what a similar vacation on land would cost. In 2003, for the first time in several years, Rickee and I decided to take a land vacation to Hawaii. We soon realized that we had been spoiled by all the cruises we had taken. Not only were the hotels extremely expensive (some as much as $550 a night!), we had the additional expense of paying for all of our meals. And just in case you have never been to Hawaii, the food is outrageously expensive, too! A dinner for two at a Hawaiian restaurant comparable to what we would have been served on a cruise ship can easily cost $100. There is no question that we could have enjoyed a 7-night Hawaii cruise for less than half of what we spent on our Hawaii land vacation.

> **Did You Know?** 8 million Americans took a cruise vacation in 2003. That is a 40% increase since 1999. Cruise travel is the fastest growing segment of the leisure travel market!

You may notice that I say *inclusive* value instead of *all-inclusive*. While some travel agents and *even some cruise lines* may imply that a cruise is all-inclusive, this can be misleading. I cover this in detail in the Chapter "Planning the Perfect Cruise" in a section titled "What is Included".

Nevertheless, the amount of money you pay for virtually any cruise will include your accommodations, entertainment, most, if not all, meals aboard the ship, and a variety of onboard activities.

Reason Two: There is a Cruise for Everyone

I am convinced that there is a cruise line and cruise ship for just about everyone. The variety of ships, amenities and cruise destinations is virtually without limit. The cruise industry has undergone an explosion of capacity in recent years. Since 1999, the number of berths[1] has grown from 148,000 to over 215,000. That means there are more choices available to consumers than ever before. An additional 20 new ships are planned for the North American market between 2004 and 2008.

There are small, intimate yachts, medium-sized ships, really big ships and MEGA ships like Royal Caribbean's Voyager-class ships and Cunard Line's Queen Mary 2. There are ocean liners, cruise ships, sailing vessels and river boats. You can even take a cruise on a cargo ship! There are ships with rock-climbing walls, ice-skating rinks and movie theatres.

There are 6-star cruises that can cost $1,000 or more per day per person, and there are some 4-star cruises as low as $50 per person per day. You can spend as little or as much money as you want, and go virtually anywhere in the world on a cruise.

---

[1] berth: A place to sit or sleep especially on a ship or vehicle. Generally refers to accommodations for one individual passenger.

There is also a wide variety of activities taking place aboard a cruise. It has often been said that you will never be bored on a cruise unless you choose to be. You can do as much or as little as you like on a cruise.

Millions of North Americans have already discovered the joy of cruise travel, and the numbers are growing rapidly. Cruise lines are expanding their fleets at a dizzying pace to meet the demand for this popular vacation option. People who never thought they would be interested in cruising are attracted by flashy television ads from the big cruise lines like Carnival and Royal Caribbean. The introduction of rock-climbing walls, ice-skating rinks, miniature golf courses and first-rate fitness centers on ships has opened the door to a whole new generation of cruise travelers.

Reason Three: Cruising is a "Hassle-Free" Vacation

To borrow a computer term, cruising is a very *user-friendly* experience. When you take a cruise, you walk onboard your ship, unpack once, and everything you need is within walking distance! You can visit several countries with multiple cultures and never see your suitcases until it is time to pack for the trip home. Try that with a land vacation. Imagine taking a Mediterranean cruise where you can wake up in a different country every day and only have to unpack once! And, you do not need to concern yourself with stressful details like "where will we eat dinner tonight?" No matter where you travel, you can always return to your floating hotel for a great meal and place to sleep. If you do choose to have lunch or dinner ashore, most ships offer complimentary concierge services that will be happy to recommend a good local restaurant. The cruise industry has done an amazing job of making your vacation as stress-free as possible.

Reason Four: A Cruise Can Take You Just About Anywhere

Since two thirds of the Earth's surface is covered by water, you can cruise to just about any destination on Earth. Most of the interesting historic destinations throughout the world were built as port cities. The reason is simple: for centuries the ocean served as the primary source for distribution of goods and materials. If your interests lie inland, there are river cruises that can take you to those destinations, as well. It is safe to assume that you could spend months or even years aboard different cruise ships and never visit all of the destinations offered on today's cruises. Those looking for a warm weather getaway can enjoy a cruise to the Caribbean; adventure-seekers can opt for a cruise to Antarctica or Galapagos Islands; those interested in history and culture can sail the Baltic region and visit St. Petersburg, Russia, Belgium and Estonia. If you have the time and the resources, you can literally travel the world on a single vessel. Several cruise lines offer World Cruises that last for 100 days or more and visit dozens of countries. The choices are as limitless as the Earth itself.

5 Mistakes That Can Ruin a Perfect Cruise

The vast majority of people we meet when we cruise have nothing but good things to say about their vacation. Occasionally, we do meet people who, for whatever reason, are not happy and not having a good time. It is always puzzling to Rickee and me that these people are on the exact same cruise we are but they are having a completely different experience.

So I have put together a list of the 5 things that people do to cause themselves to have a bad cruise experience. More importantly, I tell you how you can avoid making those same mistakes.

Mistake 1: Not Using a Good Travel Agent

As you will learn throughout this book, I am a big believer in the value of using a travel agent or, more specifically, what I refer to as a *cruise specialist*. However, as with any industry, there are good travel agents and a few bad ones. I have included an entire section of this book on Choosing and Using a Travel Agent.

After we talk with people who are dissatisfied with their cruise experience, we almost always determine that if they had used the services of a *qualified* travel agent, things would have worked out differently. In fact, of all the 5 mistakes that can ruin your cruise vacation, simply avoiding the first mistake can almost guarantee that you will avoid the other four.

With the popularity of the Internet, some people are beginning to book their cruises directly with the cruise line through the cruise line's web site. This can be a risky decision, especially for a cruise novice.

Whether you have been on 50 cruises or you are considering taking your very first cruise, there is nothing more valuable than having a good travel agent working on your behalf.

Solution: Use the services of a qualified travel agent/cruise specialist.

Mistake 2: Not Buying Travel Insurance

Nothing can ruin a cruise vacation like an unexpected emergency that can interrupt or cause you to cancel your cruise. Even though a good travel insurance policy costs only a fraction of the cost of a cruise, many people take unnecessary risks and opt not to purchase insurance.

Many people assume that a medical emergency is the only thing that can interrupt a vacation. However, there are many events that could cause you to miss your cruise and lose what monies you've already paid.

Even though these situations are rare, they are potentially devastating when and if they occur:

- You could be injured in a fall or other accident on the ship or on a shore excursion. This could require expensive medical treatment.
- A medical emergency could force you to be evacuated from the ship or from a foreign country back to the U.S.
- The cruise line could go into financial default before or during your cruise. Did you know that if a cruise line goes bankrupt during your cruise, you and the crew are put off the ship in the next port-of-call? The responsibility for return airfare is totally up to you!

- An airline delay could cause you to miss all or a portion of your cruise.
- Your luggage could be lost, stolen or damaged and cruise lines, like airlines, have strict limits on the value assigned to damaged baggage.
- You could have personal merchandise stolen or damaged on your cruise which may not be covered by your homeowners insurance.

Solution: Don't tempt fate, buy travel insurance.

Mistake 3: Selecting the Wrong Cruise

Regardless of all the information on the Internet and in print about cruise travel, you would be amazed at how many people simply choose the wrong cruise. Again, this can be avoided by using the services of a good cruise specialist.

Every cruise line attempts to target a specific segment of the cruise market. Some cruise lines consider their primary market to be Americans between the ages of 21 to 35 while others may focus on retirees. There are cruise lines whose customer mix is primarily European and others whose mix is Asian. Obviously, if you are a 22-year-old American going on a cruise for Spring break, you probably do not want to end up on a ship full of retired Frenchmen! The second-hand cigarette smoke alone might take 3 years off your life!

Even within a single cruise line, certain ships may be better suited than others for passengers with certain needs or desires. There are even specific sailings tailored for specific target markets.

There are also destinations that tend to attract different demographic groups of travelers. The Caribbean attracts a wide variety of cruisers because of its easy accessibility and warm weather, while Alaska cruises might have somewhat older and more seasoned cruise travelers.

The Internet is a great research tool that can be a tremendous help to you in choosing the perfect cruise. CruiseReport.com is one web site designed to do just that. However, *even the Internet cannot replace the knowledge and experience of a cruise specialist.*

> **Solution:** Use the Internet to do your research. Read consumer and editorial reviews of cruise ships. Do a little homework.

Mistake 4: Having Unreasonable Expectations

Many dissatisfied cruise passengers simply have unreasonable expectations. Without trying to sound redundant, your travel agent should be able to manage your expectations so you will not be disappointed with your cruise experience.

Airlines - Probably the number one complaint people have with their cruise vacation has nothing to do with the cruise line. Some people walk onboard the ship in a bad mood because there was a problem with the airline flight getting to their cruise embarkation point. Obviously, the cruise line has no control over the airlines and should not bear the brunt of this kind of complaint.

All-Inclusive - Some passengers expect the cruise to be all-inclusive and are surprised and angry when they find out they have to pay extra for certain items on board the ship. You should be aware of exactly what items are included in your cruise fare before you book a cruise.

> **Solution:** Read the section in "Planning the Perfect Cruise" the section titled "What Is Included".

Mistake 5: Looking for Problems

Then there are those people who are going to complain no matter what. In Texas we have a saying: "They would not be happy if you hanged them with a new rope." If you cruise long enough, you will undoubtedly meet someone like this. You will swear that they are complaining just for the sake of complaining. There is no vacation, cruise or otherwise, that is *perfect* in the literal sense. There is always the potential for problems to arise. Usually, these problems are very minor and roll off the backs of *normal* passengers. Cruise lines work very hard to anticipate and plan for any potential problems. We have found that crew members want passengers to be satisfied. Remember, it is in the cruise lines' best interest to make you happy so that you will tell your friends good things about your cruise experience.

> **Solution:** If you are a chronic complainer, do everyone else a favor and stay home.

Planning the Perfect Cruise

A vacation is a considerable investment in time and money. I assume you work hard for your money. If you are retired, I assume that you *did* work hard for your money. Since most folks only take two or three weeks each year to indulge in a vacation, it makes sense to invest the time and energy necessary to make the right purchase decision. Perhaps this book is an example of an investment you have made to research your cruise options.

The fun and excitement of your cruise vacation starts as soon as you begin this research. By reading this book, researching on web sites such as CruiseReport.com, flipping through the cruise line brochures, and talking with others about your cruise, you begin to mentally experience the joy of cruising before ever stepping aboard a ship.

Before you start your research, however, there are some very important things you must consider. The information in this chapter will help you focus your cruise search efforts in the right direction.

Decide On Your Cruise Budget

An important consideration in the process of finding the right cruise for you is your budget. Your budget can help you to refine your choices of cruise lines, ships and destinations.

Cruise Line Choices

Great cruise lines for budget-minded travelers:

- Carnival
- Celebrity Cruises
- Royal Caribbean
- Norwegian Cruise Line (NCL)
- Princess Cruises

Great cruise lines for those who can spend a little extra:

- Holland America
- Oceania Cruises
- Windstar Cruises
- Disney Cruise Line
- Star Clippers

Great cruise lines for those for whom money is no object:

- Crystal Cruises
- Cruise West
- Cunard Line
- Radisson Seven Seas Cruises
- SeaDream Yacht Club
- Seabourn
- Silversea Cruises

For details on these cruise lines, see the chapter on Cruise Lines.

Typically, the larger cruise lines can offer the best deals because of the simple economies of scale. Larger cruise lines usually sail bigger ships which hold more passengers. This fact alone allows them to lower their overall cost per passenger and those savings can be passed along to consumers in the form of discounts.

Destination Choices

If you are budget-minded, then the Caribbean is most likely your best choice for destination. There are dozens of ships operating year-round in the Caribbean, so you are more likely to get a better deal there than anywhere else.

Stateroom Choices

Your budget will determine the stateroom you select. Here are some general guidelines you can follow:

Inside staterooms – These are the least expensive accommodations on the vessel. There are no windows in these cabins and they may be smaller than other cabins on the ship.

Ocean View – These staterooms have windows or portholes and cost a little more than inside staterooms.

Balcony or Veranda – These staterooms cost a little more than ocean view stateroom and have their own private balcony.

Suites – These are the largest accommodations aboard a ship, and the most expensive.

The location of your stateroom can also affect the cost of your cruise. Typically, the lower the deck, the lower the price. Staterooms positioned toward the middle of the ship may also be more expensive than staterooms located forward or aft.

What is Included?

Many people board a cruise ship under the misconception that it is an "all-inclusive" package. In all but a few instances, this is simply not the case. Therefore, we think it is only fair that you know 'up front' exactly what your cruise fare will include and what will cost extra.

- Your stateroom accommodations
- Port charges
- Cabin steward/attendant
- Most, if not all meals
- Evening entertainment/Shows
- Onboard activities
- In-room television
- Room service
- Pizzeria
- Use of pool/hot tubs
- Use of fitness center
- Use of spa facilities*

*Depends on cruise line. Some cruise lines may charge $10 to $15 per day for access to steam room/sauna and locker rooms.

Not Included

- Airfare (unless purchased as part of a cruise+air package)
- Transfer costs to/from airport/ship (unless you purchase air through the cruise line)
- Alcoholic beverages
- Soft drinks/Bottled water
- Medical costs or doctor visits while on board
- Specialty restaurants (some ships)
- Ice cream (some ships)
- Incidentals
- Laundry services
- Spa treatments

www.PerfectCruiseBook.com

- Shore excursions/tours
- Photos
- Purchases in onboard gift shops
- Gratuities
- Ship-to-shore phone calls
- Casino/bingo
- Internet access
- In-room movies
- Specialty services or packages (weddings, anniversary, concierge, etc.)

> **Note:** Some luxury cruise lines do include complimentary cocktails, wine with dinner, soft drinks and bottled water. Some also include gratuities in the cruise fare.

At first glance, it may appear that there are more items *not* included in the cruise fare than are included. However, many of the items in the 'Not Included' list are purely optional (such as Bingo or Internet access). The cost of soft drinks and alcoholic beverages will vary from one cruise line to the next, but generally speaking, they cost no more than what you would expect to pay at any typical hotel or restaurant.

Rules of thumb:

1. The larger cruise line operators can offer better prices than the smaller, niche-oriented cruise lines.

2. Caribbean cruises are less expensive than Alaska, Hawaii or European cruises.

3. Cruises on smaller cruise lines may cost a little more (or a lot more) but they generally offer unique services that the larger cruise lines cannot or do not offer.

Decide When You Want to Go

Once you have decided that a cruise vacation is for you and what you want to spend for that cruise, the next thing you should consider is *when do you want to cruise?* Of course, you can take a cruise at any time of year, but some destinations may not be available during certain months.

Most people take their cruise during a normal work vacation period. For many people, this falls during the summer months when the kids are out of school. Spring Break is also a popular time for families to cruise. For this reason, cruise ships tend to fill up with families during these months, especially in the Caribbean. Therefore, if you are single or are not traveling with children, you may want to consider scheduling your vacation in the fall or winter months.

Here are some simple guidelines for choosing the time of year for your cruise vacation:

October thru April – Many ships operate in the Caribbean during this time of year. Ships that sail to Alaska and Europe in the summer months typically return to the Caribbean in late September or October. The reason for this is simple, *warm weather*. The Caribbean is warm and inviting year-round and during this time of year, it is cold in many parts of the U.S. There is nothing better than leaving your hometown where it is 21 degrees outside and, the same day, stepping on a beautiful ship in Miami where it is 83 degrees. Due to the large inventory of ships in the Caribbean during these months, your chances of getting a better price go up. Also, if you are traveling *sans kids*, you will no doubt encounter fewer families on the ship than during the summer months. You will also find ships sailing South America and Panama Canal cruises during these months.

April thru September – Alaska, Europe and Mediterranean cruises are popular during these months. The days are too short and the weather too cold in Alaska the rest of the year, so ships don't even go there until late April. Europe and the Mediterranean are also unseasonably cool in the winter months and are more popular when warm weather returns.

March, April, September and October – These months are very popular for transatlantic cruises also referred to as *crossings*. Even though Cunard does offer transatlantic cruises from New York to Southampton (and vice-versa) throughout the year, most cruise lines only offer transatlantic cruises when they are re-positioning their ships to/from Europe. You will also find many cruises during these months to/from Hawaii and the Panama Canal as cruise ships move between the Caribbean and Alaska.

Year-round – The Caribbean, Mexican Riviera (West Coast of Mexico) and Panama Canal are popular cruise destinations year-round because of the warm weather, unlike Alaska and Europe[1] which tend to be seasonal.

Decide Where You Want to Go

Once you have decided when to go, you can then decide on a destination available during that time period. In deciding on a cruise destination, it might help to consider what types of activities you enjoy. I have included a table with ratings from 1 to 10 for a variety of activities available in various destinations. Each rating is based on how enjoyable that activity is in that particular destination.

---

[1] There are cruise lines that operate in Europe year-round. However, except for the summer months, they tend to sell these cruises to the European market. Very few Americans sail to Europe in the winter months.

Warm Weather Cruising - Caribbean Style

The Caribbean is the most popular cruise destination in the world, and for good reason. The weather here is warm year-round which is perfect for sun lovers or those who need to escape the cold weather areas of North America and Canada. For Americans, the

Activity	Score
Adventure	8
Dining in port	5
Fun	9
Relaxation	8
Shopping	9
Sightseeing	6
Sunbathing	**10**

Caribbean offers the best value in cruising because there are ships sailing from a wide variety of cities such as Miami, Ft. Lauderdale, Galveston, New Orleans, Tampa, and Orlando (Port Canaveral), Baltimore, Bayonne, NJ, Los Angeles, San Francisco, Seattle, Norfolk, VA, just to name a few. Airfare to these cities from most other cities across the country is much more reasonable than, say, airfare to Acapulco. Also, with so many embarkation ports, many people live within driving distance of their cruise departure city.

Caribbean cruises are usually divided into three sub-destinations: Eastern Caribbean (St. Thomas, St. John, Nassau, San Juan, St. Maarten); Western Caribbean (Ocho Rios, Grand Cayman, Cozumel, Key West); and Southern Caribbean (Barbados, Grenada, St. Vincent, St. Lucia, Martinique, Aruba).

The Caribbean is much more than just warm weather. There is great duty-free shopping in St. Thomas, St. Maarten, Aruba and Grand Cayman. There are also tons of exciting and fun shore excursions offered in the Caribbean (see the table below).

Snorkeling
Swim with the dolphins
Atlantis submarine
Beach activities
Explore Mayan ruins
Bicycle tours
ATV tours

SCUBA Diving
Swim with the stingrays
Parasailing
Golf
Island tours
Horseback riding
Water sports

What about hurricanes? – Hurricane season in the Caribbean runs from June 1 through November 1. While it is possible that the presence of a hurricane in the Caribbean may result in a slightly rougher ride, modern cruise ships are equipped with high tech satellite warning systems which allow them to avoid the path of the hurricane. In some cases, a developing storm may cause a cruise ship to deviate from its scheduled itinerary, potentially missing a port-of-call.

The Scenery of Alaska

The best word to describe Alaska is *majestic*. The scenery visible from the ship as it sails through the Inside Passage is breathtaking. It is not uncommon to see wildlife from the deck of the ship (or your own balcony).

Activity	Score
Adventure	8
Dining in port	5
Fun	5
Relaxation	8
Shopping	7
Sunbathing	1
Sightseeing	**10**

The cruise season for Alaska begins in May and can last through late September. During this time of year, temperatures can vary from 50 to 80 degrees during the day and can fall into the 40's at night.

The two most popular itineraries for Alaska begin (or end) in Vancouver, British Columbia and end (or begin) in Seward (Anchorage), Alaska. Therefore, a northbound Alaska itinerary would begin in Vancouver and a southbound itinerary would begin in Anchorage. Another popular itinerary is the Inside Passage cruise which embarks and disembarks in Vancouver. It is much easier to obtain flights for Inside Passage cruises since you do not have to fly in or out of Anchorage.

> **Tip!** If you embark and/or disembark in Vancouver, you can fly into and out of Seattle. There is a wonderful train ride available from Seattle to Vancouver.

Things to do on an Alaska cruise:

Whale watching	Mountain bike ride
Horseback riding	Hiking
Salmon bake	Lumberjack contests
Panning for gold	Salmon fishing
Kayaking	Canoeing
Wildlife tours	Denali National Park visit
Helicopter glacier tour	Sea plane tour

Alaska Cruise Tour Package – Princess, Holland America, Royal Caribbean and Celebrity Cruises all offer optional tour packages with their cruises. These optional tours can be from three to five days in length and usually include a visit to Denali National Park and Mt. McKinley. We highly recommend these packages if you plan to visit Alaska and can afford the additional time and money. There are simply some things that cannot be seen from the ship. Royal Caribbean and Celebrity Cruises have their own custom-built rail cars for the train ride from Anchorage to Denali. Princess Cruises operates its own beautiful resort lodges in Alaska.

European Style in the Mediterranean

With so much history and diversity of cultures, the Mediterranean offers a more sophisticated cruising experience. On a Mediterranean cruise, you can literally wake up in a different country each morning. The ship's passenger mix will likely reflect a more international flavor, as well.

Activity	Score
Adventure	4
Dining in port	9
Fun	5
Relaxation	8
Shopping	**10**
Sunbathing	**10**
Sightseeing	**10**

Mediterranean itineraries are as varied as the ships that sail there. Most Med cruises embark from Lisbon, Barcelona, Piraeus (the port city for Athens, Greece), Civitavecchia (a port city about 45 minutes from Rome), Istanbul or Venice. With embarkation ports like these, you can see why most cruise passengers want to extend their vacation by a few days at the beginning and/or end of their cruise. In 2001, we spent five days in Rome before boarding

Windstar's Wind Surf in Civitavecchia for our Med cruise. For five days we walked all over Rome and had an incredible time doing it.

A typical Western Mediterranean cruise will visit ports in Italy, Spain and France. Eastern Mediterranean and Greek Isles itineraries may include ports such as the Greek islands of Mykonos, Santorini and Rhodes, Piraeus (the port of Athens), the Turkish ports of Istanbul and Kusadasi, and Venice. Some also visit Dubrovnik, Croatia, an up-and- coming new port destination. A Riviera cruise may include the ports of Monte Carlo, Nice, Cannes, Portofino, Portovecchio and St. Tropez. Many Riviera cruises will begin in Rome (Civitavecchia) and end in Nice or Monte Carlo (or vice-versa).

On your Mediterranean cruise, you will have an opportunity to visit museums and historical sights dating back for centuries. Unlike the Caribbean and Alaska where everyone speaks English, you will experience a variety of cultures and languages. Nevertheless, most everyone speaks English in addition to their native language.

> **Tip!** Spend the money on a balcony stateroom in the Mediterranean. There is nothing more memorable than sailing down the Grand Canal in Venice and enjoying the incredible view from your private balcony.

Favorite Ports – Without question, Venice is the most memorable port in the Mediterranean. Nothing can compare to the romance and history of Venice. We cannot wait to return. Istanbul, Kusadasi, Portofino, Florence, Rome and Naples are also at the top of our list of Mediterranean ports to visit again.

There are some cruise lines that sail the Mediterranean year-round (i.e. Costa), however, the prime season for Americans to sail in the Med is in the summer (from May through September). Most major cruise lines bring their ships back to the Caribbean during the winter months. April, May, June and September are the best months (in my opinion) to visit the Mediterranean. In August, there are large numbers of European tourists on vacation throughout Europe which can cause some venues to be very crowded.

Canada/ New England

From May through October, ships routinely sail from New York City, Montreal and Boston to ports in Maine, Nova Scotia, and New Brunswick. The 4 and 5- day cruises sailing from New York City are popular getaways for families and young adults, while the longer 10-day cruises tend to draw a more mature crowd.

Activity	Score
Adventure	4
Dining in port	7
Fun	5
Relaxation	9
Shopping	6
Sunbathing	1
Sightseeing	7

As you can see from our table above, there is no one thing that is outstanding about this destination compared to the Caribbean, Mediterranean or Alaska. Yet, we find ourselves going back to Canada/New England almost every year. Part of the attraction has to be New York. It is such a great city in which to spend an extra day or two before or after the cruise.

Hawaii

You can sail the Hawaiian Islands year-round. The weather there is about as perfect as it gets. Unfortunately, U.S. law prohibits ships that were not built in the United States from sailing directly to/from Hawaii from/to another U.S. port

Activity	Score
Adventure	10
Dining in port	9
Fun	8
Relaxation	8
Shopping	9
Sunbathing	10
Sightseeing	10

without visiting a foreign port. As you might have guessed, virtually all cruise ships are built outside the U.S. (France, Germany, Norway, Italy and Japan). To get around this law, cruise lines routinely make a port call (albeit a short one) in Ensenada, Mexico on Hawaii cruises which embark from California ports. Of course, this requires a 10- day cruise or longer, 5 days of which are spent sailing from the West Coast to Hawaii. Cruise lines that offer Hawaii roundtrip cruises (a cruise that embarks and disembarks from a Hawaiian port) make a short visit to Fanning Island, or some other small foreign island to comply with the law. It literally wastes about two days of a seven-day cruise to make the jaunt to Fanning Island.

There is good news for one major cruise line, however. Norwegian Cruise Line (NCL) was able to convince Congress to agree to a provision that does not require NCL ships to call on a foreign port when sailing Hawaii cruise itineraries. In exchange for this provision, NCL is required to flag the ships sailing Hawaii itineraries in the U.S., pay the U.S. taxes and comply with U.S. labor laws for the staff working on board the ships.

NCL's new Pride of Aloha and Pride of America will be sailing 7-night cruises out of Honolulu beginning in July of 2004.

NCL Pride of Aloha 7-Night Itinerary

Day	Port	Arrive	Depart
Day 0	Honolulu		8:00 pm
Day 1	Nawiliwilli	7:00 am	Overnight
Day 2	Nawiliwilli		1:00 pm
Day 3	Hilo	9:00 am	6:00 pm
Day 4	Kona	7:00 am	5:00 pm
Day 5	Kahului	8:00 am	Overnight
Day 6	Kahului		6:00 pm
Day 7	Honolulu	7:00 am	

Tip! To see what ships are sailing to what destinations in a given month go to www.cruisereport.com and click on the link titled 'Find My Perfect Cruise' in the menu bar. Use the drop-down menu to search by destination, month and/or cruise line.

Decide on the Length of Your Cruise

There are cruises available from 3 nights to as long as 120 nights. Occasionally, you will even see a 2-night cruise offered, but these are rare. The most popular cruise length is 7 nights.

3, 4 and 5-night cruises are a good choice if you have never been on a cruise and are apprehensive about whether or not you will enjoy the experience. This is also a good option for those who live within a few hours (or less) driving distance of the ship's embarkation port. If, however, you must fly across the country to meet your ship, 3 or 4 nights is hardly worth the trouble.

> **Caution!** If you choose a 3 or 4-night cruise, you will likely kick yourself later for not opting for a 7-night cruise.

7-night cruises are the most popular choice since most people take 7 days of vacation at a time. You will also find that there are more choices of ships and destinations with 7-night cruises. We have found that 7 nights aboard a ship gives you just enough time to enjoy most, if not all, of the facilities on board. You will have a day or so to unwind and relax from the flight and get into the mood of the cruise. The next four days are pure pleasure and relaxation, and the last day is spent preparing for the trip home (yuck).

10 to 14-night cruises are great for those who can afford the time away and the cost of the cruise. These longer cruises are very popular with retirees, teachers (who do not work in the summer) and people who take cruises that embark from European or Asian ports of call. Since most ships have launderettes on board, you don't necessarily need to pack more than you would for a 7-night cruise.

Back-to-back cruises allow you to cruise for 14 or more nights on the same ship, even if the ship only does 7-night itineraries. A great choice for a back-to-back cruise might be Royal Caribbean's Voyager of the Seas which does alternating Eastern and Western itineraries thru April, 2005.

Week One – Western Caribbean

Day	Port	Arrive	Depart
Day 0	Miami	---	5:00 PM
Day 1	At Sea	---	---
Day 2	Labadee	8:00 AM	4:00 PM
Day 3	Ocho Rios	9:00 AM	5:00 PM
Day 4	George Town	8:00 AM	5:00 PM
Day 5	Cozumel	10:00 AM	7:00 PM
Day 6	At Sea	---	---
Day 7	Miami	8:30 AM	---

Week Two – Eastern Caribbean

Day	Port	Arrive	Depart
Day 0	Miami	---	5:00 PM
Day 1	Nassau	7:00 AM	1:00 PM
Day 2	At Sea	---	---
Day 3	Charlotte Amalie	7:00 AM	5:00 PM
Day 4	San Juan	7:00 AM	2:00 PM
Day 5	Labadee	8:00 AM	4:00 PM
Day 6	At Sea	---	---
Day 7	Miami	8:30 AM	---

Planning Special Occasions

A cruise can be a memorable place to celebrate a special occasion. Cruise lines offer special packages for honeymooners and those who are celebrating wedding anniversaries. Your travel agent should be able to provide you with details on what packages are offered by each cruise line. Packages often include a bottle of champagne, special receptions for honeymooners, a framed photograph from the ship's photographer, a romantic breakfast in bed, spa treatments, etc. There will be an additional charge for these extras, but they are well worth it.

Getting Married Onboard

It is a myth that a ship's Captain can conduct a legal marriage ceremony. Some cruise lines will offer wedding packages where you can be married on board the ship before it leaves its port of embarkation. Your cruise line will provide a local government official to perform the ceremony, or you can provide your own. You can choose from a variety of packages whose prices vary. The ship can handle all the details for flowers, reception, photographers, etc. Your travel agent can arrange all the details for you. Many cruise lines also offer a "renewal of vows" ceremony for those celebrating anniversaries on board.

Select a Cruise Line/Ship

There are dozens of cruise lines operating throughout the world today. However, only about 35 or so are sold aggressively in North America. Since we assume that most people reading this book will be English-speaking, we will focus on those cruise lines.

> **Tip!** Before making any firm decision on which cruise line is best for you, we highly recommend consulting with a qualified cruise professional (travel agent). A professional cruise consultant will be invaluable in helping you to make this decision.

Your choice of cruise lines and ships should already be somewhat narrowed based on your budget, the destination to which you wish to cruise and the time of year. Here are some things to consider when deciding on a cruise line/ship:

Big Ship or Small Ship

There is no real definition of what qualifies as a "big" ship today. An average size ship today is twice as large as the Titanic and it was the largest ship of its day! When I took my first cruise, the SS Norway was the largest ship afloat at 70,000 tons. A few years later when Royal Caribbean introduced Sovereign of the Seas at

73,000 tons, it was considered revolutionary. Today, Royal Caribbean, Carnival, and Princess all have ships in excess of 100,000 tons. Cunard's new Queen Mary 2 is the largest ship today at over 150,000 tons!

Large ships have some advantages over small ships:

- More Activities – The larger the ship, the larger the cruise staff and the more activities you will find throughout the ship.
- More Dining Choices – The bigger ships (especially ones built after 1998) often have two or more dining venues. NCL's newest ships have up to 9 restaurants. However, some alternate restaurants on the bigger ships have a cover charge associated with them.
- Better Entertainment – There is no doubt that the bigger the ship, the bigger the production shows and generally, the better the entertainment. Certainly there are more choices of entertainment on a larger vessel.
- Less Motion – Most ships sailing today have stabilizers that greatly reduce the amount of side-to-side rolling caused by high seas. However, larger ships probably do ride smoother than smaller ships. On the other hand, some of the larger ships are also more subject to motion caused by cross winds.

Small ships have some advantages over large ships:

- Intimacy – On a smaller vessel, you are more likely to see the same people throughout the cruise and get to know them better.
- Visits to less accessible ports-of-call – The smaller ships can dock at some of the smaller, less crowded ports and islands that the big ships simply cannot get into because of their size.
- Personal service – As a rule of thumb, smaller ships have a higher staff-to-guest ratio. Because there are fewer passengers, everyone gets a little more personal attention.

- Convenience – Smaller ships are much easier to find your way around. In some cases, you may only be a few steps from the dining room, swimming pool or theater. On some of the mega ships, it might take several minutes to walk from one end of the ship to the other.
- Shorter lines – Because there are fewer passengers, getting on and off a small ship is much less stressful. You don't have to stand in long lines.

Are you traveling with children?

Cruising has become a true family vacation. Cruise lines have invested millions in recreational facilities and staff to keep kids of all ages occupied and entertained during the cruise.

As you would expect, Disney Cruise Line has done an excellent job of catering to families. However, you may be surprised to learn that many cruise lines have excellent programs for kids of all ages. Below are some cruise lines that we feel offer superior programs for kids:

- Carnival Cruise Line
- Celebrity Cruises
- Costa
- Disney Cruise Line
- Holland America Line
- NCL
- Princess Cruises
- Royal Caribbean International

For details about many of the kids programs offered by these cruise lines, check the information for the specific cruise line in Chapter 6.

When traveling with children, you may also want to consider a larger cruise ship as opposed to a smaller ship. The larger the ship the more likelihood that there will be other children on board within the same age group(s) as your child(ren). Larger ships

(70,000 tons and larger) are more likely to have video arcades and extensive kids facilities.

Are you traveling without children?

If you are not traveling with children you may want to select a cruise with fewer children on board. That does not mean you have to avoid the larger, mass-market cruise lines which do cater to a large number of families. Instead, modify the time of year you book your cruise. Holiday cruises and cruises in the summer, when school is out, are more likely to have lots of kids. Especially avoid Spring Break!

Celebrity Cruises is a large ship cruise line which, while offering programs for children, tends to cater to the adult market. Celebrity even offers several 'adult only' cruises throughout the year. Radisson Seven Seas Cruises is a luxury line that also caters primarily to adults. Holland America has only recently begun marketing to families so much of its clientele is still made up of adult couples. Oceania Cruises, Seabourn, Silversea and SeaDream Yacht Club, Star Clippers, Cruise West, Viking River Cruises and Windstar do not even offer programs for children. Therefore, if you are traveling without kids and would prefer an adult-oriented clientele, you may wish to put these cruise lines at the top of your list.

Dining Choices

Another consideration when selecting your cruise line/ship is their approach to dining. Traditionally, cruise ships offered two seatings for dinner: Main (or Early) Seating (generally starting between 6:15pm and 6:45pm) and Late Seating (starting between 8:15 and 8:45pm). With the traditional two-seating dining, you are assigned a table at which you will have dinner each evening. You will have the same waiter, assistant waiter and tablemates each night. The advantage to this type of dining arrangement is that you have an opportunity to dine with the same people each evening, make new friends and really get to know some of the other people with whom you are cruising. Since you will have the same waiter each evening, it is also common for the waiter to know your name, your drink choices and other food preferences. When we sailed on Celebrity Summit to Alaska in 2002, I informed our waiter, Sebastiao, that I was not eating starchy vegetables and would like to have an order of creamed spinach as my vegetable each evening. The other couple with whom we were sailing also ordered a Diet Coke on the first evening at dinner. From that night forward, I always had creamed spinach and our friends had Diet Cokes waiting for them when we arrived at the table. Of course, all of the afore-mentioned advantages could also turn to disadvantages depending on the people involved.

Early or Late Seating? - When booking your reservation, you may be asked if you prefer Early (sometimes referred to as Main Seating) or Late Seating. Early Seating is typically preferred by families or those who simply do not like to dine later in the evening, or who want to have their kids in bed by 10:00pm or earlier. The advantage of Main Seating is that you are usually finished with dinner by 8:00 and have plenty of time to attend the evening show and still get to bed by 10:30pm. The disadvantage of Main Seating occurs on days when the ship is in port. If you have a shore excursion that does not return you to the ship until 4:00pm or 5:00pm, you have very little time to clean up and dress for dinner. Some guests have also commented that they feel rushed with Main Seating since the dining room staff must get the dining room cleared and prepared for the Late Seating guests. With Late Seating, you have plenty of time to relax, have a drink and still get cleaned up and dressed for dinner. Late Seating is generally preferred by those who are not traveling with children and who do not mind eating later in the evening. Some ships will offer early shows for Late Seating guests (show at 7:00 and dinner at 8:30).

> **Tip!** Another advantage to booking your cruise in advance is that you get preferential treatment on dining reservations. Late Seating typically fills up before Early Seating. So if you want late seating, book early!

Join Us for Dinner? A new trend in cruising is open-seating dining. With open-seating dining, you simply go to the dining room and are seated, much like a traditional restaurant on land. The advantage to open-seating dining is that you are not required to be at the dining room at a pre-determined time. You also have the flexibility to invite new friends to join you for dinner, or simply request a table for two if you prefer a romantic dinner alone. The downside to open-seating is that you may have to wait for a table during peak periods in the dining room. You will also likely have a different waiter and assistant waiter each evening.

Personally, Rickee and I prefer open-seating dining and we are pleased that many cruise lines are going in this direction. However, since most ships offer casual dining alternatives to the main dining room, it is not as big an issue as it was back 'in the day' when there was only one place on the ship to eat dinner.

River Cruises

An alternative to a "typical" ocean-going cruise is a river boat cruise. In the U.S., Delta Queen Steamboat Company has three boats sailing the Mississippi, Arkansas, Tennessee, Illinois, Ohio, Missouri, Cumberland and Kanawha Rivers. America West Steamboat Company sails the Columbia, Snake and Willamette Rivers. Cruise West offers California Wine Country cruises on the Sacramento River and also sails the Columbia and Snake Rivers. In Europe, Viking River Cruises is the largest river cruise company in the world sailing the rivers of Germany, Switzerland, France, Holland, Austria, Belgium, Slovakia, Romania, Serbia/Montenegro, Hungary, Russia and the Ukraine. Uniworld and Avalon Waterways also offer European river cruises to these destinations. In China, you can experience a Yangtze River cruise from Viking River Cruises or Uniworld.

River cruises are a great vacation for:

- Mature adults traveling without children
- Travelers who prefer a quieter, more peaceful cruise

- Those who enjoy having all shore excursions included in their cruise fare
- Those who are more interested in the destination than the amenities and activities offered on the ship

By comparison to an ocean-going ship, a river boat is small, often only carrying 100 to 150 passengers. Because of their smaller size, river boats are much easier to embark and disembark. You never have to stand in line to get on or off a river boat. River cruises are a great way to see inland cities that are unreachable by ocean-going vessels.

What are you looking for?

I recently went back through my notes of the cruises Rickee and I have taken over the past few years. Here are just a few of my *personal* rankings in various areas of interest. This may be helpful as you decide which cruise line is best for you.

Best Fun Cruise
- Carnival Cruise Line
- Norwegian Cruise Line
- Royal Caribbean International

Best Value
- Carnival Cruise Line
- Royal Caribbean International
- Norwegian Cruise Line

Great Entertainment
- Norwegian Cruise Line
- Royal Caribbean International
- Carnival Cruise Line

Best Ships
- Royal Caribbean International (Voyager/Radiance class)
- Radisson Seven Seas Cruises (Mariner/Voyager)

- Celebrity Cruises (Millennium class)

Best Family Cruise
- Disney Cruise Line
- Royal Caribbean International
- Carnival Cruise Line

Best Adult Cruise (without kids)
- Celebrity Cruises
- Oceania Cruises
- Viking River Cruise

Best Dining Options
- Norwegian Cruise Line (Dawn, Star)
- Royal Caribbean International *Voyager and Radiance class vessels*
- Princess Cruises (Grand class ships)

Best Food Quality
- SeaDream Yacht Club
- Silversea Cruises
- Radisson Seven Seas Cruises

Best Large Ship Luxury
- Silversea Cruises (Whisper, Shadow)
- Radisson Seven Seas Cruises (Mariner, Voyager, Navigator)
- Crystal Cruises

Best Small Ship Luxury
- SeaDream Yacht Club
- Silversea Cruises (Wind, Cloud)
- The Yachts of Seabourn

Best for Romance
- Windstar Cruises
- SeaDream Yacht Club

- The Yachts of Seabourn

Best Service
- SeaDream Yacht Club
- Silversea Cruises
- Radisson Seven Seas Cruises

Best Fitness Center
- SeaDream Yacht Club
- Norwegian Cruise Line (Dawn, Star)
- Royal Caribbean International (Voyager/Radiance-class)

Best Spa Treatments
- Silversea Cruises
- SeaDream Yacht Club
- Radisson Seven Seas Cruises

Select the Right Stateroom

Choosing the right stateroom can make a big difference in your cruise experience. After all, this will be your home-away-from-home for the duration of your cruise. The first step in this process is to decide what type of stateroom accommodations you want and that your budget will allow. Here are some of your choices:

Inside/Interior – These staterooms are typically the smallest on the ship. Consequently, they also tend to be the least expensive accommodations. Because they are located in the interior of the ship, there is no window.

Outside/Ocean View – These rooms are located around the perimeter of the ship and will have one or more portholes or large windows. Portholes are usually found on the lowest decks.

Balcony /Veranda – These are the most popular staterooms on newer cruise ships. These rooms generally have a wall of glass facing the ocean with a door that leads out to a balcony. Generally, the balcony will include at least two chairs and a small table. Larger balconies may include a lounger. On some ships, the size of the balcony will reduce the size of the interior cabin space. Therefore, it is possible that an ocean view stateroom could be larger than a balcony stateroom.

Suite – Suites can range anywhere from 250 sq. ft. to over 1,400 sq. ft. depending on the ship. Suites are generally located on the mid to upper decks of the ship, are always ocean view and almost always have one or more balconies. Suites may also include separate living room and bedrooms, two bathrooms, a dining room, large screen television, CD/DVD players, etc. Some cruise lines offer butler service to suite guests.

Location - In addition to the type of stateroom, you must also be aware of the location of the stateroom. Generally, the *type* and *location* combine to determine the stateroom category. The stateroom category you select will determine the price you pay for your cruise.

Rules of thumb:

- The higher the stateroom is located on the ship, the higher the category (and the higher the price).
- Staterooms located in the middle of the ship (regardless of deck) tend to be a higher category. Staterooms located in the forward or aft (front or rear) parts of the ship will generally be a lower category.

Staterooms located in the middle of the ship are more preferable for two reasons:

1. They are more centrally located which means there is less walking required to get from one part of the ship to another.
2. There is less pitching motion the closer you get to the center point of the vessel. The more aft or forward, the more motion.

It is interesting that the higher decks are more preferred since rolling motion is more noticeable the higher you get. This is due to the fulcrum effect of a ship as it rolls from side to side. Of course, with stabilizers, there is very little rolling motion on most ships.

> **Tip!** If you want to save money, book your stateroom on one of the lowest decks available for your selected stateroom type. You will have the added benefit of less rolling motion. If potential moderate rocking does not bother you, save money by booking a stateroom at the aft section of the ship.

When booking an ocean view stateroom, you should be aware that some will have obstructed views. A common obstruction would be a stateroom with a lifeboat suspended right outside the window. In some cases, the obstruction may be minimal while, in others, the view may be almost totally obstructed. If it is enough for you to have some sunlight coming through the window in the morning, then you can save money by booking one of these obstructed view staterooms. The deck plans found in most cruise line brochures will identify these cabins.

Another consideration when selecting a stateroom is noise. You should be aware that if you book a stateroom on the highest deck available, it will most likely be positioned underneath the pool deck or lido restaurant. Late night pool parties can be a big sleep deterrent, unless of course you are at the party! Always check the deck plans above and below your selected stateroom. If you are directly underneath the disco, for example, you will probably be dancing to the beat all night long whether you want to or not. If you are in a stateroom located directly above or below a galley (kitchen), you might experience lingering cooking smells. Your best bet to avoid these issues is generally to stay in the middle of the ship.

Cruising For People with Special Needs

Rather than writing on a subject about which I know little or nothing, I asked one of our regular CruiseReport.com contributors,

Vincent Finelli, to share his thoughts on cruising for people with special needs.

We have been cruising since 1956 and just completed our 46th cruise. It is only recently, during the last five years, that we have needed wheelchair assistance. First, Mary had surgery on both knees, and then I had my fourth back surgery, which left me with nerve damage resulting in a walking impairment. Before these surgeries, we were both extremely active university faculty who traveled extensively. In the last few years we have learned several lessons in traveling for the physically challenged.

Enjoyable cruising can be done on most cruise lines with a bit of preparation and planning. First, provide your travel agent with medical proof of limitations (this can be placed on file and only done once). Second, book your cruise as early as possible since there are a limited number of wheelchair accessible staterooms. Older ships have fewer of these special needs cabins: for example, Regal Princess, like other ships of its vintage, has only 6 inside and 4 with obstructed view (10 total), while newer and much larger ships have 20 or more, like Grand Princess with 6 inside, 4 outside with obstructed view, and 12 with balcony (22 total). This holds true for Royal Caribbean International (RCI), as well. On its Voyager Class ships, there are a total of 25 wheelchair accessible cabins available in most categories. Thus, across the lines, there is an average of between 14 and 25 special needs cabins on each ship. These larger cabins provide special baths with safety rails, ramps to balconies and, only on RCI, automatic door openers. Among all cruise lines, we have found that Royal Caribbean and Princess cater more to cruisers with limited mobility.

Embarkation for all the lines that we have used (Carnival, Celebrity, Costa, Holland America, Norwegian, Princess and Royal Caribbean International) has been assisted. Upon request, ships will provide wheelchairs for embarkation and debarkation procedures. There may be a slight wait for the chair; however, priority boarding will be given. We bring our own companion chair, and electric scooters can be rented in ports. Recently, a passenger rented a scooter in Vancouver, Canada, for $300 per week, left it on board when he disembarked in Anchorage, Alaska, and Princess returned it to the rental company in Vancouver. Even though passenger assistance is given at embarkation, tendering and debarkation, during the cruise passengers are expected to be on their own.

While cruising, choose the appropriate dining times to avoid crowds. Speak with the Maitre D' about being seated at a table near the entrance to avoid having to thread a path between the tables. He can also assist with special dietary needs such as the following: Sugar free, Lactose free, Vegetarian, Kosher, etc.; however, to avoid surprises, be sure to make special dietary requests at the time of booking. At the buffets, there are crewmembers who will help with both serving and carrying trays. At the theater, either arrive early for seats down front, or utilize the reserved seats at the rear. In the solariums of Princess and RCI "Oxford Dippers" are available for lowering handicapped swimmers into the pools.

Shore excursions should be reviewed carefully since there may be some that are not appropriate for those with limited mobility. Read the brochure descriptions and avoid those excursions identified as requiring stair climbing or with an emphasis on walking. Ask at the Tour Desk about the feasibility of specific tours but, in the final analysis, each person knows his/her capabilities.

Each cruise will be unique, but depending on individual taste, one ship may be preferred over another. The cuisine, the amount of carpeting (which makes it difficult to wheel around the ship), the ship size or the proximity of wheel chair accessible cabins to elevators, and placement of restaurants and theaters are all important to people with limited mobility. We have observed that some cruise lines, like Costa, have more marble and tile flooring in public areas making wheelchair maneuverability easier.

When booking a cruise ask for the ship deck plans, so that the proper cabin can be reserved. Choose accommodations near the elevators and near the venues accessed daily. We have traveled from Alaska to the Caribbean; we have cruised the Mediterranean and the Baltic seas and taken our dream cruise to South America around Cape Horn, through the Magellan Strait. We believe most physically challenged passengers will have a wonderful experience when sailing. Cruising is our preferred style of vacation, because it is user friendly for those with limited mobility. The ship can be a destination in itself, or it can be a platform to view exotic destinations. Happy Sailing!

Vincent & Mary Finelli

Get the Best Deal

Nobody wants to pay more than they have to, regardless of how much money they have. No matter what you pay for your cruise, the chances are you will be paying a lot less than you would have 10 or 20 years ago. Actually, you will probably get a much better cruise today for less money. My first cruise on the SS Norway in 1979 cost me $1,179 for a single berth in the lowest cabin category with upper and lower bunk-style beds! The air portion was $180 roundtrip from Midland, Texas, to Miami; therefore, the cruise-only portion of the fare was roughly $1,000. For $1,000 per person today, you can get an ocean view stateroom on most ships and a balcony stateroom on many. Plus, today's ships have much better facilities, more dining options, and better entertainment. The fact is, cruising is a much better value today than 30 years ago! How is this possible?

Capacity – There are more cruise ships today than ever before. The industry has more than doubled the number of berths for the North American market since 1999. Over the past several years, cruise lines have been building new ships as fast as the shipyards can get them to float. This increased capacity has created a "glut" of cabins that the cruise lines have to fill at any cost.

9/11 – After 9/11/2001, the entire travel industry was dramatically impacted. Fears over terrorism exist to this day which causes cruise lines to lower their fares in order to fill empty cabins.

On Board Revenue – The cruise lines have learned that once they get people on board their beautiful new floating resort hotels, these people will spend money. In many cases, passengers will spend more on board the ship than they did for their cruise in the first place. Soft drinks, alcoholic beverages, casino gaming, bingo, shore excursions, spa visits, onboard shopping, etc. are all profit centers for the cruise lines.

Tips for getting the best deal on your next cruise:

1. **Use the services of a travel agent who is a cruise specialist.** Look for an agent who is a CLIA Certified ACC (Accredited Cruise Counselor), ECC (Elite Cruise Counselor) or MCC (Master Cruise Counselor)[1]. Note: If you don't already have a cruise specialist, you can search for one on the CruiseReport.com web site.

2. **Book your cruise in advance** to take advantage of early booking discounts. Typically, booking 9 months to a year in advance will get you the maximum discounted fare. You will be required to make a deposit to hold your reservation.

3. **Make your deposit with a credit card**, preferably American Express. Your credit card company will protect you in the unlikely event that the cruise line gets into financial trouble.

> **Important!** After you make your deposit, always request the cruise line confirmation number from your travel agent (within 24 to 48 hours). This is your assurance that payment was made to the cruise line and that you do, in fact, have a reservation. Most cruise lines allow you to check your reservation online through their web site using your confirmation number.

4. **Have your travel agent check for last minute deals** before you make your final payment (typically due 60 days prior to sailing). Most cruise lines will honor the new, lower rate for those who booked earlier at a higher rate. Just as with the airlines, *you* have to ask for the credit. The cruise line will not offer it automatically. A good travel agent will keep on top of the changing prices and advise you if the price is lowered.

---

[1] The Official trade organization of the cruise industry, Cruise Lines International Association (CLIA) works to ensure the highest caliber of cruise sales expertise and service for cruise vacationers. ACC, MCC and ECC designators indicate an agent has completed various phases of a comprehensive CLIA certification program.

www.PerfectCruiseBook.com

5. **Ask your travel agent about special perks.** Perks might be offered by certain credit card companies, or a consortium[1] to which the travel agent belongs.
6. **Ask about a group rate.** Your travel agent may have access to special pricing based on a *Group*[2] organized through their agency or consortium.
7. **Book your own airfare.** Typically, the air arrangements offered by the cruise lines are more expensive than if you book your own airfare on the Internet. However, there are some other things to consider if you book your own airfare, such as the additional cost of getting from the airport to the ship.
8. **Buy good travel insurance.** You never know when or why your plans might change. A medical or family emergency may require you to cancel your cruise. Without insurance, your entire cruise fare could be at risk. (See the section on Travel Insurance).
9. **Book your next cruise while on board the ship.** Virtually every cruise line now has a 'cruise consultant' on board the ship when you sail. They want your repeat business and they are willing to give you an additional discount to get it! Most cruise lines will offer a 5% discount for booking your next cruise before you leave the ship. All that is required is a deposit (again, use your credit card!) to hold your reservation.

---

[1] A 'consortium' is an association of travel agents which negotiates special deals with cruise lines and tour operators for the benefit of their members. Some consortiums get perks from cruise lines for their agencies' customers such as shipboard credits, cabin upgrades, special shore excursions, private bridge tours, etc.

[2] Group Space refers to a block of cabins that a travel agent has reserved with the cruise line in advance. Cruise lines will offer the travel agent incentives and discounts to get them to commit to selling a certain number of cabins on specific sailing dates.

> **Important!** If you book your next cruise on board the ship with the cruise line, you should always make sure that they have the name and address of your travel agent. This way, your travel agent will get credit for the new booking and can intervene on your behalf if it becomes necessary.

Booking a Last Minute Deal

We have all heard stories about people who booked their cruise three days before the ship sailed and got an incredible bargain. The truth is that people on most cruise lines (like airlines) do pay varying rates for the exact same accommodations. By following the guidelines covered in this chapter, you greatly increase your chances of getting the best deal.

Cruise lines, especially the larger cruise lines, monitor the availability of cabins on their ships every day and may adjust rates accordingly. Some cruise lines adjust these rates several times during a single day! For this reason, the rates that are printed in the cruise line brochure, or even on a web site, could be outdated before they are published. Only a travel agent will have access to the real, up-to-the-minute price for a particular cabin on a particular ship.

It is certainly possible to get a better price on a cruise if you are available to go on a moment's notice. If there is space available on a ship within 30 days of sailing, some cruise lines will do some deep discounting. However, by waiting until the last minute, you give up something in return for the possibility of a better price. First, you may not get on the ship at all because all the cabins were sold. Second, if you do book a last minute reservation, you will have to take whatever accommodations are available.

If these limitations are acceptable to you, let your travel agent know that you are interested in last minute deals offered by the cruise lines. Agents receive dozens of faxes and emails every day from cruise lines trying to fill empty cabins before the ship sails.

However, if you are like most people and need time to plan and schedule your vacation, the last-minute deal is not a good option. Also, the difference in price between a last-minute deal and an advance booking discount is minimal, if any. In our opinion, your best bet is to book far in advance and have your travel agent keep tabs on the cruise line for better prices before your final payment is due (giving you credit for the difference if a lower price becomes available). By booking in advance, you have the advantage of *knowing* you will get on board and you will have a better selection of cabins. Some cruise lines even dole out stateroom upgrades based on how far in advance you booked your cruise.

> **Warning!** Booking a last-minute deal on a cruise is not the panacea you might expect. At best, you will have to take whatever cabin is available. You will be last on the list for any possible upgrades. You will not be able to plan your vacation because there is no guarantee that any space will be available when you want to go.

Getting a Cabin Upgrade

Paid Upgrades – Some cruise lines will, from time to time, offer the opportunity to upgrade to a higher cabin category by paying an additional fare.

Guarantee Fare – In some cases, a cruise line will offer what is referred to as a "guarantee" on a particular cabin category. This is especially true if they happen to be sold out of the category that you are trying to book. What this means is that you will pay the fare for the category you select and will be guaranteed a cabin in that category or higher. The downside of booking a guarantee is that you will not be assigned your stateroom until you check in at the pier. On the upside, you may be upgraded if no cabins are available in your selected category.

Cabin upgrades are rare, especially on a ship that is sailing at or near capacity. Even on a guarantee fare basis, you are only "guaranteed" to get the category for which you paid. When upgrades are given, they are generally given to those who booked early or to passengers who have previously sailed with the cruise line. Seldom would you ever get upgraded from an inside stateroom to an ocean view or balcony stateroom.

Paying with a credit card

We highly recommend that you use a major credit card when you book your cruise. There are several logical reasons for this:

Payment Options – Your credit card company may allow you to pay off your cruise over time, easing any immediate financial burden.

Protection from Default – In the unlikely event that you pay for your cruise and the cruise line goes out of business before your sailing date, your credit card company may offer protection for your investment. Of course, your best protection from default is a good travel insurance policy.

Upgrades and Perks – Some credit card companies, in conjunction with certain cruise lines, offer special perks. For example, if you are an American Express Platinum Card member, you can get a shipboard credit (up to $300 per stateroom) on several cruise lines. Other perks might include private tours of the bridge, dinner with a ship's officer, a special gift or a cabin upgrade (if available).

> **Important!** Check with your credit card company to find out the exact procedures required to receive any perks and benefits they may offer with various cruise lines.

Airlines Miles/Rebates – If you have a credit card that gives you airline miles for your purchases, then you will earn miles for the money you spend on your cruise! If you use a rebate card such as Discover, you can get a percentage back on the amount you spend. In essence, this is like receiving an additional discount.

If you do not have a credit or debit card and are forced to pay with a money order or cashiers check, it will most likely have to be made out to the agency you are using instead of the cruise line. If you pay in this manner, you have no real protection in the event the agent you have chosen turns out to be less than ethical.

How to Get a Free Cruise

What if you could go on a cruise and not pay a penny? Well, if you are willing and able to put together a group of people to go on a cruise, you might just be able to earn a free cruise for yourself. Some cruise lines will offer travel agents a free berth (space for 1 traveler sharing a stateroom) for every 10 or so berths sold as part of a group booking. The industry term for this free berth is a *TC* which stands for Tour Conductor.

Cruise lines offer TC's to travel agents who pre-book a block of staterooms on a specific sailing. If a cruise line has a ship with a lot of available space, they may offer 1 for 10, which means one free berth (or TC) for every ten berths sold. In layman's terms, for every ten passengers sold they will allow the eleventh passenger to go for free. As the ship begins to fill up, they may modify this policy to 1 for 12 or 1 for 15. Therefore, if you plan to put together a group, you will get your most lucrative deal the farther out you block your group space.

By now you may be asking yourself, "So how would I get 10 other people (or more) to take a cruise?" Well, I am glad you asked. Here are just a few examples of groups that routinely take advantage of cruise line group programs:

- Family reunions
- Sales incentive trips
- Military Veteran reunions
- Religious groups
- Civic groups
- Professional groups (medical, legal, etc.)

Become a Group Leader

To become a group leader, you need to find a travel agent who is experienced in working with groups. Start by asking them, "Have you ever put together any group cruises?"

Make sure your travel agent understands that if you spearhead the promotion of the cruise to your group, that you expect to be compensated with a TC (a free berth) for every X number of berths sold. If your group is large enough, say more than 30, you may tell your agent that you only expect a maximum of two TC's which would give you a free cruise for two people.

For example, let's say you have the ability to put together a group of 100 people for a cruise. If the cruise line is offering 1 for 10, your group would get 10 free berths (5 staterooms based on 2 people per stateroom). If you take two of the TC's to get a free cruise for you and a traveling companion, that leaves 8 TC's. You may wish to take the value of the remaining TC's and use the value of the free berth(s) in the form of a discount to the group of 100. This will ensure that your group is getting a much lower cost per person than if they booked the cruise on their own.

Promoting Your Group Cruise

Your travel agent will be able to help you in the promotion of the cruise to your group or organization. Your agent should be able to obtain some assistance from the cruise line, depending on the size of your group. On large groups, the cruise line may even prepare special mailers for marketing and promotional purposes.

Special Functions

Most cruise lines will offer some form of onboard services for groups. Larger ships will even have a group coordinator as part of their permanent staff. Depending on the size of the group, you may be able to arrange private cocktail parties for your group during the cruise, private ship tours, tours of the bridge, etc. These vary by cruise line and by ship. Make sure you ask your travel agent for details.

Meeting Facilities

If your group needs to conduct meetings or presentations during the cruise this is not a problem. Check with your travel agent to make sure the ship on which you will be sailing offers the appropriate audio visual equipment and meeting space.

Choosing and Using a Travel Agent

I have already told you that I am a big believer in using a travel agent to book a cruise vacation. You may find it peculiar that an "Internet Guy" like me would not be in favor of simply going online and booking a cruise on the Internet. First of all, this 'do everything yourself' on the Internet did not come about as a result of consumer demand. This new culture has been forced on consumers by corporations who see the Internet as a way to reduce their cost of doing business.

> **Tip!** Selecting a good travel agent who is a cruise specialist will have more impact on your having a *perfect cruise* than any other decision you make.

Allow me to illustrate. Today, virtually all of the airlines require that you book online (or by calling the airline's toll-free number). Back 'in the day', you used to call your travel agent, tell him where you wanted to go, and he would use the agency computer to research and find the best deal. The airline paid the travel agent a commission for handling the transaction and everybody was happy. The airlines were not too keen on the idea that the travel agents were so good at their research that they could find a better deal for you than the airline thought you should have. The way the airlines looked at it, why should they pay a commission to someone who is ultimately going to cost them a larger, more profitable sale?

> 88% of cruise passengers use a travel agent to book their cruise and surveys conducted by CLIA show that 74% of the consumers who did were satisfied with their travel agent.

The airlines, in their infinite wisdom, decided a few years ago that if they could eliminate the commissions they were paying to travel agents, they could not only save the 6% or so in commissions they were paying, but that their customers would be buying higher priced tickets (since there would be no seasoned professional to assist them in getting the best deal.) Surely this would save the airlines and return them to profitability. Well, you know the rest of the story.

- The travel agents lost their commissions and thousands went out of business as a result.
- The traveling public no longer has an advocate to assist them in getting the best airfare deal.
- You are now required to do your own research online, or call the airline's toll-free number to make a reservation[1].
- The airlines continue to lose money at a dizzying pace.

When the cruise industry was just getting started in the 70's (after the hit TV show The Love Boat), it turned to travel agents to sell the cruise product to consumers. Up until that time, travel agents were primarily in the business of issuing airline tickets to business travelers. With an airline ticket there was not a lot of "selling" involved. Basically, the travel agent was an "order taker" and ticket processor. Over the past 30 years, the travel business has changed dramatically. As the airlines were gradually phasing out commissions, the cruise industry began to explode. Smart travel agents soon learned that they could make a lot more money selling a cruise vacation worth $2,000 or more at 12% commission than a $300 airline ticket at 3%.

---

[1] There are still a few die-hard full-service travel agencies who will, for a fee, make airline reservations.

Today, the cruise industry has grown to the point that it can literally sustain thousands of travel agencies who sell nothing but cruises. The biggest challenge facing travel agents today is lower cruise prices which result in lower commissions.

All of that being said, here are some of the reasons I believe in using a travel agent to purchase your cruise:

- It does not cost anything to use a travel agent because they are paid a commission by the cruise line.
- You will probably save money because a good travel agent has the right "connections" and knows how to get the best deal. Remember, travel agents do this for a living so they are always receiving special offers from the cruise lines that we, the consumers, may never see!
- You have an advocate who can intervene on your behalf if there is a problem.
- You have someone to call if there is a problem. Try calling a reservation agent at a cruise line for help once you have booked your cruise. Good luck!

Perhaps the most important decision you can make in the process of planning your cruise vacation is the selection of a qualified professional cruise consultant. Technically speaking, *any* travel agent can book a cruise for you. However, many travel agents are not professional *cruise consultants*.

A professional *cruise consultant* will be familiar with a variety of cruise lines, ships and destinations. He or she will be able to help you make the right decision based on your personal likes and dislikes. Best of all, they will be able to get the best deal for you.

> **Tip!** Using a cruise consultant/travel agent does not cost you anything. They are paid a commission by the cruise line so the price you pay for your cruise is the same whether you use a travel agent or not.

Perhaps the best reason to use a professional cruise consultant is to have an advocate on your side that has some leverage. If a problem arises between you and the cruise line, you are just a single customer. If, however, your travel agent does hundreds of thousands or millions of dollars in business with the cruise line, they can intervene on your behalf and, suddenly, you have a better chance of getting a resolution in your favor.

Generally, there are three types of travel agencies selling cruises.

1. **Full-service Agencies** offer a wide variety of business and leisure travel services. In addition to booking cruises, they may also book airline tickets, land vacations, Las Vegas trips, etc. If you choose to go to a full service agency, there should be one or more cruise specialists within that agency with whom you can work.

2. **Cruise-only Agencies** sell nothing but cruises. More and more cruise-only agencies are home-based. Thanks to the Internet, some agents have found they no longer require the expense and hassle of a commercial office location.

3. **Online Travel Agencies** do business solely through their web site. Most travel web sites are owned and operated by either a full-service agency or a cruise-only agency (agencies that only sell cruises and do not sell airline tickets, hotel packages, land tours, etc.). Many agencies have gone to the online business model to reduce their expenses and most are legitimate, trustworthy professionals. However, when working with an online travel agency, you should check to see if their web site has been certified by either PITA (The Professional Internet Travel Alliance) or The Better Business Bureau.

Here are some guidelines to consider when choosing a professional cruise consultant:

1. **Look for an agent who is an Accredited Cruise Counselor (ACC), Master Cruise Counselor (MCC) or Elite Cruise Counselor (ECC) with CLIA.** This indicates that this travel agent has invested the time and energy to specialize in cruise vacations.

2. **Your cruise consultant should be a top producer with the cruise line you are booking.** By being a top producer, he or she will be more familiar with the cruise line policies and will have the *ear* of the cruise line should a problem arise. A top producer may also be able to negotiate a better rate or possible upgrades and other perks.
3. **Look for an agent who is responsive to your needs.** Did he or she call you back when promised? Do they follow-up promptly when you have questions or concerns?
4. **Some states require licensing and registration for 'sellers of travel'.** You may wish to ask your travel professional for their state license number.

As mentioned previously, some travel agents today are *home-based*. This should not be a deterrent to selecting them as your professional cruise consultant. Some of the best and brightest travel agents have decided to work from home.

If you have a good travel agent that has served you well in the past, don't change! As we say in Texas, "If it ain't broke, don't fix it." However, if you do not already have a travel agent, you can find one by accessing www.PerfectCruiseBook.com and clicking on the link "Find a Perfect Cruise Specialist". From there you will be able to locate a cruise specialist based on area of specialization or one located in your city/state. We recommend looking for an agent based on specialization, not location. Every specialist listed in the CruiseReport.com database has a web site, an email address and a toll-free phone number.

> **Note:** It is no longer necessary to do business with a travel agent in your local area. The Internet may not be the best tool for booking a cruise, but it is great for working with your travel agent! Look for an agent who can best meet your needs, not one that has an office close to where you live.

Tips on Working with a Travel Agent

Your travel agent/cruise specialist is the best resource you can have when it comes to experiencing the Perfect Cruise. However, it might be helpful to know how to get the most out of your travel agent.

Do your research – Use books such as this one and web sites like CruiseReport.com to identify the type of cruise you are interested in. Before you call or contact a travel agent, you should have already determined the following:

- The destination to which you want to cruise
- The month and year you want to cruise
- The price range you want to spend on your cruise
- Who will be taking the cruise
- One or two cruise lines in which you are interested

Armed with this information, your travel agent can immediately focus on how to get you the best deal and make any alternative recommendations for other cruise lines that may better suit your needs.

Quote Request Form – If your travel agent has a web site (and they should), they probably have some sort of quote request form on that web site. Completing this online form can be a real time-saver for both you and your travel agent because it collects a lot of information the agent will need when contacting the cruise line on your behalf. It saves you time because you can complete the form at your leisure and are not limited to calling the agent and delivering the information over the phone during business hours. If you would prefer, you can fax a quote request form to your travel agent.

Get what you want – It is common for a travel agent to suggest alternate cruise lines which may be very similar to the one(s) you have requested. However, some travel agents may only be trying to book you on a different cruise line because they earn a higher commission from that cruise line. This is why it is important to work with a travel agent you trust and with whom you genuinely enjoy doing business.

Comparing Prices

As you begin shopping for your cruise, you may choose to shop and compare the price and services of two or more agencies. This is a common practice and can be a valuable way to determine where you want to do business.

You may notice a discrepancy in the pricing of a cruise between two agencies. You may wonder why one cruise is less or more expensive than the other. Here are some possibilities:

> **Need a travel agent?** Go to www.PerfectCruiseBook.com to locate a Perfect Cruise Specialist for your next cruise!

Not Comparing Apples to Apples – Make sure that both agencies are comparing the exact same cruise line, cruise ship and cabin category on the same sailing date. Prices can vary from one week to the next. Also, if you get a quote on Monday from Agency A and wait until Thursday to get a quote from Agency B, it is very possible the rates have changed. Don't write off Agency A just because you found a "better deal." Three days later, Agency A may be able to offer the same or better deal.

Incomplete Pricing – Make sure that you are quoted your cruise fare inclusive of all taxes, insurance, transfers and port charges. Also, make sure to ask if there are any additional handling fees or delivery charges (for tickets, documents, etc.) that do not appear in the quote. If you are using cruise line airfare, make sure you get comparable air quotes from each agency.

Group Space – If the agency has reserved a block of cabins in advance at a reduced rate, they may choose to pass their group space savings on to you in the form of a discounted cruise fare.

Rebates - Some travel agencies will offer to rebate a portion of their commission in order to offer a more competitive price. This is a common practice among the larger agencies that derive most of their business through toll-free phone numbers and large web sites.

These agencies work off of volume, opting to make a smaller percentage of profit on a larger number of sales.

A lower price is not always the best determining factor when selecting an agency. You should never sacrifice service and/or a good working relationship just to save $50 or $100 on a $2,000 vacation. Remember, if there is a problem, you want to be able to call this person and have him or her be responsive to your needs. If they are not making any money on the deal, or feel like they had to give up all of their commission just to make the sale, how willing are they going to be to step in and help?

> **Rule of Thumb** – You don't always get what you pay for, but you almost never get something that you don't pay for.

Booking Online

There are literally hundreds of web sites where you can book your own cruise online. Basically, they fall into three categories:

Cruise Line Sites – Some cruise lines allow you to book directly with the cruise line through their web site.

Mega-Sites – Expedia, Travelocity and Orbitz. These web sites are basically online travel agencies which are paid commissions by the cruise lines. These companies have large marketing and advertising budgets. That does not necessarily make them the best place to buy your cruise.

Travel agent web sites – These are independent travel agents who have implemented booking technologies on their own smaller web sites (small in comparison to the mega-sites).

I am not a big fan of booking a cruise online. Why? Because I cannot come up with a compelling reason to do so. Remember, you are not buying a book or computer memory. This is your vacation we are talking about!

I highly recommend using the Internet for doing your research. Check out itineraries, ship information, read consumer and editorial reviews, even requesting a quote. But when it comes time to doing the actual booking, I prefer to pick up the phone, call a toll-free number and have a cruise professional do the booking for me. Remember, online booking is designed to save the agent or the cruise line time, not *you*. I suppose if you have a booking emergency at 4:00am and you absolutely cannot wait until business hours to book your cruise, then you could argue that online booking is a reasonable option. I, personally, have never had to book a cruise at 4:00am.

I would never book a cruise directly with a cruise line web site because, as I stated earlier, I have no advocate in the event of a problem. Booking online with one of the Mega-Sites, in my opinion, is not much better than booking with a cruise line. Sure, you may save a few bucks on the cruise, but an operator in a telemarketing phone bank located in India[1] is not going to be your advocate if there is a problem.

It is important to note that the price you are quoted from an online booking system may *not* be the best price available. The only way to know for sure that you are getting the best deal is to work with a professional travel agent. There may be group rates or other offers available that are not reflected in the online pricing tables.

I suppose if I were forced (and I would have to be) to book online, I would do so with a travel agent web site. At least with a travel agent site, I would have access to a live person if a problem were to arise.

---

[1] Travelocity recently announced that it was moving its call center operations to an off shore telemarketing company in India.

> **Tip!** Why waste your time? Find a good travel agent who is a cruise specialist and talk with them on the phone, meet with them in person, or email them your questions. Let them do the work of booking. *Use the Internet for research.*

Travel agents who understand their business and their customers realize the value of a personal relationship. Unlike buying a book or a piece of computer memory, buying a cruise is an emotional purchase. It is not simply a transaction like an airline ticket. The vast majority of customers appreciate a little hand holding, guidance and frankly, service.

Booking Directly with a Cruise Line

Once you've decided which cruise is best for you, it is time to book it. Some cruise lines will now allow you to book directly through their web site or via their toll-free phone number. This was virtually unheard of 20 years ago when cruise lines referred all inquiries back to a travel agency. While you might think that circumventing the travel agent and the associated commissions will result in a better deal, you would be wrong. In fact, chances are you will pay *more* by booking direct than by using a travel agent.

When you book direct with a cruise line's toll-free number, you may be talking to a minimum-wage employee working in a telemarketing operation. There is no incentive for that person to find you the best deal or the best cabin on the ship. They have no vested interest in having you call and ask for them the next time you book a cruise. Your travel agent, on the other hand, *does* have a vested interest in your repeat business. Therefore, they are *motivated* to research the best deal for you. Some might argue that since the travel agent's commission is based on the sale amount they are more likely to sell you a more expensive cruise. However, our *experience* has been just the opposite. A *good* travel agent will recognize that your long-term repeat business and word-of-mouth advertising is far more valuable that a little extra commission on one sale.

Since 75% of all cruises are sold through travel agencies, cruise lines cannot afford to offer better pricing direct to consumers. To do so would violate their primary distribution channel. If a cruise line decided to do this, the travel agent community might just decide to stop selling that brand. This is possible because there is a lot of competition among cruise lines (unlike the airlines). Therefore, you will not get any better price by going directly to the cruise line than by using a travel agent. The money the cruise line saves on paying the travel agent commission drops to *their* bottom line, *not yours*.

The question you have to ask yourself is not "W*hat do I gain by booking direct?*" The real question is "What could I lose?"

1. You may not get the best deal available.

2. If the price drops on your cruise between the time you book and the final payment date, the cruise line will not graciously inform you and lower your rate. A good travel agent will check the rates periodically and adjust your fare to any lower rate being offered.

3. If a problem arises, you do not have an advocate to go to bat for you with the cruise line.

So, when should you book directly with a cruise line? There really is never a reason to do so. However, if you live within driving distance of the ship you are cruising on and just want a 3 or 4-day getaway cruise, booking direct may not do any harm. Besides, you are probably only talking about spending a few hundred dollars. However, if you are talking about your dream vacation or plan to spend $1,500 or more, why risk it? Use a professional.

Airfare and Transfers

Unless you plan to drive to the port where your ship embarks, you will need to purchase airfare and make arrangements for transportation from the airport to the port and from the ship back to the airport for your return flight. The cruise lines refer to this transportation as a "transfer."

If you purchase your air travel from the cruise line, they will typically include the transfers in the price. Even if the airfare is a little more expensive than what you can get on the Internet, it still may be a better deal because of the included transfers. It really depends on the port of embarkation. For example, if your ship embarks in Port Everglades in Ft. Lauderdale, the cost to take a taxi to the ship is around $7 because the port is only minutes from the airport. In Miami, however, it can cost $25 or more to get from the airport to the ship ($50 roundtrip). So, if the airfare from the cruise line is $30 more than what you can get on the Internet for a cruise that embarks out of Miami, the cruise line air, with transfers, is a better deal.

There is another slight advantage to buying your airfare from the cruise line. If your flight is delayed or cancelled, the cruise line will cover the cost of getting you to the next port-of-call where you can get on the ship. If your flight is slightly delayed, they may even delay the ship leaving the pier until your flight arrives. This is especially true if there are a lot of cruise passengers on your flight.

Also, when you use the cruise line's transfers, your luggage will be automatically picked up at the airport and transported to the ship. After you claim your bags at baggage claim, a cruise line representative will take your bags and they will be delivered to your stateroom.

If you choose to purchase your own airfare, make sure that your flight will arrive at the embarkation port city in plenty of time for you to get to the ship. We think you should allow at least 3 hours from the time your plane lands until the time the ship is scheduled to leave. Of course, this depends on the port of embarkation.

> **Tip!** For first or second time cruisers, we highly recommend that you buy your air tickets from the cruise line to reduce the hassle and eliminate potential problems.

For example, let's say that your ship is scheduled to depart Miami at 5:00pm. You should plan to arrive in Miami no later than 2:00pm. That will give you plenty of time to claim your luggage, locate a taxi or meet your pre-arranged transfers, and still allow a little time for airline delays.

If you purchase your own airfare, you can usually still purchase transfers from the cruise line (through your travel agent). This will cost anywhere from $25/pp to $100/pp depending on the port of embarkation. The cruise line will have a representative in most cities who will meet you at the baggage claim area to direct you to the transfer van or bus.

Buying Travel Insurance

There is really no good reason not to purchase travel insurance. Can you afford to lose your deposit or your entire cruise fare in the event of an emergency or unforeseen event? Some people think that travel insurance is only valuable for elderly travelers or those with serious medical conditions that might impact their cruise. That can be a costly misconception. Here are just a few things that could happen to you:

- A medical or family emergency could prevent you from being able to take your cruise.
- Your home could be severely damaged by fire or flood within a few days of your scheduled departure causing you to miss your cruise, or this could happen while you are at sea.
- Jury duty or a court appearance could interrupt your cruise.
- You could be involved in accident on the way to the airport.
- The cruise line could experience a problem (such as going into bankruptcy) which would cause you to miss your trip and potentially lose your cruise fare.
- An airline scheduling or flight problem could occur causing you to miss all or a portion of your cruise.

- You could experience a medical emergency while on your cruise that could result in costly medical care or even costly evacuation from the ship via helicopter or boat.

At the very least, a travel insurance policy should cover (1) the cost of your cruise and air fare if you are forced to cancel your cruise, or the cruise is interrupted; (2) the cost of medical evacuation from the ship via helicopter or boat; and (3) medical expenses that may be incurred during your vacation that are not covered by your personal medical insurance policy.

> **Tip!** In most cases it is better to buy travel insurance from an independent company through your travel agent as opposed to the insurance offered by the cruise line. The independent insurance companies provide more coverage and are generally less expensive.

Trip insurance is typically based upon the total cost of your vacation (airfare and cruise). Of course, you can purchase less protection if you wish. For example, if your total cruise and air costs are $6,000, you could purchase a total of $4,000 in coverage and take the $2,000 risk yourself. This could lower your insurance costs and still cover you for most of your outlay.

Example Policy: "Cruise Guard" policy from Travel Guard Insurance:

- 2 Passengers
- $4,000 total coverage
- Royal Caribbean International 7-night Caribbean
- Texas resident
- Cost: $212

The coverage offered by this insurance plan is as follows[1]:

- **Trip Cost: Trip Cancellation** - covers you if you cancel your trip for a covered reason.
- **Trip Cost: Trip Interruption** - covers you if you interrupt your trip for a covered reason.
- **$600: Trip Delay** - Reimburses you up to $200 a day for additional accommodations or travel expenses if you are delayed for more than 12 hours.
- **Trip Cost: Missed Cruise Connection** - $200 per person per day covers meals and accommodations expenses.
- **$3,000: Lost, Stolen, or Damaged Baggage & Personal Effects** - Reimburses you if your baggage is lost, damaged, or stolen while you are on your trip.
- **$500: Baggage Delay** - Reimburses you for the purchase of essential items if your baggage is delayed or misdirected for more than 24 hours.
- **$25,000: Sickness Medical Expenses** - Covers necessary medical expenses up to one year after the sickness or injury, provided you sought initial medical treatment while on your trip.
- **$25,000: Accident Medical Expenses** - Covers necessary medical expenses up to one year after the sickness or injury, provided you sought initial medical treatment while on your trip.
- **$100,000: Emergency Medical Transportation** - Covers evacuation and transportation to the nearest adequate medical facility. Travel Guard® Assistance Offers emergency assistance for your peace of mind anywhere in the world.
- **Livetravel / En Route Assistance** - 24-hour hotline to make emergency travel changes, such as rebooking flights, hotel reservations, tracking lost luggage and more!

---

[1] Source: www.travelguard.com web site – July 2004

- **Live messaging -** Relay of any e-mail or phone message to family, friends or business associates.
- **Emergency Cash transfers -** Assistance in coordinating an emergency cash advance.
- **Pre-trip advisories -** Around-the-clock access to passport, visa, inoculation and vaccine requirements; travel advisories; embassy and consulate contacts; travel health advisories; weather and currency information — all for your planned destination.
- **Roadside Assistance —** 24-hour hotline for towing and flat tire assistance; fuel, oil and fluid delivery; lock-out, battery and collision assistance.

It should be noted that your policy will only reimburse you for your actual cost of your cruise. Therefore, you should not purchase a $5,000 policy if you cruise only cost $2,300. The insurance company will reimburse you for your total cruise fare less any refund paid by the cruise line.

Some insurance companies will offer different types of coverage under separate policies. This allows you to purchase only the insurance that you feel you need. However, most companies offer complete insurance packages (like the one from Travel Guard in the previous example). We highly recommend that your policy cover trip cancellation/interruption and medical emergency evacuation. The cancellation/interruption should cover the insured traveler and companion(s) against potential loss resulting from death, injury or serious illness. It is common for most policies to also protect you from loss in the event of death, injury or illness of a close family member.

The "Cruise Guard" policy used as an example offers the following coverage:

- Trip Cancellation
- Trip Interruption
- Missed Connections
- Trip Delay

Some occurrences will be remedied with a 100% cash refund while others are remedied with 100% cruise credit toward a future cruise. You should check your individual policy for detailed information on how remedies are handled.

> Coverage and rates may vary by state. Ask your travel agent for a quote for your particular cruise and your state of residence.

Every policy will outline the situations that qualify for cancellation/interruption coverage. You should check to make sure your policy will cover the following situations:

- Death, injury or illness
- Traffic accidents on the way to the airport or from the airport to the ship
- Fire, flooding or other disasters at your home

If you have a pre-existing medical condition (one for which you have received treatment within the 60 or 90 days prior to purchasing the policy), you should check to make sure that your policy covers you. Pre-existing conditions can also apply to a family member at home whose death or illness may cause you to cancel your cruise. Therefore, if a family member at home dies during your cruise as the result of a pre-existing condition, your trip interruption coverage may not reimburse. To be safe, you should question your insurance company and request confirmation in writing if you have such concerns.

You should also be aware of a policy's interruption/cancellation coverage in the event of "operator failure" or "default". Some policies may narrowly define "default" or failure as bankruptcy. However, it may be that a cruise line or airline can go "out of business" or, at the very least, be unable to fulfill your cruise vacation without having officially filed for bankruptcy. Businesses fail every day without filing bankruptcy; they may simply close their doors. Most policies will not provide any coverage in the event that your travel agent's business fails. This is another reason that you should always verify that your credit card charges are run directly with the cruise line, not the travel agent's merchant account. You may think that the possibility of a cruise line going out of business is extreme, but I could name five cruise lines that I know of that have gone out of business in the past 3 years alone!

Emergency medical evacuation coverage will pay the costs of transportation from the ship to a location where quality medical care can be obtained. In some parts of the world, you may not care to receive medical treatment from sub-standard medical facilities. Once your insurance company verifies your medical condition, they will authorize evacuation, the method of which is generally arranged by the insurance company.

We always purchase insurance from Travel Guard through our travel agent. I use the link on the travel agent's web site to get to the Travel Guard site and purchase the insurance directly. I find that to be the easiest way for me to buy it and my travel agent still gets credit for the insurance sale. We have found Travel Guard's coverage to be as good as, or better, than any other company and they do pay their claims! We had a situation on a Silversea cruise recently where Rickee fell on some stairs and broke two toes on one foot. This required a trip to the ship's doctor and two shots. The total bill was over $100 (which was fair). We submitted the paperwork to Travel Guard and within 3 weeks we received a check to cover all of the costs of her treatment.

Two of my clients, who were also friends of ours, had always declined travel insurance. A few years ago they decided to book a Northern Europe cruise.

This time I strongly encouraged them to purchase the travel insurance, and they agreed to do so. Just a few days before the cruise, the wife learned that she was pregnant. During a shore excursion in St. Petersburg, Russia, the wife began to have serious cramping and pain and was rushed from the tour to a clinic where it was determined that she had experienced a miscarriage and would require emergency surgery. As she was taken to a local Russian hospital, the cruise ship departed St. Petersburg for its next port of call (which is their policy). Since my clients had been in St. Petersburg on a group visa purchased by the cruise line, they were now in the country illegally!

Fortunately, my friend remembered that he had purchased the Travel Guard insurance and called Travel Guard's worldwide toll-free number to see if they could help. The Travel Guard representative was able to get a Russian interpreter in the U.S. to communicate with the hospital on my client's behalf. They also contacted the U.S. consulate to arrange for a visa during their stay. After the surgery, the hospital demanded full payment before they would release the wife and said that they would accept his American Express card. After another call to Travel Guard, my client was told to relax and that the money would be wired directly to the hospital. Afterwards, sensing that the couple was weary from their ordeal and that the wife may still be in some pain after surgery, Travel Guard arranged and paid for two First Class airline tickets for them to fly back to the U.S.

Three days after my clients returned to the U.S., a Travel Guard representative called them to see how they were doing. Travel Guard then contacted me to let me know that, in addition to the medical costs they had covered, they had also reimbursed the client for the missed portion of the cruise. The total amount of the claim was over $15,000.00. This is just one of many stories that emphasizes how valuable travel insurance is for our clients.

Michael & Sharon Czarnecki
Bon Voyage Cruises, Inc.

Here are some good travel insurance companies that you can check out online, or through your travel agent. You should always go with the company that your travel agent recommends. Again, they are familiar with that insurance company and can intervene with them on your behalf.

Travel Guard	www.travelguard.com
Travel Insured	www.travelinsured.com
CSA Travel Protection	www.csatravelprotection.com
Access America Service Corporation	www.accessamerica.com
Travelex	www.travelex-insurance.com

Extending Your Cruise Vacation

Many people desire to extend their vacation to include additional time in the port of embarkation or disembarkation. This is often referred to as "pre-cruise" or "post-cruise" extensions. Pre-cruise and post-cruise extensions offer a lot of advantages.

- By flying into the port of embarkation a day or two early, you avoid the worry of flight delays and you have more flight time options available to you.
- By staying a day or two after your cruise disembarks, you avoid the mad rush of cruise passengers crowding the airport to go home.
- You have an opportunity to relax and unwind from the flight for a day or so before boarding the ship.
- You get to see the sights of the city of embarkation/disembarkation. These sights are often missed without a pre/post package.

When you think about it, extending your cruise by one or more days makes a lot of sense, especially when you are traveling a great distance. For example, if you are going on a Mediterranean cruise and have to fly to Europe, you might as well stay a few extra days and see some of the European cities, right? After all, how often do you get to Europe?

If you decide to extend your vacation prior to or at the end of your cruise, you must decide whether to purchase a pre/post package from the cruise line or make the arrangements on your own. In most cases, you can save a tremendous amount of money by making your own hotel and transfer arrangements. Cruise line pre/post packages can be very expensive. The only exception to this "rule" would be Alaska cruise tours. The Alaska cruise tours are generally a good value because the price includes all of your excursions as well as your hotel and transfers.

> **Tip!** Aside from Alaska cruise tours, you will save money by making your own pre-cruise and post-cruise hotel and transfer arrangements. Your travel agent may offer this service, or you can do it yourself on the Internet.

If you plan to make your own hotel arrangements, check out Hotels.com. We have used them on several occasions and have found their 4 and 5-star hotels to be quite a good value. If you are planning a stay in London, England, check out LondonTown.com.

Things to Know Before You Go

Identification Requirements

Cruise lines require that you bring a valid, government-issued photo I.D. with you before you will be allowed to board the vessel. A state driver's license is not sufficient identification because it does not offer any proof of citizenship. The most common forms of identification accepted are a U.S. or Canadian passport, a government-issued birth certificate, or a military ID. Birth certificates issued by a hospital are not acceptable.

> **Warning!** Using a birth certificate as a form of identification may only be accepted for cruises which embark in U.S. ports of call. It is advisable that you always have a valid passport, just to be safe.

If you already have a passport, make sure that the expiration date is at least 6 months after the date of your cruise departure date. This is especially true for cruises which embark at ports outside the U.S. If the expiration date is less than 6 months from the date of embarkation, you should renew your passport before you leave for your cruise.

> **Important!** Check with your particular cruise line or travel agent to find out what is required for identification purposes.

For detailed information on obtaining a U.S. Passport, go to the following web site:

http://travel.state.gov/passport_services.html

If you plan to use your birth certificate for identification, it must be an original with a raised seal. A simple photocopy may not be acceptable.

Dress Code

You may be wondering what you are supposed to wear on your cruise. Dress codes vary from one cruise line to another. The luxury cruise lines tend to have more formal dress codes. The 'contemporary' or mass-market cruise lines have much more relaxed dress codes.

During the daytime (before 6:00pm) just about anything goes. You can wear shorts, sandals, and a t-shirt anywhere on the ship. You can even wear a swimsuit and sandals just about everywhere except the dining room. Ladies should wear a cover up over their swim suits when not at the pool.

After 6:00pm, the mood of the ship changes and, generally speaking, shorts are not acceptable in the ship's public areas. On most ships, men can get by with nice slacks and a shirt with a collar (not a t-shirt). Even on formal nights, there will always be somewhere on the ship where casual clothing is acceptable. If you plan to attend the formal events, a tuxedo is not required. A dark suit and tie will suffice.

Your daily cruise newsletter will state the dress code for that day. Typically, the night of embarkation is casual and the second night is formal (usually the Captain's Welcome party). The last night of the cruise is always casual.

In recognition of an increasingly less formal society, some cruise lines have done away with 'Formal Night' altogether. SeaDream

Yacht Club, Windstar Cruises and Oceania Cruises are among the lines that have gone the more casual route.

Cruise Ship Safety

One question many people ask is "Is cruising safe?" Since 9/11 there have been news reports about cruise ships being the target of terrorists and of "massive" outbreaks of the Norwalk virus. If you believe everything you read in the newspapers and see on television, you might never go on a cruise! Here are some facts about cruise ship safety that you should know[1].

> "During the last two decades, North American cruise lines have maintained the best safety record in the travel industry, while transporting more than 60 million people throughout the world." International Council of Cruise Lines

Cruise Ship Security

By far, cruising is the safest way to travel. When you consider the risks involved in other forms of travel, this becomes pretty obvious. Even something as simple as a road trip carries greater risks. Your odds of getting killed or injured in an automobile accident are hundreds or thousands of times greater than if traveling on a cruise ship.

It should comfort you to know that cruise lines had U.S. Coast Guard-approved security plans in place before the events of September 11, 2001, and within hours of the attacks, cruise ships implemented their highest level of security.

---

[1] The information was received from literature provided by the International Council of Cruise Lines (ICCL).

Cruise ship security measures include:

- 100% screening of all passenger baggage and carry-on baggage.
- Intensified screening of passenger lists and passenger identification.
- Restricted access to any sensitive vessel or terminal areas.
- Stringent measures to deter unauthorized entry and illegal activity.
- Notice given to U.S. Coast Guard 96 hours before entering U.S. ports, and passenger and crew identification information submitted to federal agencies.
- Coast Guard established security zone around cruise ship.

Most cruise ships today will issue you a photo ID card when you board the ship. Many times this card will also be used as your room key and/or on board charge card. You must show this card whenever you leave the ship in port and re-board the ship. This measure insures that nobody who is not a passenger is getting onboard the ship in a foreign port.

In addition to passenger security measures, the cruise lines require a comprehensive screening process for all prospective employees. U.S. Embassy personnel conduct background checks before issuing work visas to non-U.S. citizens.

Crime aboard cruise ships is rare. One reason may be that the ship is a closed environment. If you steal something, there is nowhere to run and hide. The punishment for a crew member caught (or even suspected) of stealing is severe. Most cruise lines will summarily discharge the crew member at the next port-of-call and it becomes the crew member's responsibility to figure out how to get home from there. Even though burglary is rare, most cruise ships provide safes in every stateroom for valuables, or you can have the purser's desk store your valuables in their safe. Every ship has one or more security officers available onboard. Larger ships will have an entire staff of security officers.

Cruise Ship Sanitation

News reports of Norwalk virus (Norovirus) outbreaks on cruise ships have been blown completely out of proportion. It is interesting that the Centers for Disease Control & Prevention (CDC) reported that of the Norovirus outbreaks from 1997-2000, only 10% were contracted in vacation settings which includes resorts and cruise ships.

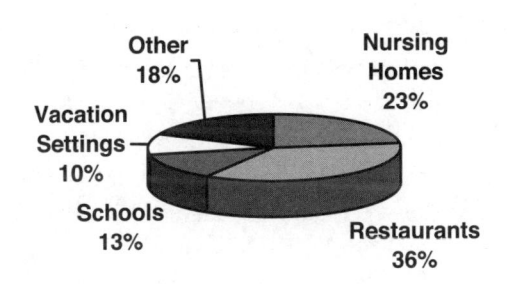

- Other 18%
- Nursing Homes 23%
- Vacation Settings 10%
- Schools 13%
- Restaurants 36%

Norovirus outbreaks from 1997-2000

In 2002, there were 23 million cases of Norovirus reported on land in the U.S., representing 8% of the population. 1 in 12 people were diagnosed with some form of the virus. During the same period, there were approximately 2000 cases reported in the cruise industry out of 7.5 million cruising passengers. That represents only 0.025% of the cruising population translating to only 1 in 4000 on cruise ships compared to 1 in 12 on land.

The fact is that cruise ships have an excellent reputation for preventing Norwalk and other viruses. In the early 1970's, the U.S. Centers for Disease Control and Prevention (CDC) established the Vessel Sanitation Program (VSP). This program was designed to assist cruise lines in the development and implementation of comprehensive sanitation programs. The CDC provides cruise lines with operational guidelines, reviews plans, and conducts on-site inspections on all new-build ships and renovations.

Every ship that has a foreign itinerary (calls on any port outside of the U.S.), carries 13 passengers or more, and calls on a U.S. port is subject to two unannounced inspections every year by VSP staff. The ships must meet or exceed criteria established in the VSP Operations Manual and score 86 or above on a 100-point scale. The scores can be viewed on the CDC web site at www.cdc.gov/nceh/vsp/.

Motion Sickness

The fear of motion sickness causes many to avoid taking a cruise. Today's modern cruise ships are extremely stable. In fact, it is not uncommon for people to be unaware that the ship is moving at all. Part of the reason for the smooth ride is that cruise ships are equipped with stabilizers. These long, wing-like structures extend outward from the vessel (under the water line) and can reduce the amount of side-to-side rolling motion by up to 90%.

> **Tip!** If motion sickness is a concern for you, make a visit to your local pharmacy where you can purchase medication to prevent motion sickness in the form of pills, patches and even wrist bands. Every ship also has an ample supply of motion sickness pills available at the reception desk, just in case.

Electrical Outlets

Since most cruise ships are constructed in Italy, Japan, Norway or Germany, they are designed to European electrical standards. However, most staterooms will have at least one 110 volt U.S. standard outlet in the stateroom and one in the bathroom. The one in the bathroom is only for use with an electric razor, *not* a hair dryer or curling iron. Since most ships provide hair dryers in the cabin, that is not a huge issue.

The single 110 outlet is usually located at the desk area. If you are like me and have a digital camera, video camera, laptop computer and walkie-talkies and cell phone, you will soon grow frustrated trying to figure out how to get the myriad of battery chargers all hooked up at the same time. The solution is a $10 mini power strip with 4 power outlets. You can buy these at just about any office supply or Wal-Mart and they don't take up too much space in your luggage.

If your cruise is taking you to Europe and you plan to stay a few extra days, it is a good idea to invest in a set of international plug adapters. Most computer and digital camera transformers will operate on 220 or 110, so as long as you can plug them into the outlet, they will work properly.

> **Tip!** Read the transformer label before plugging in to a foreign outlet to make sure it will operate on both 110 volt and 220 volt.

Enjoying Your Cruise

The responsibility for having a *perfect* cruise does not fall solely on the cruise line or your travel agent. A little preparation and planning can have a tremendous effect on the quality of your vacation experience. Also, by knowing what to expect once you get onboard, you will be armed with information that many passengers only gain after taking several cruises.

Packing for your Cruise

Most cruise lines will provide you with a guideline of what types of clothing you should pack based on the length of the cruise and the destination to which you will be cruising. You can also find this information in the cruise line's brochure or on their web site.

However, there are some little-known packing secrets that can make your cruise much more enjoyable.

Less is more. Most people, especially women, tend to pack way too many clothes for a cruise. Keep in mind that most cabins don't have a lot of closet and storage space. Also, cruising is much more casual than it was thirty years ago. Gone are the days where everyone dresses up for dinner each evening. The typical 7-night cruise will include two *formal* nights with the remainder being informal or casual.

- Formal – Men wear a tuxedo or jacket and tie. Ladies wear cocktail dresses, gowns or dressy slack suits.
- Informal – Men wear a jacket (tie optional). Ladies wear dresses or pantsuits.

- Casual – Men wear slacks and shirt with collar. Ladies wear dresses or slacks.

On most cruise ships today, what one wears on formal evenings is rather loosely enforced. American society is much more casual (sadly) than it once was. Of course, if you enjoy dressing up for dinner, you will not feel out of place if you choose to do so.

> **Rickee's Tip!** Most of my cruise wardrobe has been purchased at Chico's, a wonderful women's clothing store. (www.chicos.com). Their wrinkle-resistant, wash and wear 'Travelers Collection' consists of lots of mix-and-match separates made from a fabric that is not only nice-looking, but also truly pack-able. When I pack, I fold or roll my Chico's clothes and they come out of the suitcase without showing even the slightest hint of a wrinkle. I usually take a pair of black pants, a black skirt and a black jacket and accessorize with jewelry and different colored tops from the collection. This means I only have to pack one pair of shoes for evening wear. Check it out. It's a great store!

During the day, casual is the way to go. You can go anywhere on the ship before 6:00pm wearing shorts, sandals and a t-shirt. However, most cruise lines do not allow bare feet or swimsuits in the dining areas (except the Lido buffet near the pool) at anytime during the day. So ladies, make sure you take a cover up for your swim suit unless you want to change clothes before you eat lunch.

> **Warning!** No bare feet or swimsuits are allowed in the dining room for lunch on most ships. Shorts, t-shirts and sandals are generally acceptable.

Here is a quick list of things you should be sure to pack:

- SPF 30 sun block (even in Alaska)
- Tuxedo (optional) – Some cruise lines, such as Windstar and SeaDream Yacht Club, are 'Country Club Casual' every night, so you would never need a tuxedo. Also, a few cruise lines offer onboard tuxedo rental.
- Jacket, tie & dress shirt (gentlemen)

- Cocktail dress or formal gown (ladies)
- Shorts and t-shirts
- Swimsuit and cover-up
- Sweater or light jacket – It can sometimes get cold in the ship's theater and dining room.
- Deck Shoes or tennis shoes (comfortable)
- Exercise clothes
- Extra pair of glasses or contact lenses
- Sunglasses
- Hat, visor or cap
- Prescription medications
- Small first-aid kit with Band-Aids, antibiotic crème, Benadryl, etc.
- Names and addresses of friends and family to whom you wish to send postcards from the ship or foreign ports
- A fold-up tote bag to use to transport your purchases home
- Passports
- Travel alarm clock
- Photocopies of credit cards and passports
- Camera and film (You can buy film onboard most ships and can have your film developed onboard, too.)
- Walkie-talkie (optional)
- Small power strip – Useful for recharging multiple items from a single power outlet.
- Name, address and phone number of your travel agent
- Travel insurance documents
- Personal care products – Most ships will provide soap, shampoo, conditioner, and body lotion (as do most hotels), so packing these is optional. Check with your travel agent to find out if your cruise line offers these amenities.

Relax: In most cases, if you forget something minor, you can purchase it onboard the ship. Most ships have gift shops that sell sundries, film, batteries and even clothing on larger ships.

More Packing Tips for the Caribbean/Panama Canal

The sun is extremely powerful in the Caribbean and you can easily get sun-burned. Don't take this advice lightly; take a good sun-block with high a SPF rating of 30 or more. You don't want to spend a moment of your cruise soaking away sunburn pain in a tub of cold water. A wide-brimmed hat is also advisable. Sunglasses are a must.

Warning! You can get severely sun-burned just sitting around the pool for 30 minutes without protection.

More Packing Tips for Alaska

You may be surprised to learn that you can get sunburned in Alaska just as easily as in the Caribbean! If you are a snow skier, you know that the reflection of the sun off of snow can be very bright and damaging. If you plan to visit any glaciers in Alaska, you should pack sun-block.

There is a lot of breathtaking scenery in Alaska so take along one or more pair of good binoculars. You will be amazed at how much wildlife you can see from your own balcony or from the decks of the ship. If you have a 35mm camera, take a good telephoto or zoom lens.

The weather will most likely be cool so pack a light to medium weight jacket. Be prepared to dress in layers. It is often cooler in the mornings and evenings and can get warm in the afternoons. Check the cruise line documents to see what the expected temperatures will be during your cruise.

Tip! It is often rainy in Alaska so pack a couple of fold up rain ponchos that can easily fit over your existing clothing. It is also a good idea to take along a portable umbrella for each traveler.

Before you leave

Within three weeks of the sailing date of your cruise, you should receive your cruise tickets and other documentation from the cruise line or from your travel agent.

> **Important!** If you have not received your documents within three weeks of sailing, you should contact your travel agent.

Be sure to carefully read all of the documentation that you received from your travel agent and/or the cruise line. It contains lots of valuable information regarding what to pack and what to expect from your cruise experience. Here are some things you should check for in your documents:

- Make sure all airline tickets are included (if you purchased air through the cruise line) and that they are for the proper flight times and dates. Also check your seat assignments.
- Check your cruise tickets to make sure your name(s) are spelled correctly (matching your passports).
- Check the stateroom/cabin assignment.
- Make sure the sailing date is correct.
- Make sure the transfer vouchers are included (if you purchased transfers from the cruise line.)
- Check for any pre-cruise or post-cruise vouchers. These may include optional tours or hotel room nights you purchased from the cruise line or from your travel agent.
- Check your travel insurance documents to verify all information is correct.
- A "Welcome Aboard" brochure is usually included so that you can become familiar with your ship. Read it.

> **Important!** Some cruise lines request that you pre-register for your cruise before boarding the ship. This can be done through the cruise line's web site. Check your documents to see if this is a requirement.

Luggage Tags

Your documents will include some colored luggage tags. These tags will be used by the ship's porters to identify your luggage and deliver them to your stateroom. You should fill out all requested information on the back of the luggage tags completely. Make sure to include your stateroom number in the proper place on the tag.

If you are using the cruise line's transfers from the airport to the ship, you should place the tags on all luggage before you leave home (even hand-carried luggage).

If you are *not* using the cruise line's transfers to the ship, *do not* place the tags on the luggage before leaving home. Some cruise lines will have personnel at the airport to pull luggage off the baggage claim carousel based on the colored tags. You do not want your luggage mixed in by accident. Instead, you will need to take the completed luggage tags with you in your carry-on bag so that you can tag your luggage once you have retrieved your bags at the destination airport.

Tip! Be sure to remove all other airline and cruise line tags and stickers from your luggage before leaving home.

Information to leave behind

In the unlikely event of an emergency, it is a good idea that you leave some information with friends and family before departing for your cruise.

- A copy of the cruise itinerary with ports-of-call.
- The names and phone numbers of the various port agents for each port being visited (if this information was included with your cruise documents).
- The ship-to-shore phone number and fax number so that you can be reached aboard the vessel. This information should be included in your cruise documents, or can be found on the cruise line's web site.

- Your email address (assuming the ship has Internet access) or the ship assigned email address (check your documents for details).
- Your airline flight departure/arrival times and flight numbers.
- If you are staying at a hotel prior to the cruise or after the cruise, you should include any hotel information.

Get To the Airport Early

It would be a shame to miss your cruise just because you were late getting to the airport and missed your flight. Don't take any chances. You should check in for your flight at least one hour prior to departure time for domestic flights. On international flights, you should arrive at least 2 hours before your flight. Many airlines will overbook flights (sell more seats than the plane has). That means even though your ticket is paid for, you may not get a seat on the flight. The only way to ensure that you get on the flight is to show up early and check in to get your boarding pass.

Boarding the Ship

Now it is time for one of the most exciting parts of any cruise…getting onboard! The hassle of packing, getting to the airport, squeezing into the airplane seat and enduring little or no airline meal is about to pay off!

Airport Arrival

When you arrive at your destination airport, you are going to head immediately for baggage claim to meet your cruise line representative and claim your checked luggage. Back 'in the day' before increased airline security measures, cruise line representatives would actually meet you at your flight arrival gate and escort you to baggage claim. However, only ticketed passengers are now allowed in the gate areas of airports in the U.S.

When you arrive at baggage claim for your flight, look for a uniformed cruise line representative. Typically, he or she will be holding a sign with the name or logo of the cruise line. If you are using the cruise line's transfers to the ship, the representative should have your name on a list and will give you instructions on what to do. Typically, they will ask you to identify your luggage and show them your transfer voucher. You will then be escorted to a waiting motor coach or van. Be prepared to wait up to an hour before actually departing the airport. In some cases, the cruise line will wait for other flights to arrive so that the buses will be full before leaving.

Embarkation Process/Checking-in At the Pier

When you arrive at the pier, you will be directed to the check-in area. Some cruise lines will offer early embarkation for passengers who arrive prior to the stated embarkation time. Typical embarkation time is 3:00pm on cruises which are set to sail at 6:00pm. However, we have been allowed to board some ships as early as 12:30pm. Some cruise lines, however, are more rigid and stick to a strict embarkation schedule. Actual embarkation times can vary from one sailing to another. A lot depends on when the ship was cleared by U.S. Customs and how long it took to get everyone off the ship from the last cruise.

The check-in process at the terminal is fairly straightforward. There may be some documents that you need to fill-out and hand in to the representative, much like checking into a hotel. You will need to give them your passports (or other proof of citizenship), a major credit card (to cover any charges you make onboard), your cruise tickets and any other documents that have been previously requested. Don't be alarmed if the cruise line does not return your passports to you at this time. Many cruise lines will retain the passports until you disembark the ship at the end of the cruise. This is a common practice and should not be cause for alarm. This is why we recommend making photocopies of your passports to keep with you at all times.

> **Note:** It is common practice for most cruise lines to retain your passport in their care while you are onboard the vessel. This is not a cause for alarm.

The cruise line will then present you with (1) your stateroom key; (2) a boarding card and, (3) a charge card to be used for all onboard charges (cruise lines do not accept cash or credit cards for purchases made onboard the ship). On newer ships, you may get a single card (per person) which will serve as all three.

Welcome Aboard Photo

Once you have received your boarding card/room key, it is time to get onboard! Most cruise ships will have a ship's photographer on or near the gangway to take your picture. Your embarkation photo can be a great keepsake, so drop your carry-on bags, comb your hair and smile! Like all photos taken by the ship's photographer, you are under no obligation to purchase the embarkation photo.

Once your photo has been taken, you will most likely enter one of the ship's public areas (like the main lobby of a hotel). There will be ship's crew members there to greet you and direct you to your stateroom.

> **Note:** If you embark the ship early, you may not be able to go directly to your stateroom. This is because your room attendant needs time to get your room cleaned and prepared.

If the cruise line allows you to embark early, say around 1:00pm or so, it is possible that you may not be able to go directly to your stateroom. Typically, the ship will offer a buffet lunch or snacks during this time period. This is also a great time to explore the ship.

Changing Dining Room Reservations

One of the first things you should do when you get on board the ship is to check your dining reservations to make sure that they meet your approval. On most ships, the maitre d' will be available during embarkation to make changes to dining arrangements. He or she should have a printed layout of the dining room to which you are assigned showing your assigned table.

Cruise ship dining rooms have tables that seat from 2 to as many as 10 guests. It may not be possible for the maitre d' to accommodate everyone's special seating requests. However, the earlier you check with him/her, the better your chances.

If your ship offers two seatings (early and late) for dinner, make sure you are assigned to the one you requested when making your reservations.

Note: On ships that offer open-seating dining, it is not necessary to check with the maitre d' during embarkation. You will simply go to dinner whenever and with whomever you wish.

Now is also a good time to make advance reservations for dinner in any of the alternate dining restaurants onboard (if your ship has these venues).

Booking Tours and Excursions

Some cruise lines now offer you the opportunity to pre-book your shore excursions weeks before your cruise. However, most people book shore excursions once they board the ship. After you have verified your dining room reservations, you should head to the shore excursion desk (sometimes referred to as the tour desk) and book your shore excursions. Even if you are not sure you want to take a particular excursion that's scheduled for a few days into the cruise, go ahead and book it. Most cruise lines will allow you to cancel your reservation 24 hours before the ship arrives at the port where the excursion takes place (you should check with the Tour Desk to confirm the cancellation policy.)

Popular tours will sell out quickly so we highly recommend making your shore excursion reservations soon after you board the vessel.

Muster (Lifeboat Drill)

Every cruise ship is required to conduct a formal lifeboat drill, or "mustering", within 24 hours of passenger embarkation. In most cases, the drill will be conducted prior to the ship leaving port. Your cruise staff will provide ample instructions on the procedures for the drill. Every stateroom aboard a ship is assigned a muster station, a location on the ship to gather in the event of an emergency. On some ships, the muster stations are located in public lounges and bars; on others muster stations may be located outdoors on a specific deck adjacent to where your assigned lifeboat is located. During the drill, the Captain will announce from the bridge that the muster operation is about to begin, after which you will hear seven short blasts of the ship's whistle followed by one long blast. The "7 short 1 long" is the signal to return to your stateroom, gather your lifejacket and go immediately to your muster station.

In the event of a real emergency, you should also take any medications with you and dress in warm clothing. If you are unable to get back to your stateroom to retrieve your lifejacket, there are plenty of extra lifejackets at your muster station. Every lifeboat is designed to hold from 75 to 150 passengers and each is stocked with plenty of fresh water and food rations.

Fortunately, emergencies aboard cruise ships are extremely rare. But cruise lines take these drills very seriously and so should you.

Cruise Ship Dining

Dining is an important part of any cruise vacation. The cruise industry has a well-deserved reputation for providing guests with incredible dining choices. It has been said that on a cruise you can eat up to 7 meals a day if you work at it. You simply cannot have a great cruise without having a great dining experience!

Breakfast

There is no better way to start each day than with a hearty breakfast. Most of today's ships offer a wide variety of breakfast choices. Breakfast times vary from ship to ship, but generally they will begin serving between 7:30am and 8:00am. Early-risers can usually find coffee, tea and a selection of pastries somewhere on the ship as early as 6:30am. You can choose to dine in the main dining room where you will be served breakfast from a substantial menu, or you can enjoy a breakfast buffet on the Lido[1] deck. Many ships offer omelet stations where you can have eggs cooked to order, or a fresh omelet made with the ingredients of your choosing. Undoubtedly, there will be a huge selection of fresh fruit, cereals, scrambled eggs, bacon, ham, sausage, potatoes, pancakes and more. And of course, there will muffins, pastries, breads, croissants and doughnuts. The dining room offers a more sedate and relaxed setting for breakfast than the Lido buffet. Typically, the dining room is not as crowded or busy as the breakfast buffet. Here your waiter will take your order from the breakfast menu. And don't be shy, if you want Eggs Benedict with a side order of bacon and two banana pancakes it's perfectly permissible.

On Radisson Seven Seas Cruises, you can have a New York strip steak and eggs for breakfast in the dining room. Or, opt for my personal favorite, baby lamb chops and eggs.

Perhaps the best way to enjoy breakfast is in your underwear. No kidding. Most ships offer complimentary room service for breakfast. You may even find a breakfast menu order card that you can leave on your door each evening before you go to bed to have

---

[1] The term Lido comes from the British definition 'a recreational facility including a swimming pool'. Therefore, the Lido deck on a cruise ship refers to the deck where the pool is located.

breakfast delivered to your stateroom the next morning. Imagine dining on pastries and coffee while sitting on your private balcony as you watch the sun rise out of the ocean.

Lunch

When lunchtime rolls around, you will find your dining choices are even greater than those at breakfast! Lunch service will begin sometime between 11:30 and 12:30 depending on your ship. If you plan to spend your afternoon at the pool, you may want to check out the Lido buffet. Here you are likely to find a variety of salads, breads, sandwiches, hot entrees and desserts. With the exception of the salad bar, the selections on the buffet will change daily. It is not uncommon to see a carving station with a different roasted meat each day. Fresh pasta stations are also popular. Many ships have a poolside grill where you can get freshly grilled burgers, hot dogs, chicken sandwiches and fries.

If you prefer a more formal setting, you can enjoy lunch in the ship's dining room. As with breakfast, your waiter will present a lunch menu (which changes daily) from which you can order whatever you like.

> **Tip!** There is nothing that says you cannot eat lunch in the dining room, run up to the Lido deck and scarf down the best of the buffet, then go out to the pool grill and have a burger!

On Royal Caribbean's Voyager Class vessels (Voyager of the Seas, Explorer of the Seas, Adventurer of the Seas, Mariner of the Seas), there is a Johnny Rocket's diner where you can get a great Johnny Rocket's burger, hot dog, fries and/or onion rings topped off with a delicious milkshake. If you miss it for lunch, don't worry, they stay open until 11pm!

Carnival Spirit's Lido buffet has a variety of ethnic food stations preparing everything from pizza to Chinese food to Mexican food to Mediterranean cuisine.

On NCL's Norwegian Dawn, a poolside barbeque was available almost every single day offering grilled burgers, hot dogs, chicken and pork ribs (my personal favorite).

Silversea Cruises offers fresh Sushi on their Lido lunch buffet every day.

Afternoon Tea

This timeless British tradition has been preserved by most cruise lines. Afternoon tea takes a variety of forms depending on the ship and cruise line. Typically, afternoon tea is served at approximately 4:00pm in one of the ship's lounges. Traditional "formal" tea will offer brewed tea served by waiters or waitresses wearing white gloves. Traditional scones[1] and clotted cream are offered as well as other pastries and finger sandwiches. Oceania Cruises offers one of the most elaborate afternoon tea services we have seen. A choice of teas followed by a rolling cart filled with decadent delights can leave one feeling too guilty (and too full) to go to dinner.

Some of the larger ships have turned traditional afternoon tea into more of a 'snack time' with a choice of sandwiches, ice cream, pastries and a variety of beverages.

Dinner

At dinner, the cruise ship pulls out all the stops to give you a memorable dining experience each evening. If you are dining in the ship's main dining room, you will enjoy a different experience each evening. Menu choices change throughout the cruise so you will have an opportunity to try a lot of new, exciting dishes.

---

[1] A scone is a small, rich biscuit-like pastry or quick bread.

A 'typical' cruise ship dinner menu will have from four to six courses offered as follows:

- Appetizers
- Salads
- Soups
- Pasta
- Main Course
- Dessert

Some cruise lines combine the soup and salad as a single course and some do not offer a separate pasta course. Regardless of the number of courses, you are certain to have enough to choose from. It is perfectly acceptable to order an item from each course, or you can mix and match however you prefer. For example, you may want two different appetizers and no soup. Remember, this is *your* vacation; you can have whatever you want! If you have a difficult time deciding between the Prime Rib and the Lobster, order both! I have never had a cruise line refuse an order for an extra entrée. When I cruised on Royal Caribbean's Explorer of the Seas with my brother, we ordered a pasta dish each evening to share between us *in addition* to our main courses.

Good Etiquette – Do not be late for dinner if you have assigned seating, especially if you are seated at a table with other guests. It is not polite to make others wait for you to arrive before they order their meal. If you plan to dine elsewhere one evening, let someone at your table know in advance so that they can inform the waiter.

Each menu will offer multiple choices within each course category. There may be two or three appetizers, two salads, two soups, and three or four main courses offered. Typically, there will be a beef, chicken, lamb or pork, and seafood dish each evening. There is always a vegetarian selection available. If you do not see anything on the menu that interests you, most cruise lines offer some standard items which are always available.

Some standard 'always available' choices might be:

- Steak
- Grilled chicken breast
- Baked potato
- Spaghetti with tomato sauce
- House salad or Caesar salad

Most ships today also offer a 'healthy' menu for those on low-fat or low-sodium diets.

> **Tip!** If you have special dietary requirements, you should inform the cruise line 30 to 60 days prior to sailing.

You will find that your waiter will usually go out of his or her way to make sure you are satisfied. Part of the reason for this is that their livelihood depends entirely on gratuities. Most cruise line waiters are not paid a salary or an hourly wage. They are given room and board and they make their living on the tips they receive from their dining customers. Don't feel sorry for them. There are people standing in line in many countries to get these jobs. A good waiter on a cruise ship can earn a very nice annual income (possibly tax free) and have a clean, safe work environment. The waiter and his or her assistant are well aware of the fact that their income for the week will be directly related to how satisfied you are with the service they provide. Even though they cannot control how the food comes out of the galley, they will be the first one to offer to make a replacement if something is not to your liking. You could say that they are your *advocate* when it comes to dining.

> **Tip!** Ask your waiter to make a suggestion for dinner. He or she knows what 'looks good' in the galley that evening and they will generally steer you in the right direction. Remember, they have a vested interest in your satisfaction.

If you enjoy a bottle of wine with your meal, your waiter can provide you with a wine list. Some ships have one or more Sommeliers (wine stewards) who specialize in selling wines. The Sommelier will bring you a wine list and can make suggestions based on the selections available on board. There should also be a few wines available by the glass. The wine prices are generally comparable to any restaurant on land[1]. If you order a bottle of wine with a meal and do not finish the bottle, most ships will store the wine for you so that you can enjoy it the next evening. This is true in most ship lounges as well. If you purchase a bottle of wine in port and bring it to the table, the ship may charge a corkage fee.

Alternate Restaurants

Some newer ships offer other upscale dining choices as an alternative to the main dining room. Typically, these restaurants will charge a nominal service charge from $12.50 per person to $25 per person. In our experience, these alternate restaurants generally offer better quality food and service than what is available in the main dining room. The reasons for this are fairly obvious. It is easier to control quality when you only serve 100 to 200 guests per evening in a smaller setting. The main dining room may serve as many as 3,000 people each evening.

You will need advance reservations for these alternate restaurants and embarkation time is a great time to make these reservations.

> **Tip!** It is always easier to get a reservation in an alternate restaurant for the first night or last night of the cruise. Most passengers don't even think about dining in other venues until the second or third day of the cruise.

I should emphasize that these restaurants are completely *optional*. You are not required to pay for any meals on a cruise ship. I have heard some passengers complain that the cruise lines have decreased the quality of the meals served in the main dining room so that you now have to pay to get the same quality meal that used to be included in your cruise fare. This is simply not true. I have

---

[1] Wine with dinner is complimentary on Radisson Seven Seas Cruises, Silversea Cruises, Seabourn and SeaDream Yacht Club.

not noticed any significant decrease in the quality of food served in main dining rooms over the years. Let's face it, you simply cannot serve 2,000 to 3,000 meals in an hour and have gourmet quality food. That being said, the food served in most cruise ship dining rooms is surprisingly good and always plentiful.

The new breed of upscale alternate restaurants is definitely a step up from main dining. In fact, some of the best meals we have had on land or sea have been in these venues. We have never had a meal in one of these restaurants that was not well worth the service charge.

> **Recommendation** – If your ship offers an upscale alternate restaurant, treat yourself to the experience one evening.

Here are some of the alternate restaurants we can highly recommend:

- Carnival Spirit – Nouveau Supper Club
  2002 Best Alternate Dining at Sea Award Winner from CruiseReport.com
- Holland America Zuiderdam – Odyssey Restaurant
- Royal Caribbean Explorer of the Seas – Portofino Grill
- Royal Caribbean Serenade of the Seas – Portofino Grill
  2003 Best Alternate Dining at Sea Award Winner from CruiseReport.com
- Royal Caribbean Serenade of the Seas – Chops Grille
  2003 Best Alternate Dining at Sea Award Winner from CruiseReport.com
- Radisson Seven Seas Mariner – Signatures Restaurant
- Silversea Silver Wind – Saletta Restaurant
- Radisson Seven Seas Voyager – Signatures Restaurant
- NCL Norwegian Dawn – Le Bistro
- NC Norwegian Dawn – La Trattoria Italian

Midnight Buffet

The midnight buffet is a long-standing cruise tradition that is quickly slipping away on most cruise lines. Typically, the dining room staff prepares a selection of desserts, sandwiches and salads. However, once during the cruise there might be a Gala Midnight Buffet which is a culinary spectacular. Take your camera along with your appetite. The ice sculptures are unbelievable!

24-Hour Room Service

Just about every cruise line offers a 24-hour complimentary room service menu. For those with late night munchies, you may be able to get pizza, cookies or sandwiches delivered to your stateroom. We enjoy an order of cheese and crackers delivered to the stateroom around 4:30pm each afternoon. When we watch a movie in the stateroom, we have even been known to order popcorn from room service. A few cruise lines will extend their room service menu to include items from the evening's dinner menu during evening dining hours.

Low-Carb Cruising

Just because you are on the Atkins® or South Beach Diet® does not mean you have to avoid taking the vacation of a lifetime. In fact, I am convinced that a cruise is the best vacation for low-carb dieters.

Unfortunately, Americans equate cruising with gorging. Most people think that gaining 7 to 10 pounds during a cruise is acceptable. For years the cruise industry has attracted passengers to its ships with promises of 7 meals per day or more. Certainly, the temptation to overeat and overindulge is amplified on a cruise. Not only is food available 24 hours a day, but it is included in the price of the cruise. Some people feel 'cheated' if they do not eat themselves into a coma at every opportunity; otherwise, they paid for something they did not get.

Therefore, to enjoy your cruise without sabotaging your weight management/loss program requires a completely different frame of mind. Fortunately, you have probably already undergone a significant change in thinking by committing yourself to a low-carb lifestyle. So when preparing for a low-carb cruise, there are really two things that you have to keep in mind:

1. Define a plan for limiting the carbs during your cruise.

2. Accept that cruising without carbs can be enjoyable. You don't have to have the pies, cakes and breads to have a great time on a cruise. Look at it this way, it is better to be on a low-carb lifestyle and on a cruise than on a low-carb lifestyle and at home!

How to Limit Carbs During Your Cruise

It is actually very easy to limit carbs while on a cruise. Since starting the Atkins' Diet in July of 2002, I have been on more than 15 cruises. During that time, I have been able to successfully lose 35 pounds and keep the weight off. The great thing about a cruise is you have so many choices of proteins and vegetables that it is actually easier and more enjoyable to adhere to a low-carb regimen on a ship than on land.

Plan Ahead - Pack Low-Carb Snacks

> **Tip!** Take a couple of the low-carb candies to dinner each evening to eat as your dessert.

There are so many great low-carb snacks available on the market now, especially the candies and breakfast bars. I always pack a half dozen Advantage™ (Atkins) food bars for every cruise. I sometimes will eat these for breakfast instead of bacon and eggs. The new low-carb Russell Stover candies are delicious and very easy to pack. Keep the candy in your in-room refrigerator to prevent it from melting.

Eat Breakfast in the Dining Room - Rather than going to the breakfast buffet on the Lido Deck, try going to the main dining room for breakfast. Here you can order from a set menu and just about every cruise ship will offer you a fresh, delicious omelet. Go ahead and pack it with ham, onion and cheese if you want, it is all legal! A side order of bacon or ham is a delicious addition. Remember, it is all paid for, so enjoy. If you love Eggs Benedict, GO FOR IT. Just don't eat the English muffin. The eggs, Hollandaise sauce and Canadian bacon are all legal. On Radisson Seven Seas Cruises, Silversea Cruises and SeaDream Yacht Club, you can even order a breakfast steak or baby lamb chops to accompany your omelet.

Save the Buffet for Lunch - Most ships offer a buffet lunch on the Lido Deck (near the pool). There are all kinds of low-carb items you can enjoy on the lunch buffet. There are lots of salad options, just avoid the pasta salads and fruit salads which tend to be full of carbs. There is almost always a carving station with roast beef, lamb, turkey or pork. There will also be a selection of green vegetables.

Things to look for:
- Carving station
- Green salads
- Green vegetables (spinach, green beans, etc.)
- Whole grain rolls or bread
- Bouillon or broth

Things to Avoid:
- Croutons
- Sweet dressings like French, 1000 Island, etc.
- Pasta salads and pasta in general
- Potatoes
- Desserts
- Breads other than whole grain
- Creamy soups
- Pizza

Be sensible

One misconception about a low-carb diet is that you can eat all the steak, butter, cheese and eggs you want and still lose weight. While that is true in theory, it is not a healthy low-carb lifestyle. If you want to load up on large quantities to satisfy your hunger, do it with green vegetables and salads, not fatty beef and eggs. It is better to have an 8-oz Rib Eye with lots of salad and green beans than a 16-oz. Rib Eye and no vegetables. A great cruise lunch might consist of a huge chef's salad with lots of lettuce, cheese, eggs, ham and turkey. Top it off with a balsamic vinegar and oil dressing, (or bring your own low-carb dressing) and you have a filling and satisfying lunch!

> **Tip!** If a food item is white or yellow, it is probably full of carbohydrates. For example, white flour, bread, corn, potatoes, sugar, yellow squash are all high in carbs. As a rule of thumb, substitute something green for something white or yellow!

Don't Be Afraid to Ask for Something Special - You might be surprised to learn that cruise lines are generally very willing to fulfill special requests in the dining room. This is something I take full advantage of, especially at dinner each evening. Every cruise line dining room has a Maitre d' or Dining Room Captain and they are a low-carb dieter's best friend. Take a few minutes to meet with the maitre d' when you board the ship and let him know that you do not eat starchy vegetables and would like to have green vegetables with dinner each evening. In some cases, they may not be able to fill your request the first evening, but should be able to do so every night thereafter.

During an Alaska cruise on Celebrity Summit, our waiter brought me creamed spinach every evening without my having to ask a second time. Impressive for a ship with 2,500 passengers! On some of the smaller ships, like Silversea Silver Wind and SeaDream Yacht Club, I was able to get even more specific about how I like the spinach prepared with garlic and mushrooms!

On the larger ships with assigned seating, your waiter is your ally. He knows that his gratuity is based on how satisfied you are when you leave the table each evening. If you tell him what you want, he or she should work extra hard to make sure your wishes are met. If he or she does not, ask the head waiter to move you to another table. Cruise lines, by and large, want to you to be a satisfied customer, but they are not good at reading your mind. Don't be afraid to ask for something if you do not see it on the menu.

- Request green vegetables each evening from your waiter or maitre d'
- Order a Caesar salad each evening
- At the pool grill, ask for two hamburger patties with no bun (and skip the fries!)
- At the bar, ask for Michelob Ultra (low-carb beer) or Miller Lite

Watch What You Drink - I always drink more alcoholic beverages on a cruise than I normally drink. I think this is partially because I do not have to drive home from the bar! However, some drinks can be loaded with carbs. Avoid all frozen drinks such as Margaritas, Pina Colada, Daquiri, etc. Even a Mojito has a lot of sugar in it. White wine is better than red and even a glass of champagne won't completely blow your regimen. Hard liquor has no carbs, but I don't know of any diet that recommends excessive amounts of hard liquor.

Drinks to avoid:
- Frozen drinks
- Mojito
- Tonic drinks (Gin & tonic, Vodka tonic, etc.)
- All soft drinks with sugar
- Lemonade
- Bailey's, Sambuca, Kahlua, or any 'dessert' drinks (they are pure sugar)

Drinks to enjoy:
- White wine
- Champagne (in moderation)
- Hard liquor (scotch, vodka, gin, etc.)
- Diet soft drinks
- Diet or sugar-free tonic
- Club soda
- Water
- Iced tea

If you enjoy mixed drinks with tonic (i.e. Gin & Tonic or Vodka Tonic) ask the bartender if they offer diet or sugar-free tonic. Regular tonic is full of sugar and has a very high carb count. You may even consider bringing a 6-pack of diet tonic onboard with you. You should not have any problem getting this through security. If they say anything, tell them that it is a dietary requirement.

Enjoy Low-Carb Snacks - Another thing I enjoy is having a before-dinner snack around 4:30 each afternoon. This is especially important if I am dining later than 7:00pm. Just about every cruise line offers a cheese and cracker plate from room service. The cheese makes an excellent low-carb snack to tide you over until dinner. Sometimes we will take our cheese and wine onto our balcony and enjoy it along with the view.

On the luxury lines, you can get your cheese plate delivered just about anywhere on the ship. Get to know your bartender at your favorite lounge and let him know that you want a cheese plate every afternoon when you come in for your favorite beverage. Silversea, SeaDream and Radisson Seven Seas are all great at handling this type of request.

Beware of "No Sugar Added" Desserts - Don't be suckered in by the 'no sugar added' or 'zero-zero' claims on desserts and assume that these desserts are low in carbs. Just because the galley does not add sugar does not mean that there is no sugar in the dessert. If you are really disciplined, you could order a 'zero-zero' ice cream, eat about two or three bites and push the rest away. Why play with temptation? A good dessert alternative is a decaf Cappuccino (if you like coffee). A better choice is to bring your own low-carb candy to dinner with you each night to enjoy with coffee or tea.

Use the Fitness Center - One of the best features of virtually every ship sailing today is the fitness center. Most ships offer lots of cardiovascular equipment, fitness classes, weight machines and free weights. By exercising just 30 to 45 minutes every day during your cruise, you can stave off a lot of your hunger pangs and feel better about yourself to boot. Regular exercise is a vital part of a healthy low-carb lifestyle (or any lifestyle for that matter).

Treat Yourself One Night - If you are tempted to blow it, pick one night late in the cruise itinerary and designate it as your "night to celebrate". Perhaps the last formal night would be a good choice, when the Chef will most likely prepare his most exotic dishes. If you are going to blow it, you might as well enjoy a chocolate soufflé or cherries jubilee, right? Remember, once you go over your grams per day carb limit, the additional carbs are really insignificant.

The logic behind selecting a night near the end of the cruise is that there is not much time left in case you become tempted to blow your diet for the rest of the cruise!

You Can Cruise and Lose - You might be surprised to know that you can enjoy a substantial amount of food on your cruise and actually lose weight! Imagine how good you will feel when you get home from your vacation and are not carrying an extra 7 to 10 pounds.

Captain's Welcome Reception

The Captain's Welcome Reception is traditionally held on the second evening of the cruise and is a great opportunity to get dressed up, make new friends, and meet the Captain. Traditionally, this has always been a formal event and many cruise lines still adhere to this tradition. However, cruising is much more casual than it was 20 or 30 years ago. It is generally acceptable for men to wear a dark suit and tie instead of a tuxedo to these events. Ladies should wear long dresses or cocktail attire. Of course, you should check your cruise line documents for details on attire for your particular cruise.

The reception is usually held in one of the ship's lounges or in a large public area. You can enjoy music from the ship's orchestra, and complimentary cocktails and hors d'oeuvres. You may have an opportunity to have your picture taken with the Captain by the ship's photographer as you enter the reception.

The reception is usually held in the early evening and is often followed by the Captain's Welcome Aboard Dinner. The meals served on 'formal' nights are usually a little more elaborate than the dinners served on other nights.

The Nightlife

You may be wondering what there is to do on your cruise after dinner. Needless to say, today's cruise ships offer a variety of activities and entertainment options after the sun goes down. For obvious reasons, there are a lot more nightlife options on a large cruise ship than on a small one. It is not uncommon for a ship to have as many as 10 lounges/bars open from 6:00pm until after midnight. Here are just a few of the things that you can do on your cruise before returning to your stateroom.

Theater show – All but the smallest ships will have some evening entertainment. Larger ships will have production shows that rival Las Vegas productions. There is a different show each evening. On a seven-night cruise, there will usually be two or three 'production' shows performed by the ship's troupe of singers and dancers. The other evenings may feature top comedians, magicians, acrobatic acts, solo musicians and jugglers. One evening (generally toward the end of the cruise) is reserved for the passenger talent contest. If your cruise has a passenger talent show, don't miss it!

Casino – You can always stop by the ship's casino to make a donation if you are the gambling type. The slots are Rickee's weakness. OK, so I play the one-armed bandits myself. You may be surprised to find how well-equipped your ship's casino is. Some of the larger ships have hundreds of slot machines along with Black Jack tables, Roulette wheel, Craps table, and Caribbean Stud Poker.

Cigar lounge – There is nothing quite as relaxing as sitting in a big leather chair with a great cigar sipping on a glass of cognac. Cigar lounges are a relatively new feature on most new ships. Michael's Club on Celebrity Cruises' ships is a model cigar lounge that even offers hand-rolled cigars!

Champagne Bar – Royal Caribbean ships feature a special Champagne Bar which is a beautiful and relaxing place to enjoy a glass or bottle of your favorite bubbly. Of course, you can order champagne in any bar or lounge on any ship, but it is nice to have a lounge dedicated to the sparkling wines. Remember, if you order a bottle and do not finish it, the ship will keep the bottle chilled for you to enjoy the next day.

Music, music, music – If you enjoy listening to live music, then you are in the right place. You will find a variety of musical acts in the various lounges throughout the ship. You will probably be able to select from Jazz, Classical, Country & Western, Latin and Big Band. Some musical acts will appear in the same lounge each evening so you will have an opportunity to visit different lounges and hear each musical act at least once during your cruise. Or, you may find a favorite lounge or act and go back each night.

Ballroom dancing – There is almost always somewhere on every ship where you can try out your favorite salsa, tango, cha-cha or waltz steps to the music of a live band. Many ships also have dance hosts and instructors who give lessons as part of the ship's daytime activities.

Disco – You can dance the night away to the beat of the disco on most large ships. The disco is a great place to let your hair down and let it all hang out (so to speak). It is not uncommon for the disco to stay open until the wee hours of the morning.

Dance under the stars – If you prefer a more romantic way to dance, why not join the band out by the pool and dance under the stars. There is nothing like it anywhere else in the world.

Moonlight walk – Of course, you don't have to dance at all. Sometimes a quiet, romantic walk around the Promenade Deck is the perfect end to a perfect evening. Even on a ship with 3,000 other passengers, you will be amazed at how easy it is to find a quiet, romantic spot under the stars.

Hot tub – I have never done this myself, but I have seen it done. Some ships keep their hot tubs open until midnight and it looks like a fun way to soak away dinner before going to bed. However, keep in mind, swimsuits are required!

Big screen movie – Many ships will feature a recent hit movie in their onboard theatre or in one of the lounges. On Celebrity Summit, we could not find a seat for an 11pm showing of My Big Fat Greek Wedding (2002).

Sing-along bar – A trademark of Carnival ships is the sing-along bar. Here you can sit at a bar surrounding a piano and request songs from the piano player. Everybody can sing along and have a great time.

Karaoke – My personal, all-time, favorite thing to do at night on a cruise ship is watch people get up and attempt to sing in front of other people. Of course, I don't have the courage to do it myself, but it is great fun to watch. If you have ever wanted to try out for American Idol, here is your chance to practice in front of a live audience.

Daytime Activities Onboard

There is probably no other place in the world where there are as many different activities going on at one time as on a cruise ship. You will never be bored on a cruise unless, of course, you choose to be.

Go ashore – By far the most popular daytime activity on a cruise is exploring the various ports where the ship stops during the cruise. When your ship is in port, you can take a ship-sponsored shore excursion or simply go ashore and wander around on your own. In many Caribbean and Alaskan ports, the ship docks literally right in town.

> **Caution** – You should always check with the ship's tour desk to inquire about the safety of 'going it alone' in a port. Most of the time this is not an issue, but it is always wise to ask.

Stay in shape – You may want to work off some of the extra eating you will no doubt do aboard your cruise by spending some quality time in the ship's fitness center.

Take a fitness class* – Your ship's fitness instructor will offer a variety of fitness classes throughout the cruise. You will probably be able to choose from yoga, Pilates, kick-boxing, stretching, walking, abdominal workout, etc. These classes are a great way to stay in shape and meet new friends. Be aware that some cruise lines charge a fee for these classes.

Enjoy the spa – Why not pamper yourself with a world-class spa treatment?

Go online – You could go to the Internet café and check your email, or your stock portfolio.

Relax by the pool – Throw on your swimsuit and head to the pool.

Wine tasting* – Many ships offer one or more wine tasting sessions throughout the cruise. Sometimes, a fee is charged for this activity.

Lectures* – The daily port lecture is a great way to learn about the next day's port-of-call. Many ships offer enrichment lectures conducted by professionals from a variety of fields.

Play team trivia* – Want to test your knowledge? Team trivia is a great shipboard activity and the competition gets pretty heated. If you are good at Trivial Pursuit, you should give this a try.

Dance lessons* – Why not learn a few new steps from your on board dance instructors?

Art auction* – If you are an art enthusiast, a collector, or just want a new piece of art for your home, the art auctions at sea offer great bargains and are a lot of fun. Sometimes you even get a free glass of champagne just for attending.

Read a book – Of course, you don't have to do anything if you don't want to. You could just go to the ship's library, pick out a good book, find a nice quiet spot (say, on your private balcony perhaps?) and read.

Play cards or board games – Most ships have a card room set up with tables and chairs conducive to a friendly game of cards. Usually, a large assortment of board games is also available.

Take Bridge lessons – Bridge lesson for all levels of expertise are sometimes offered.

* These scheduled activities typically last for 1 hour or less.

Going Ashore

One the great features of a cruise is the ability to visit new destinations and experience new cultures. Depending on your itinerary, your ship should stop in as many as 4 or 5 ports during a 7-night cruise and more on longer voyages.

In some ports the ship will be docked. This is convenient because it allows you to simply walk off the ship and begin exploring. Some docks are located within walking distance of shops, restaurants and other points of interest while others may require a short taxi or shuttle ride to get to town. There are some ports where large ships cannot dock and must remain anchored a mile or more from shore. In these ports, you are required to tender[1] to shore. Most cruise ships will use two or more of their lifeboats to conduct the tender operations. On a large ship, it can take two or more hours to get everyone ashore since each tender only holds 75 to 150 people.

The first thing you have to decide is whether you want to go ashore on your own, or as part of a ship-organized shore excursion. Your ship will offer several different shore excursion experiences for each port. Here are just a few of the possible shore excursion opportunities you might choose:

- Mountain bike riding
- Horseback riding
- Hiking
- ATV tour
- Four-wheel Drive tour
- Helicopter tour
- Glacier tour (Alaska)
- Nature walking tour
- Shopping tour
- Island tour by bus
- Whale-watching (Alaska, Southern Caribbean, Hawaii)
- Swimming with the dolphins
- Swimming with stingrays

Tip! When you take a ship's shore excursion, you never have to worry about getting back to the ship late and being left behind. The ship will wait for all guests on ship-organized shore excursions to return before leaving for the next port-of-call.

---

[1] Tender - A vessel attendant on other vessels, especially one that ferries supplies between ship and shore.

As you can see, there are a lot of choices to suit every type of interest. And this is just a small sampling of the shore excursions offered. Of course, you may simply want to get off the ship and walk around town, do some shopping and have lunch at a local restaurant. Or, you may want to hire a taxi and get a private tour of the island or port city.

> **Our Recommendation** – If you are a first-time cruiser or are cruising to a port for the first time, purchase one of the ship's shore excursions. The hordes of vendors awaiting your arrival in port to aggressively peddle their wares or offer private tours can sometimes be a little overwhelming.

Whenever you choose to venture out on your own in a port, you should be aware of several things:

1. You are in a foreign country (most likely) so you should be aware of the local customs. You can get information about this from the ship's Tour Desk.

2. Always carry a photocopy of your passport with you when in a foreign country.

3. Take one credit card and leave the others locked in the safe in your stateroom.

4. Only take as much cash as think you will need for the day. Check with the Purser's office on your ship to determine if the merchants will accept U.S. dollars or if you need to exchange some money into local currency.

5. Leave your flashy jewelry in the safe in your stateroom.

When going ashore on your own, it is *your* responsibility to get back to the ship before its scheduled departure time. Trust me, if you are not back on time, the ship will leave without you. It will be *your* responsibility to get transportation to the next port-of-call so that you can re-join the ship.

> Most, if not all, Caribbean ports will accept US dollars.

Dining Out in Port

One of the exciting things to do when on a cruise is try out the local cuisine of some of the places you visit. Of course, you can eat on the ship for free, but you may want to try something a little different and unique. The ship's Tour Desk or Concierge should be able to recommend good local restaurants for you to try. Chances are the ship visits the port regularly and the crew eat out when they go ashore.

You should always exercise caution when eating in a foreign country as health regulations vary greatly. If you are eating at a known chain restaurant (like Carlos and Charlie's or T.G.I. Fridays) you are probably safe no matter where you are. Always drink only bottled water, soft drinks or beer. Never drink tap water in a foreign country. Bon appetite!

> **Tip!** Always take a bottle of water with you when you go ashore. Never drink the local water in foreign ports. Check with the Tour Desk for local restaurant recommendations before eating in port.

Duty-Free Shopping

One of the most popular activities on any cruise (especially in the Caribbean) is duty-free shopping.

In our opinion, the best Caribbean ports for duty-free shopping are:

- St. Thomas
- Phillipsburg, St. Martin
- George Town, Grand Cayman
- Cozumel, Mexico

The term "duty-free" actually refers to the fact that the goods are free of taxes in the country where you are buying them. This does not necessarily mean that the items are duty-free when you get back to the United States.

Your purchases are subject to U.S. duty if you exceed your standard exemption when you bring the merchandise back into the U.S. at the end of the cruise. Every U.S. citizen is allowed to bring a certain amount of purchases back into the U.S. exempt from taxes. Remember, items purchased on the ship count in your duty-free total.

Articles sold in duty-free shops are meant to be taken out of the country; they are not meant to be used, worn, eaten, drunk, etc., in the country where you purchased them.

The standard allowance for a U.S. citizen was recently raised to $800 for duty-free goods if you are returning from anywhere other than a Caribbean Basin country or a U.S. possession such as the U.S. Virgin Islands (St. Thomas, St. John, St. Croix), American Samoa or Guam. This can include 1 liter of alcohol if you are over the age of 21, 1 carton of cigarettes and 100 cigars. This $800 allowance is *per person including infants and children*. Family members who live in the same home and return together to the United States may combine their personal exemptions. This is called a *joint declaration*. This comes in handy if one person in the family has exceeded their personal limit and the others have not. By combining the exemptions, no duty has to be paid as long as the total to be declared is under the allowed limit.

Allowances for what you can bring back are different depending on what country you visit. For example, for certain destinations (including Antigua, Aruba, Bahamas, Barbados, Belize, the British Virgin Islands, Costa Rica, Dominica, Dominican Republic, El Salvador, Grenada, Guatemala, Guyana, Haiti, Honduras, Jamaica, Montserrat, Netherlands Antilles, Nicaragua, Panama, St. Lucia, St. Kitts and Nevis, Saint Vincent and the Grenadines, and Trinidad and Tobago), the duty-free allowance is $600 and 2 liters of alcohol as long as one liter was produced in one of these countries.

Because Puerto Rico is part of the U.S., goods purchased there are entirely duty-free. You can bring back $1,200 worth of goods duty-free from the U.S. Virgin Islands, American Samoa or Guam. This includes 1,000 cigarettes, but 800 of them must have been acquired in one of these U.S. insular possessions. Similarly, you may include five liters of alcoholic beverages in your duty-free exemption, but one of them must be a product of an insular possession. Four may be products of other countries. Any goods purchased in Mexico and Canada can also be brought back to the U.S. duty-free or at a reduced duty rate.

If you visit more than one country, the duty-free situation can get complicated. For example, if you shop at an island with a $600 duty-free allowance and then travel to the U.S. Virgin Islands, you will be taxed on anything exceeding $600 in purchases from the first island, but then can spend another $600 in the Virgin Islands since the duty-free limit there is $1,200.

While you are shopping, keep in mind that certain items are not allowed to be brought into the United States. If you are caught with any of these items, the items will be confiscated; you could face a stiff fine, and in the case of Cuban cigars, even criminal charges. Some of these forbidden items are:

- Live animals
- Items made from endangered species such as anything made of elephant ivory, items made from sea turtles, items made from coral reefs, items made from crocodile skin or furs from specific kinds of exotic cats
- Fresh meat
- Fresh produce
- Cuban cigars
- Antiques (items over 100 years old sold without the proper permit)
- Cultural artifacts (unless items are accompanied by an export permit issued by the country of the item's origin)
- Narcotics, including drugs that are legal here with a prescription
- More than $10,000 in currency

The U.S. Customs Service offers all kinds of information about what you can and can't bring back into the country as well as lots of help understanding all the rules and regulations dealing with bringing items into the country. Visit the Customs Service web site at www.customs.gov where you can order the booklet *Know Your Customs Before You Go, Customs Hints for Returning U.S. Citizens.* You can also write to U. S. Customs Service, P.O. Box 7407, Washington, D.C. 20044, to request a copy of this booklet and further information.

Cruise Line Recommended Shops

Many cruise lines offer a Port Shopping Guide listing 'recommended' merchants who are 'backed' by the cruise line. Cruise lines charge these merchants to advertise in the cruise lines' shopping programs. These merchants will be mentioned frequently during your port shopping talks. The cruise line will offer to guarantee any purchases made from these merchants for 30 days after your cruise. For example, if you buy gold or jewelry, then return home only to find that your new diamond is actually a piece of glass, the cruise line will make sure you get a suitable replacement or refund. While this program can offer a lot of 'peace of mind' to cruise passengers shopping for the first time outside the country, it does limit you to a specific group of merchants. Merchants pay the cruise lines to be a part of this marketing program. Actually, they pay a substantial amount to participate. Plus, the merchants must agree to repair or replace any items within 30 days of the purchase date. So in reality, it is the merchant who is guaranteeing the purchase.

The downside to the cruise line marketing programs is that only the bigger merchants can afford to participate. Some of the smaller shops, which are quality merchants, can be passed over. One such merchant is Ballerina Jewelers in St. Thomas and St. Martin. On our first cruise in 1997, Rickee purchased a diamond tennis bracelet and a multi-colored gold bracelet from Ballerina. The sales people were professional, helpful and not pushy. We even receive Christmas cards from Ballerina every year. Each time we return to St. Thomas or St. Martin, we stop by to say hi, do a little shopping or have our jewelry cleaned (for free!). One of Ballerina's owners said they had to stop participating in the cruise line marketing programs because of the cost. Shop around and compare prices before you buy.

Be aware that incredible savings are not a sure thing. Sometimes you can by an item for less at home. Do your research before you cruise to see what an item would cost in the U.S. I purchased a watch from a reputable dealer over the Internet and paid less than I could have bought the watch for in the Islands. Of course, this won't work for handcrafted items made locally on each island.

Staying Connected

For decades one of the obstacles that prevented busy people from taking a cruise was the inability to communicate with people at home or at the office. For as long as I can remember, cruise ships have always had ship-to-shore telephone technology, but it is very expensive. A typical ship-to-shore phone call can cost as much as $7.95 per minute!

In addition to ship-to-shore phone calls, almost every ship today has Internet access. Generally, there are several computer terminals located in an Internet café which can be accessed 24 hours a day. On Royal Caribbean's newest ships, there are Internet terminals located throughout the ship in various public locations. As you might imagine, there is a charge for Internet access. A typical charge is around 50 cents per minute, with some cruise lines charging as much as 95 cents per minute. Some cruise lines offer discounts for purchasing 100 minute or more packages. Regardless of the cost, it is a fraction of the cost of a ship-to-shore phone call and makes sending and receiving email while at sea a reality. Connection speeds are about what you would expect from an average dial-up Internet account, not too fast. But, the technology seems to be improving all the time.

NCL offers Wi-Fi[1] wireless Internet access on its newest ships. You can use your Wi-Fi compatible laptop to access the Internet in various "hot spots" around the ship. On Norwegian Dawn, I was able to work using my laptop in the coffee bar each morning. If you do not have a Wi-Fi card, NCL will loan you one to use while on board. There is an additional fee for Wi-Fi access. Some other cruise lines are experimenting with Wi-Fi, so you can probably expect to see it showing up on other ships in the near future.

Note: Other cruise lines are beginning to add Wi-Fi. Seabourn recently announced Wi-Fi on their yachts and Carnival offers it on some of their ships.

Oceania offers Internet access from your stateroom through a dial-up system. Basically, you use your modem to dial into the ship's network which connects you to the Internet. The onboard technician will set everything up for you on your laptop. Again, there is an additional fee for this service.

Another popular form of communication is the cell phone. Some cell phone providers actually have service in Caribbean ports of call and, of course, most all cell phones have service when you travel in Alaska. The phones do not work once the ship gets too far from land, but while the ship is docked, you can call home for a lot less than it would cost you to use the ship-to-shore radio phone.

New Technology! We have heard rumors that soon cruise ships will be equipped with new technology to allow your cell phone to function no matter where the ship is.

---

[1] Wi-Fi stands for **Wi**reless **Fi**delity and is meant to be used generically when referring to any 802.11 network. In layman's terms, Wi-Fi refers to a wireless network.

Winning in the Casino

Cruise ship casinos have come a long way in the past 20 years. As you might expect, the bigger the ship, the bigger and more elaborate the casino. Today's cruise ship casinos offer all of the most popular games:

- Slot machines (quarter slots & dollar slots)
- Poker machines
- Black Jack
- Craps
- Roulette
- Caribbean Stud Poker

Royal Caribbean's Casino Royale is one of the liveliest places on the ship in the evenings. You really feel as if you are in a Vegas casino! NCL and Carnival have slot player's clubs that allow you to earn credits to purchase merchandise based on the amount of play. They also have a modern ticket pay system where the slot machine spits out a ticket with a bar code signifying your winnings (when you cash out of a machine). You can take the ticket to the cashier to exchange for money, or insert the ticket into another machine and keep playing! No more dirty hands from scooping up quarters.

The main difference between a cruise ship casino and Las Vegas is the complimentary cocktails. On the cruise ship, there aren't any. You will have to pay for your drinks as you play, that is, of course, unless you are cruising with one of the luxury cruise lines that does not charge for drinks.

The main question we get all the time is, "Can you win in a cruise ship casino?" The answer is YES. I won a $750 jackpot from a quarter slot machine on Silversea Cruises' Silver Whisper. Ten minutes later, the lady playing next to me hit a $500 jackpot. On Celebrity Mercury, I won $1,100 on a quarter slot machine. On Carnival Spirit, Rickee won a $400 jackpot on a dollar slot machine. One evening we watched a lady hit a $1,000 jackpot on a quarter poker machine with a Royal Flush. The very next night, the same machine hit another Royal Flush for $1,000. I have never won at Craps on a cruise, but I have seen others win. As for Black Jack, your odds of winning on a cruise ship are as good as in any Las Vegas Strip casino. Now, I must also admit I have lost money in cruise ship casinos, as well. But the fact remains, you CAN WIN.

> **Tip!** When you hit a big jackpot on a slot machine, quit while you are ahead. It is the only way to walk away a winner.

If you are new to the world of casinos, never fear. Most cruise ship casinos will conduct classes during the day on how to play the various games. Some ships also have slot and Black Jack tournaments throughout the week which are a lot of fun.

Casinos are not all about winning. This is just another form of entertainment. Take as much money in with you as you can afford to lose and when it is gone, walk away and have fun somewhere else on the ship.

Bingo

If you enjoy bingo, you will love cruise ship bingo. The cruise staff will conduct bingo games just about every day (and sometimes twice a day) of the cruise. The only exception is when the ship is in port. Local laws prohibit cruise ships from running gambling operations while the ship is in port. This includes the casino games.

Anyone can play bingo, even kids! However, most ships require that someone over 21 accompany a child playing a bingo card. Prizes are paid in cash and generally get bigger as the week goes on. Royal Caribbean's Snowball Jackpot is the richest we have seen. A percentage of each day's bingo take is held back for a winner-take-all grand finale game on the last day of the cruise. We have seen jackpots as high as $10,000!

Radisson Seven Seas Cruises pays out 90% of the take from bingo in the form of prizes. The ship retains 10% for the crew welfare fund.

Smoking Policy

Everybody has a strong opinion about smoking. If you are a non-smoker, you probably hate the smell of cigarette and cigar smoke. Rickee falls into that category. She is extremely sensitive to smoke. I don't like being around smoke, but I can deal with it. If you are a smoker, you may be wondering if you will be able to smoke on the cruise, or at least *where* you will be allowed to smoke.

Every ship has different smoking policies so you have to check with your cruise lines' web site or refer to the documentation they send you for accurate information. However, there are a few general guidelines that every cruise line follows.

The following areas are always non-smoking areas:

- Restaurants and dining rooms
- Theater/show lounge
- Movie theater
- Elevators and hallways
- Public gathering areas (lobby, etc.)

Generally, most interior areas are non-smoking unless otherwise designated as smoking. Smoking is allowed in the staterooms of most cruise ships.

> **Caution!** Never dispose of a cigarette butt over the side of the ship or off of your balcony. The wind could draw the embers or burning cigarette butt back into an open balcony door and cause a fire. In fact, never throw anything over the side of the ship.

Most ships will designate smoking areas in bars and lounges. However, some bars/lounges may be strictly non-smoking venues. It seems that in most ship casinos, smoking is allowed everywhere. Many ships have a cigar lounge where cigar and pipe smoking is permitted. There are also areas on the upper decks outdoors where smoking may be permitted.

Cruise Booze

One of the great things about a cruise is that you can drink as much alcohol as you like and not have to worry about driving home. As long as you can make it back to your stateroom without passing out, you should be OK. That is not to say that you should drink to excess or become obnoxious. If you do, the ship will ask you to 'step away from the bar'.

It seems that no matter where you go on a cruise ship there is a bar. That is because the sale of liquor is a major source of onboard revenue for the cruise lines. Drink prices can vary from one cruise line to another, but generally the prices are in line with any restaurant bar on land. You can expect to pay $4.50 to $6.00 for a mixed drink, $2.00 to $2.50 for a beer, etc. Premium brands will cost more.

Some cruise lines offer drink cards allowing you to pre-purchase a set number of drinks. However, these often do not include frozen drinks like Margaritas, Daiquiris, Piña Coladas, etc.

If you would like to enjoy a cocktail in your stateroom, you may find the cruise line to be a little less accommodating. In fact, if you attempt to bring your own liquor on board a ship, there is a very good chance it will be confiscated and held in safe-keeping until the end of the cruise. The reason is simple: they want you to buy your drinks from them. Each cruise line has a different policy regarding in-room liquor.

On Holland America Zuiderdam, they allowed liquor purchased from the onboard liquor store to be consumed in the staterooms. There was a small premium added to the cost of the liquor, but it was still cheaper and more convenient than purchasing the bar drinks.

There are also different rules in place for guests occupying larger suites. On the Grand Princess, our mini-suite's mini-bar was stocked with small bottles of complimentary liquor and mixers.

On Seabourn, Silversea and Radisson Seven Seas Cruises, each guest will have two complimentary bottles of liquor (of the guest's choice) placed in the suite on the day of embarkation.

Many of the luxury cruise lines include complimentary cocktails, wine and champagne in the cost of the cruise fare. Imagine an open bar every night where you can enjoy your favorite libation without having to worry about signing a bar ticket! Silversea, Seabourn and SeaDream Yacht Club all offer complimentary cocktails, wine and champagne throughout the ship. Radisson Seven Seas Cruises offers complimentary wine with dinner each evening. On its World Cruise, Radisson Seven Seas offers complimentary cocktails throughout the ship.

Getting the Perfect Tan

Sun worshippers equate the quality of a cruise with the quality of the suntan they go home with. Until just recently, Rickee was one who would gladly spend hours each day basking in the sun. If you love the sun and seek the perfect tan, a cruise is definitely for you.

The secret to getting the prefect tan on a cruise is not that difficult. You put on your swimsuit, slap on the suntan lotion and lay down outside, right? The secret lies in how to get the perfect tan and *enjoy the process.*

Avoid sunburn – Don't even think about spending any time in the sun in the Caribbean without wearing sun block. We are from Texas and I can tell you that the sun in the Caribbean is much more damaging than the sun in Texas or even Florida. The closer you get to the Equator, the harsher the sun becomes. If you look at a world map, you will see that your Caribbean, Panama Canal or South American cruise will take you dangerously close to, if not directly over, the Equator. Even in the Mediterranean, the sun is extremely strong. Another reason for the harshness of the sun is that the air is 'cleaner' out at sea. In our home town of Dallas, Texas, the pollution forms a haze which blocks some of the sun's rays. There is no such protection out on the ocean. If you are dark-skinned already, you should wear no less than SPF-15; everyone else should wear SPF-30 or SPF-45. Children should always be protected with SPF-45. Even with SPF-30, you will be able to get a tan if you stay in the sun long enough.

> **Tip!** Always use SPF-30 or SPF-45 and don't forget to put it on your ears, nose and tops of your feet.

Protect your eyes - You are going to need a good pair of sunglasses. The sun can be dangerously bright, especially as it reflects off of the water and the white painted surfaces of the ship.

> **Tip!** Buy a waterproof, floating neck strap for your sunglasses and keep them around your neck at all times during the day.

Protect your feet - It is always a good idea to wear a pair of sandals or other suitable deck shoes when walking around the pool area or public decks of the ship. The first reason for this is to prevent slipping on a wet surface. The second is to prevent cutting your feet on sharp objects like broken glass or metal.

Take your towel with you – Many ships today will place two pool towels in your stateroom. These towels are larger than a normal bath towel and are usually colored. Each cruise line handles towels differently. Some cruise lines still allow you to discard wet towels in large bins on the pool deck. Other cruise lines ask you to return the wet towels to your stateroom to be collected by your cabin attendant. Some cruise lines even charge you if you fail to return the towels. Your cruise line will have information in your stateroom regarding their policy on pool towels.

Take a beach bag – It is a good idea to take a small beach bag with you to the pool. You can keep your book, sun block, tissues, and room key in the bag. You can also leave the bag on your pool lounge chair to "mark your territory" if you need to go to the restroom.

On sea days, get to the pool early – If you want a lounge chair by the pool, you had better get out there early, especially on a sea day (a day when the ship is sailing and not in port).

www.PerfectCruiseBook.com

Pool Etiquette – It is extremely poor etiquette to "save" lounge chairs for others by placing towels or books in the chairs to make them look occupied. Most cruise lines prohibit this as it is not fair to other guests.

On a ship with 2,000 or 3,000 passengers, you can imagine how crowded the pool area(s) can get when the ship is at sea and everyone is onboard. Unless you just have to be near the pool, look for a secluded spot on one of the decks above the pool deck either forward or aft of the pool area. Don't hesitate to drag a lounge chair to a secluded area (as long as it is not in the middle of a traffic area).

Tip! The best days to lay by the pool are when the ship is in port. Why? Because everyone is off the ship on a shore excursion and you can have the pool to yourself! This is a secret of die hard sun worshipers.

Shopping Onboard

You may be surprised to find that your cruise ship has a virtual mini shopping mall right on board! It is common for larger ships to have several shops selling a variety of items. You may be even more surprised to learn that some of the prices on board are competitive with prices on some Caribbean islands.

Here are just a few of the items you can purchase on many cruise ships:

- Gifts and souvenirs
- Sundries
- Snacks
- T-shirts
- Logo shirts, caps and other logo merchandise
- Fine jewelry and watches
- Formal wear, dress shirts, ties, socks
- Crystal and porcelain
- Perfume and cologne
- Spirits

As with all purchases on board the ship, anything you buy in one of the shops must be charged to your shipboard account (using your room key/account card). All purchases made on board the ship are considered foreign purchases made outside the U.S. so duty-free shopping rules apply.

Laundry

The last thing you want to think about on a cruise, or any vacation for that matter, is doing laundry! Nevertheless, cruise lines realize that this is a necessary evil. Most modern cruise ships offer launderettes with washing machines, clothes dryers and irons and ironing boards. Most cruise lines will charge a nominal fee for using the launderette and will provide you with soap and fabric softener.

Virtually all cruise lines also offer laundry services (for a fee) and some even offer dry cleaning. The system works much like any hotel. You place your items to be laundered in a bag, fill out a form, place the form in the bag and leave the bag on your bed, or call your stateroom attendant to pick it up for you. Your cleaned and pressed items are usually returned within 24 hours.

Art Auctions

The popularity of art auctions has been growing steadily in the cruise industry over the past ten years. Virtually every cruise ship now has an onboard art director who conducts auctions on days when the ship is "at sea". The art director is usually not an employee of the cruise line. Instead, he or she works for a major art gallery that has a contract with the cruise line to conduct the auctions.

Art auctions can be surprisingly fun and a great way to save money on quality artwork. You can find original works from internationally recognized artists such as Peter Max, Erté, Picot, Medvedev, Salvador Dali, Krasanansky, Steynovitz, and Linda LaKinff just to name a few. There is also a selection of animation art and sports memorabilia.

Auctions are held in one of the ship's lounges and will be announced in your daily schedule. Participating is easy, just show up at the auction, sign up and get a bidding card. The art director will generally be very helpful in explaining the rules and the auction is very casual. Don't worry about accidentally rubbing your eyes and having that mistaken for a bid of $10,000. In fact, you don't have to bid on anything if you don't want to. Sometimes we go just to see the art and watch what other people are buying.

The art gallery claims that you can purchase art on board a cruise ship for 50% to 70% less than on land. Part of the reason is low overhead. Instead of an expensive display gallery on land, the gallery takes samples of the art on cruise ships and simply pays the cruise line a percentage of every sale. You pay for the artwork with a credit card and the artwork is shipped to your home directly from the gallery's warehouse. We have purchased several pieces through Park West Galleries (on a Carnival cruise and on Silversea Cruises). Everything arrived on time and in good condition.

Enrichment Lectures

Your cruise will most likely feature a series of enrichment lectures conducted by various experts in their respective fields. Lectures will typically last only an hour or so and they are a great source if interesting information. Smaller cruise ships have really embraced enrichment lectures as a form of daytime activity. While on Seabourn Pride, I enjoyed a lecture series from a gentleman who had been the head of NASA's space photography program for 25 years. He was the guy who actually mounted the cameras in the Mercury and Apollo space capsules before each mission. It was a fascinating series of lectures with an amazing slide show of photos from space.

On Radisson Seven Seas Voyager, we attended a lecture on "How to Self-Publish Your Book". This lecture was actually part of the inspiration for my writing and publishing "The Perfect Cruise".

Often the cruise line will invite a lecturer who will offer a lot of historical perspective on the islands or ports your ship will be visiting. These lectures can be very interesting and informative and can serve as a great reference point for you while you are on your various shore excursions.

Your cruise line may also replay the lectures throughout the day on one of the ship's TV channels. This allows you to benefit from the lecture, even if you were busy doing something else during the time the lecture took place.

Tipping Guidelines

Every cruise line has its own guidelines for tipping employees. You should refer to the documentation you received with your tickets for detailed information. However, there are some general rules which apply to all cruise lines. Even though you are not legally *required* to leave gratuities, you *should*. Cruise line employees, especially the housekeeping and dining room staff, work extremely long hours. Waiters, assistant waiters, and dining room managers routinely work from 6:00am until past midnight 7 days a week! Waiters and assistants typically work for little or no salary. Their livelihood depends solely on the tips they receive. The cruise line provides them with room and board, but the employees have to pay for such things as their own medical care and dry-cleaning of their uniform.

However, don't feel sorry for them. There are long lines of people in foreign countries waiting for these jobs. A good cruise ship waiter can make a very nice living, in many cases tax free, and see the world at the same time! Even assistant waiters can make a decent wage and have the opportunity to become a full-fledged waiter. Remember, these employees have very few expenses. It is conceivable that a cruise ship waiter could work for 5 years and retire from the cruise industry with earnings in the six figure range to start a new life.

Tipping is a personal matter. However, here are some general guidelines that you can follow:

- Waiter - $3.50 per day/per person
- Assistant Waiter - $2.00 per day/per person
- Cabin steward(ess)/attendant - $3.50 per day/per person
- Head waiter - $1 per day/per person

That totals $10 per person/per day. Not bad when you consider that you are dining in the ship's restaurants three or four times each day and your cabin steward(ess) tends to your room at least twice each day.

I should emphasize that these are *minimum amounts to tip* in my opinion. You can, and should, tip extra for those employees whom you feel have gone out of their way to give extra special service. If you request and receive something special from the head waiter or maitre d', you should take care of him or her with a tip.

Traditionally, gratuities are given on the last evening of the cruise. Your cabin steward(ess) will leave several envelopes in your stateroom on the next to last night of the cruise in which you can place your tip money. You can take your gratuity envelope to dinner with you to give to your wait staff on the last night of the cruise. You can leave your cabin steward's(ess) gratuity envelope on the pillow or desk before you vacate the cabin on the final day. Or, you can present the envelope to him or her personally on the last day of the cruise. Either is acceptable.

Bar Staff - Typically, all bar tabs include a 15% gratuity which is automatically added into the total. You can, of course, tip extra if you receive exceptional service from a bar waiter or waitress.

Spa and Salon Gratuities - It is customary to tip your stylist or manicurist 15% if you receive treatments in the salon. The same is true of a massage therapist after a massage.

Tour Guides – Tipping a tour guide on a shore excursion is completely at your discretion. If the guide does an excellent job, we will typically tip them $5 per person and $2 per person for the bus driver.

Reverse Gratuity Policy

Some cruise lines have instituted a new policy of automatically charging gratuities to your onboard account as soon as you board the ship. Some people like this new system and others do not. I do not like it. I like to personally give my gratuities to the staff on the last day (or, sometimes, throughout the cruise).

One advantage of having the gratuities automatically included in your onboard account is that it removes the concern over having enough cash left over at the end of the cruise to leave gratuities. You will simply pay it on your credit card as part of the overall onboard account.

On the downside, I think it could reduce the quality of service you receive in the dining room. Why? Because the wait staff assumes they are getting the gratuities regardless of their performance. When gratuities are held until the end of the cruise, the wait staff is very careful to make sure you get excellent service. After all, their livelihood depends on it.

If you are sailing with a cruise line that automatically includes gratuities on your shipboard account and you wish to leave gratuities the 'traditional' way on the last day of the cruise, you can go to the Purser's Office on the first day of the cruise and request that those charges be removed from your account. If you wish to use the automatic bill method, you can have the Purser's office adjust the amounts up or down on the final day of the cruise to reflect whatever gratuities you feel the staff deserves.

Gratuities Included Cruises

Some cruise lines include gratuities in the cruise fare. If you are sailing on these cruise lines, you have already paid the gratuities as part of your cruise ticket.

Cruise lines that include gratuities in the cruise fare are:

- Seabourn
- SeaDream Yacht Club
- Silversea
- Radisson Seven Seas Cruises

As you might expect, the cruise fare for these cruise lines is quite a bit more expensive than the typical "mass-market" cruise lines. On these cruise lines, you will never see an employee soliciting for gratuities. When we sailed on Silversea Silver Whisper, I had to practically force the masseuse to accept a $20 tip for an excellent massage.

> Holland America and Windstar have a "No Gratuities Required" policy which is much less solicitous than other cruise lines. You can, of course, offer gratuities but the choice is yours.

Disembarkation

Without question, the worst part of any cruise is disembarking. Not only do you have to leave the best vacation of your life, but the process of getting 500 to 3,000 people off a ship in a relatively short period of time can be chaotic. Unlike embarkation, where guests come aboard over a 4 or 5 hour period of time, disembarkation usually begins between 8:00am to 10:00am. Passengers have to get off the ship to make early flights home, and the ship's crew has to get everything cleaned up for the next group of passengers which will begin embarking as early as noon.

The disembarkation process begins a day or two before the end of the cruise when you will be asked to submit information about your return flight, or post-cruise package. You will be issued colored luggage tags with the color determined by the time your flight departs. On the morning of disembarkation, passengers will be allowed to disembark in groups based on the tag colors. Obviously, passengers with early flights will be placed in the first group to disembark. Typically, passengers with post-cruise hotel stays are among the last to disembark. You will also be given U.S. Customs declaration forms (if disembarking in the U.S.).

On the last evening of the cruise, you will be asked to place your checked luggage outside your stateroom before midnight. This is so the crew can collect the luggage and take it off the ship the next morning for Customs to check the bags. You will retrieve your luggage after you disembark the ship. You are allowed to carry hand luggage off the ship.

> **Tip!** A word of caution: when packing, don't forget to keep out the clothes that you intend to wear the next morning!

On the morning of disembarkation, most ships will begin serving breakfast earlier than normal. This is to allow guests with an early disembarkation time to enjoy one final breakfast before leaving the ship. Disembarkation will usually commence around 8:00am depending on the port and the Customs officials. Again, each ship handles disembarkation differently. On some ships, you will be asked to go to one of the lounges to collect your passports and turn in your U.S. Customs forms to Customs officials. On others, you will take your Customs form with you off the ship and present it to Customs officials as you enter or leave the cruise terminal.

U.S. Customs – You will be given a U.S. Customs Form 6059B to complete before arrival in the U.S. A family living in the same household is required to complete only one form. On this form, you are required to declare everything you brought back that you did not take with you when you left the United States. This includes:

- Items you received as gifts such as wedding or birthday presents.
- Items you brought home for someone else.
- Items you bought in duty-free shops including duty-free shops on the ship.
- Items you acquired (whether purchased or received as gifts) in the U.S. Virgin Islands, American Samoa, Guam, or in a Caribbean Basin country that are not in your possession when you return. In other words, if you acquired things in any of these island nations and asked the merchant to send them to you, you must still declare them on your Customs declaration form.

You must state on the Customs declaration the total amount, in United States currency that you actually paid for each item. The price must include all taxes. If you did not buy the item yourself - for example, if it is a gift - get an estimate of its fair retail value in the country where you received it. If you bought something on your trip and wore or used it on the trip, you still have to pay duty on that item. You must declare the item at the price you paid or, if it was a gift, at its fair market value. It is a good idea to save all receipts for items you purchase during your cruise vacation. This will make it easier for you to fill out your Customs form when the time comes.

If you do not declare something that should have been declared, you risk forfeiting it. Failure to declare your purchases when you are over the limit is a serious offense and you face fines and penalties if you are caught. If in doubt, declare it. Be aware that under U.S. law, Customs officers are authorized to search luggage, cargo, and travelers. That's why it's a good idea to pack all the items you purchased in the same bag, if possible, and have the purchase receipts handy.

If you happen to go over your allowed exemption amount, you will be charged duty on those items above the allowed exemption amount. A flat rate of duty will be charged on the next $1,000 worth of merchandise above the exemption amount. Any dollar amount beyond this $1,000 will be dutiable at whatever duty rates apply.

U.S. Immigration – When going through U.S. Immigration at the pier or onboard the ship you will usually be asked if you are a U.S. citizen and the immigration officer will look at your passport. That's about it, pretty painless.

Once you exit the ship you will enter the pier luggage area where you will locate and claim your luggage. The luggage will be sorted by tag color to make finding your baggage easier.

> **Tip!** Wrap your luggage with a bright ribbon, or tie a bright pink or yellow ribbon onto your luggage handle. You will be able instantly to spot your bag among the sea of luggage.

Cruise Etiquette

One of the most exciting and pleasurable experiences you will encounter on any cruise is the new friends you will make. A cruise vacation is unique in that it presents all kinds of opportunities to meet interesting people from all walks of life in one place. Over the past few years, Rickee and I have made many new friends on various cruises, many with whom we plan to cruise again in the future.

With very few exceptions, cruise passengers tend to be happy, fun-loving people. And since everyone is on vacation, it is a relaxed and cheerful environment. On rare occasions, and I do mean rare, there is someone who, for whatever reason, does not understand or adhere to what I like to refer to as proper etiquette when it comes to cruising. So, for that rare individual or individuals, I offer the following guidelines to follow when on a cruise:

1. **Don't smoke in non-smoking areas.** A ship is a relatively confined space, unlike a hotel or resort. If you smoke, please do so in the designated areas only.

2. **Don't slam stateroom doors.** This applies to hotel rooms and cruise ship staterooms. Cruise ship cabins have relatively thin walls, so noise and vibration can very easily travel from one cabin to the next. When exiting or entering your stateroom, be careful not to allow the door to slam shut. Also, if you have a balcony stateroom, make sure you do not allow the wind to slam the balcony door shut especially early in the morning or late at night.

3. **Control your children.** Everyone loves kids, but when your kids are running up and down the hallways after 10 pm at night, enough is enough!

4. **Call room service to pick up dirty trays.** Cruise ship hallways are narrower than those in a hotel. Please do not set your tray in the hallway. If you call room service, they will be happy to come pick the tray up from your cabin.

5. **Show up on time for dinner.** If your cruise has assigned seating and you are assigned to a table with other guests, be on time for dinner. It is not fair to make others wait for you to order.

6. **Bathrobes and slippers are for your cabin.** Please do not feel obligated to parade around the public areas of the ship wearing nothing but a bathrobe. It may sound ridiculous, but we have seen it more than once.

7. **Don't save lounge chairs at the pool.** Most cruise lines prohibit this, but are hesitant to enforce it. If you have friends joining you at the pool, make sure they show up and get their own chair.

8. **Be on time for tours and shore excursions.** Don't make others wait for you. Chances are, they will leave without you if you are not where you should be on time.

9. **Be courteous in your stateroom.** Remember, stateroom walls can be thin and sound travels easily. Refrain from slamming closet doors, bathroom doors, or leaving your television volume on loud late at night or early in the morning.

10. **Swimsuits are not for the restaurant.** Again, most cruise lines have rules against bare feet and swimsuits in the restaurants. But, we have seen it. If you are coming from the pool, wear a cover up or shorts and sandals or deck shoes.

11. **Adhere to the dress code.** If the dress code is formal, follow it! Otherwise, don't go to the formal functions. There are always casual activities you can enjoy if you are averse to dressing formally. Formal on most cruise ships nowadays only means a dark suit and tie. Tuxedos are always optional.

12. **Don't bring kids to late comedy shows.** Typically, the late comedy shows on cruise ships are for adults only. Yet, we have seen people sit their 9-year-old kids right on the front row at 11:00pm at night. This really throws the comedian off when he has adult material and cannot do his or her act. Generally, kids should not be in the lounges after 10:30pm (my rule, not the cruise lines').

13. **No babies or small children in the hot tubs.** This is really a sanitation issue as well as a safety issue. Cruise lines have rules against this, but again, I have seen people with *babies in diapers* in the hot tub, within 12 inches of a sign strictly stating that it is prohibited for children that young to be in the hot tub. Cruise lines cannot police these areas 24 hours a day.

Viking River Cruises can take you to exotic destinations like China. Here we take a breather after walking up the Great Wall. Viking River Cruises' Century Star 2004

I present an award to the Chief Housekeeper aboard SeaDream II for Best Relaxation Cruise.
SeaDream Yacht Club 2004

Who says that you cannot win big in a ship's casino? I have the picture to prove it! A $750 jackpot in Silver Whisper's casino.
Silversea Cruises Silver Whisper 2002

There is nothing more fun that cruising with friends. Michael and Sharon Czarnecki, our travel agents and good friends, relax before dinner on Oceania Regatta.
Oceania Cruises' Regatta 2003

Small ships often allow you the opportunity to visit the bridge. Rickee shares a moment with Captain A. Corsario aboard the bridge of Silver Whisper. Silversea Cruises' Silver Whisper 2002

Why not join us for a sunny day in St. Barts? The weather is always perfect here..
Windstar Cruises' Wind Surf 2003

Rickee says there is nothing more romantic that sailing the Mediterranean aboard a Windstar ship under full sail. If you are looking for a romantic, small ship experience, Windstar is a great choice.
Windstar Cruises' Wind Surf 2003

Taking a ride on a Segway Human Transporter is just one of the unique experiences you can enjoy aboard a SeaDream Yacht Club cruise.
SeaDream Yacht Club SeaDream II 2003

You can get 6-star treatment aboard Seabourn's yachts. Here we enjoy a word with Seabourn Pride Captain Rodahl.
The Yachts of Seabourn - Seabourn Pride 2002

One of the great things about a cruise is the amazing food and dining. Aboard Oceania Cruises' Regatta, there are four separate restaurants from which to choose. I think you should try them all!
Oceania Cruises - Regatta 2003

Just because you are on a 6-star luxury ship does not mean there's no fun! Here, Rickee is snatched from the audience to become part of the show on Silver Whisper. Silversea Cruises' Silver Whisper 2002

The 6-star luxury ships of Silversea give you an opportunity to dress up and socialize with some of the most successful people in the world. Cruise Director, Colin Brown welcomes we to the Captain's Farewell Party..
Silversea Cruises' Silver Wind 2004

Our good friends, Brian and Ellen joined us for a 12-night Rhine and Moselle River cruise. Here, they take a moment to relax and enjoy the scenery in Switzerland.
Viking River Cruises – Viking Danube 2003

The highlight of any SeaDream Yacht Club sailing is the Caviar and Champagne In-The-Surf barbeque and beach party. Two of SeaDream's finest keep Rickee's glass filled with Champagne!
SeaDream Yacht Club – SeaDream II 2004

The Perfect Cruise

There is nothing like a warm day at the beach in the sunny Caribbean. The water is Emerald green and 85 degrees.
Radisson Seven Seas Cruises – Seven Seas Voyager 2004

Cruise Lines

This section of the book is designed to give you some background information on each of the *most popular* cruise lines. For additional information, you can check www.CruiseReport.com. Of course, there are more cruise lines operating than the ones listed here. However, these 22 cruise lines represent 98% of the North American cruise market.

You will notice a star rating next to the name of many cruise lines listed. The open open stars (☆☆☆) represent ratings that have been provided by readers of CruiseReport.com in the reviews they have submitted to the web site. The solid black stars (★★★) identify our CruiseReport.com *editorial* ratings. If Rickee and I have reviewed a cruise line, we always will give your our rating. Otherwise, we offer you the ratings given by our web site readers.

Carnival Cruise Lines ★★★

Pros: Inexpensive, lots of fun, great value, lots of music and entertainment options, well-equipped fitness centers, festive atmosphere

Cons: Lots of announcements and solicitations, inconsistency in food quality and service, long lines for buffets and shore excursions, large crowds

Clientele: Young adults, families, singles, first-time cruisers

CruiseReport.com Awards:

- Best at Sea – Fun Cruise
- Best at Sea – Value Cruise
- Best at Sea – Alternate Dining (2002)

Profile

Carnival is the definitive "mass-market" contemporary cruise line. Carnival operates 22 ships with more new ships promised for the future. The parent company, Carnival Corporation, now owns Holland America, Costa Cruises, Seabourn, Cunard, Princess, and Windstar cruises. This makes Carnival Corporation the largest cruise operator in the world with 70% of the cruise market. Carnival has recently introduced new departure ports in the U.S. including Galveston, Texas, New York, Los Angeles, and Jacksonville. Carnival claims that their target market is "anyone", but the ships' décor, activity and atmosphere seems to focus on 25 to 45 year old singles, couples and families. However, anyone "young at heart" can enjoy a Carnival cruise.

Our Experience (5 Cruises)

The only way to describe a Carnival cruise is "fun", pure and simple. Notwithstanding the upscale, alternate dining venues (on

Spirit and Conquest-class ships), the food is pretty average. Dining rooms can get very spirited as waiters and assistants dance to loud music to entertain you during dessert. Glamour is replaced with flash and over-the-top neon décor reminiscent of a Las Vegas casino. Staterooms are larger than cruise industry average and are comfortable. The best Carnival feature is its unbeatable value.

Destinations sailed by Carnival ships:

Alaska
Bermuda (special voyages)
Canada/New England
Hawaii
Europe

Bahamas
Caribbean
Panama Canal
Mexico

Carnival Cruise Lines' 2004 Fleet				
Vessel Name	Inaugural	Tonnage	Length	Guest Capacity
Carnival Conquest	2002	110,000	952	2974
Carnival Destiny	1996	101,353	893	2642
Carnival Glory	2003	110,000	952	2974
Carnival Legend	2002	88,500	963	2124
Carnival Liberty	NA	NA	NA	NA
Carnival Miracle	2003	88,500	963	2124
Carnival Pride	2001	88,500	963	2124
Carnival Spirit	2000	84,000	963	2124
Carnival Triumph	1999	102,353	893	2758
Carnival Valor	2004	110,000	952	2974
Carnival Victory	2000	101,509	893	2758
Celebration	1987	47,262	733	1486
Ecstasy	1991	70,367	855	2052
Elation	1997	70,367	855	2052
Fantasy	1990	70,367	855	2056
Fascination	1994	70,367	855	2040
Holiday	1985	46,052	727	1452

Carnival Cruise Lines' 2004 Fleet				
Imagination	1994	70,367	855	2052
Inspiration	1995	70,367	855	2052
Jubilee	1986	47,262	733	1486
Paradise	1998	70,367	855	2052
Sensation	1993	70,367	855	2052

Dining

Carnival Cruise Lines' Total Choice Dining offers a lot of dining flexibility. In addition to the Main Dining Room, with up to 4 separate assigned seatings, there is the Lido Restaurant which offers a casual, buffet-style dining alternative. Carnival's Spirit and Conquest class ships feature upscale alternative restaurants. To dine in one of these restaurants, you must make a reservation and you will pay a nominal surcharge.

Your dining options also include:

- Spa Carnival selections
- Sushi Bars and European-style cafés
- 24-hour pizzeria
- Frozen Yogurt and Ice Cream
- Complimentary 24-hour room service

Kid's Program - Camp Carnival

Under the friendly supervision of Camp Carnival's specially trained counselors, your kids are kept entertained with games, arts and crafts, parties, talent shows, storytelling, scavenger hunts, pool parties, pizza-making and more. Camp Carnival's activities are divided into four age groups as follows:

- Toddlers 2 to 5[1]
- Juniors 6 to 8
- Intermediates 9 to 11
- Teens 12 to 15

Camp Carnival provides:

- Specially trained youth counselors
- Age-specific children's activities
- Teen shore excursion program
- Evening babysitting for a nominal fee

---

[1] Carnival will accept children in diapers but parents must provide staff with diapers and supplies. Check with Carnival or your travel agent for more details.

Celebrity Cruises ★★★★★

Pros: Surprising value, excellent dining, classy feel, beautiful ships, no annoying announcements

Cons: Entertainment could use improvement

Clientele: Primarily adult couples 40 and older

CruiseReport.com Awards:

- Best at Sea – Interior Décor (Celebrity Summit 2002)

Profile

Celebrity Cruises was started in 1989 and quickly became a popular alternative to the mass-market cruise lines of that time. Celebrity's aim was to offer a premium cruise product at an affordable price. They succeeded. In 1997, Celebrity was purchased by Royal Caribbean International and continues to operate as a separate brand. Celebrity ships are easily recognizable from a distance with their distinctive blue and white hull and odd-looking "X" mark on the smoke stack. The interiors of Celebrity's ships are filled with interesting and unique artwork set against a classy, contemporary décor that is sophisticated and stylish. Celebrity has distinguished itself among large ship lines with a reputation for exceptional dining. Celebrity offers butler service in its suites, 24-hour Internet café, complimentary use of bathrobes, Martini bars and Michael's Lounge, the ship's cigar bar. Interestingly, some of the best cruise values can be found on Celebrity. Anyone looking for a large ship with sophistication at a reasonable price should consider Celebrity.

Our Experience (2 Cruises)

We have enjoyed two cruises on Celebrity. We continue to be amazed at how they deliver such a high level of service on a large ship, but they do. Thankfully, Celebrity adheres to a strict "no announcement" policy (other than necessary announcements from the bridge) which makes for a much more relaxing cruise experience. Dining on Celebrity is a noticeable step-up from other large cruise ship companies. Celebrity is best suited for the adult crowd, 35 and up. About the only area of improvement we could find was in the entertainment department which, frankly, did not live up to the rest of the ship. Fortunately, Celebrity has recently teamed up with Cirque du Soleil to provide entertainment on its ships. We look forward to sailing Celebrity again to see how this spices up the entertainment.

Destinations sailed by Celebrity ships:

Alaska
Bermuda
Caribbean
Hawaii
Mexico
Panama Canal
South America

Bahamas
Canada
Europe
Mediterranean
Pacific Northwest
Scandinavia
Pacific Coast

Celebrity's 2004 Fleet				
Vessel Name	Inaugural	Tonnage	Length	Guest Capacity
Century	1995	70,606	815	1750
Constellation	2002	91,000	965	1950
Galaxy	1996	77,713	866	1870
Horizon	1990	46,811	682	1354
Infinity	2001	91,000	965	1950
Mercury	1997	77,713	866	1870
Millennium	2000	91,000	965	1950
Summit	2002	91,000	965	1950
Celebrity XPedition	NA	2,329	296	98
Zenith	1992/99	47,255	682	1374

Dining

Celebrity features the gourmet cuisine of world-renowned Master Chef Michel Roux.

- **Main Restaurant** - Dramatic two-story main restaurant presents soaring ocean views, soft music and exquisite settings of china, white linen and crystal -- with attentive, yet unobtrusive service from their European-trained staff. Full menu breakfast and lunch are served in an open-seating style. Two seatings are offered at dinner with menus that change each evening.
- **Poolside Grill and Café** – Buffet-style breakfast and lunch is served each day as well as gourmet-style pizza.
- **Specialty Restaurants** (Millennium, Infinity, Summit and Constellation) - Innovative new specialty restaurants offer a distinctively elegant atmosphere, featuring tableside service and the French culinary art of flambé, the intimacy of a dine-in wine cellar and the open atmosphere of a demonstration kitchen.
- **24 Hour Complimentary Room Service**

Kid's Program

Celebrity Cruises offers onboard entertainment and activities for children and young adults. The four-tiered supervised youth programs are specially created for children ages 3-17 with entertainment and activities designed for each group. Each morning a daily program lists the day's activities, games, parties and more. Special areas are set aside for "kids only," such as the Shipmates Fun Factory, teen centers and pools. Celebrity has a staff of specially trained and educated youth counselors.

Costa ☆☆☆

This cruise line has not been reviewed or rated by CruiseReport.com editors.

Pros: Italian theme, Europe itineraries year-round

Cons: Service can be inconsistent, language barriers[1]

Clientele: Adult couples, mostly European clientele on European itineraries, more Americans on Caribbean itineraries

Profile

Costa is "Cruising Italian Style" and is a great choice for those who love anything Italian. The ships are large and their newest ships are virtually identical to Carnival's Spirit-class vessels. Costa is the largest cruise line in Europe. All but two Costa ships sail Europe year-round. There are two Costa vessels in the Caribbean during winter months. Costa's two newest ships, Costa Fortuna and Costa Magica are the lines' largest at 105,000 tons each. Costa ships are modern and include all of the facilities you would find on any large cruise ship. If you are looking for a taste of Italy and prefer traveling in a European setting, Costa is a cruise line to consider.

Our Experience (None)

Unfortunately, we have not had the opportunity to sail on Costa as of the writing of this book.

Destinations sailed by Costa ships:

Caribbean	Northern Europe
Mediterranean	Transatlantic

---

[1] As reported by contributors to the CruiseReport.com web site

Costa's 2004 Fleet				
Vessel Name	Inaugural	Tonnage	Length	Guest Capacity
Allegra	1992	28,430	617	820
Costa Atlantica	2000	85,619	960	2114
Costa Classica	1991/2002	53,000	722	1308
Costa Europa	1986/2002	53,000	797	1494
Costa Fortuna	2003	105,000	NA	NA
Costa Magica	2004	105,000	NA	NA
Costa Marina	1990/2002	25,558	570	84
Costa Mediterranea	2003	86,000	960	105
Costa Romantica	1993	54,000	722	1356
Costa Tropicale	1982/2001	36,000	659	1017
Costa Victoria	1996	75,166	824	1928

Dining

Costa offers the tradition two assigned seatings for dinner each evening.

- **Main Restaurant** – Breakfast, lunch and dinner are served in the main restaurant daily with lunch and dinner menus changing each day.
- **Lido Buffet** – A poolside buffet is available for breakfast and lunch each day.
- **Complimentary room service**

Kid's Program

Costa Cruises runs an onboard entertainment program for three age groups during the Caribbean season and for the Mediterranean peak season. The extent of the program is dependent upon the number of children on each sailing.

- Kid's Club - age 3 (out of diapers) - 6
- Junior's Club - age 7 -12
- Teen's Club - age 13 – 17

The Costa Atlantica and Costa Victoria Caribbean sailings offer a group baby-sitting service for children ages 3 years (out of diapers) and older. A nominal charge applies and this service must be pre-arranged. No in-stateroom baby-sitting is available.

In addition, on Caribbean sailings, Costa offers a 'Parents Night Out' program where on two nights parents can enjoy an evening alone while their children enjoy a special dinner buffet and activities planned just for them.

Source: www.costacruises.com

Cruise West ★ ★ ★

Pros: Excursions included, intimate ships, great service

Cons: Can be pricey, little or no onboard entertainment

Clientele: Mature active adults, seniors and retirees

Profile

Cruise West is a small ship operator that puts an emphasis on getting "up-close and personal" with the destination. The company founder, Chuck West, virtually pioneered the Alaska tour industry when he founded Westours in 1946. Westours was sold to Holland America Line in 1971. In 1986, Mr. West formed yet another Alaska tour company which eventually became Cruise West. It is common for Cruise West to have an onboard lecturer to provide details about the ships' destinations throughout the cruise. Socializing with other passengers is primary evening entertainment on a Cruise West ship after spending a day of exploring wildlife and nature on shore.

Our Experience (1 cruise)

Cruise West was our very first small ship cruise and we were a little apprehensive about the small ship experience. We were joined by our good friends, Brian and Ellen, for a 5-day California Wine Country cruise on the Sacramento River sailing out of San Francisco There were only about 68 passengers aboard, but we had a great time and became immediate fans of small ship cruising. The all American crew was friendly and the service was great. All excursions were included in the cruise fare, so while it may seem expensive, Cruise West is actually a good value. We are anxious to try these small ships in Alaska. The benefits of a small ship would really be appreciated when trying to get close to the glaciers and wildlife!

Destinations sailed by Cruise West ships:

Alaska
Baja Mexico
British Columbia
California Wine Country
Costa Rica and Panama
Columbia and Snake Rivers

Vessel Name	Inaugural	Tonnage	Length	Guest Capacity
Pacific Explorer	1995		185	100
Sheltered Seas	NA	NA	90	70
Spirit of '98	1984	NA	192	96
Spirit of Alaska	NA	NA	143	78
Spirit of Columbia	NA	NA	143	78
Spirit of Discovery	NA	NA	166	84
Spirit of Endeavor	1983	NA	217	102
Spirit of Oceanus	NA	NA	295	114

Cruise West's 2004 Fleet

Dining

Cruise West offers a single-seating dining room system. Breakfast, lunch and dinner are all served in the main dining room. Open-seating allows you to dine with whomever you wish at the assigned time. Early-riser coffee and pastries are available in the lounge each morning. We found the food to be delicious.

Kid's Programs

Cruise West has no structured programs for children.

Crystal Cruises ☆☆☆☆☆

Pros: Impeccable service, great entertainment, alternate dining options, world-cruise, complimentary soft drinks

Cons: Expensive, assigned seating in main dining room, gratuities and liquor not included

Clientele: Upscale professionals, adult couples and families, seasoned travelers

Profile

Crystal promises to offer small-ship luxury and impeccable service on ships which have all of the facilities of a large ship. Crystal offers passengers of mass-market cruise lines a logical *upgrade path* to the next level in service. Crystal is renowned for its extensive lecture series. Other features include complimentary use of the ships Laundromats on each deck; a business center with A/V equipment; loaner laptop computers; gentlemen hosts; an Asian speciality restaurant; an Italian specialty restaurant.

Our Experience (None)

Unfortunately, we have not had the opportunity to sail on Crystal as of the writing of this book.

Destinations sailed by Crystal ships:

Africa	Alaska
Asia	Australia/New Zealand
Canada	Caribbean
Europe	Hawaii
Mediterranean	Mexico
Panama Canal	Scandinavia
South America	South Pacific
U.S. East Coast	

Crystal's 2004 Fleet				
Vessel Name	Inaugural	Tonnage	Length	Guest Capacity
Crystal Harmony	1990	49,400	790	940
Crystal Serenity	2003	68,000	790	1080
Crystal Symphony	1995	51,044	792	940

Dining

Crystal Harmony, Crystal Symphony and Crystal Serenity each feature an exceptional variety of dining options.

- **Crystal Dining Room** – Located in the heart of the ship just off the Crystal Plaza, the Crystal Dining Room is beautifully appointed, with sweeping ocean views by day and a magnificent ambiance at night. The gracious European-trained waiters and internationally acclaimed chefs provide regionally inspired dishes and classic continental cuisine. Two seatings are offered each evening and open seating at breakfast and lunch.
- **Lido Café** - features a casual ambiance with breathtaking ocean views, and the buffet-style indoor/outdoor café offers breakfast and lunch as well as late-morning bouillon service and luncheon buffets.
- **Trident Bar & Grill (Harmony & Symphony) & Tastes (Crystal Serenity)** - Daytime snacks, a lunchtime hamburger/hot dog grill, sandwiches, specialty burgers and a full bar are available. Early-and late-riser breakfast is also served here. Casual dining is available here each evening.
- **The Bistro** - A casual eatery for coffee, croissants and pastries in the morning and bistro snacks (cheeses, pates) in the afternoon.
- **Kyoto** (Crystal Harmony) - This Japanese restaurant features a sophisticated ambiance. Traditional dishes are created by a staff of renowned Japanese chefs.

- **Jade Garden** (Crystal Symphony) - Innovative Asian cuisine prepared with a contemporary flair. Dishes are inspired by the exotic array of traditions and ingredients of the Orient. Specialty selections from Wolfgang Puck's Chinois restaurant are also offered.
- **Silk Road and The Sushi Bar** (Crystal Serenity) - This specialty restaurant features Asian cuisine, offering signature dishes created by internationally renowned Japanese master chef, Nobu Matsuhisa.
- **Prego** (all ships) – Offers elegant dining with a spectacular view and unique Italian cuisine. Enjoy authentic regional Italian cuisine, with signature creations by Piero Selvaggio, owner of the renowned Valentino restaurants in Los Angeles and Las Vegas.

Kid's Program

Crystal offers a children's playroom and babysitting services on all cruises. During holiday cruises and selected sailings, additional children's activities are offered under the supervision of experienced Junior Activities Directors.

The Crystal Junior Activities Program is three-tiered:

- 3-7 year olds
- 8-12 year olds
- 13-17 year olds

Children under the age of six months are not permitted on board without a signed waiver by parent(s).

Hours of operation vary depending on the itinerary and number of children on board.

Activities are determined by the age and the number of children on board. On those sailings with Junior Activities Directors, a detailed schedule of events is created at the beginning of each cruise. Once on board, you'll receive Surf Runner, or Teen Scene, the teenagers guide to special activities, the daily newsletter for kids with details for the following day's schedule and other pertinent information.

Fantasia is a children's playroom offering tables and chairs for arts and crafts, popular Sony PlayStation® game titles, a large screen television set and board games. Crystal Symphony and Crystal Serenity also feature a teenager's video arcade, Waves. The Library offers children's books and children's videos or DVDs for enjoyment in staterooms.

For a small fee, all vessels offer in-stateroom baby-sitting. Guests should contact the concierge on board for this service at least 24 hours in advance.

Source: www.crystalcruises.com

Cunard (not rated)

This cruise line has not been reviewed or rated by CruiseReport.com editors.

Pros: British hospitality, history, ocean liner mystique

Cons: Expensive, formal

Clientele: Mature adult couples and singles, British and American mix

Profile

Since 1840, Cunard has been known for its grand ocean liners like Queen Mary and Queen Elizabeth. When transatlantic cruising was the only way to get from Europe to the New World, Cunard was the undisputed leader. In 1969, when Cunard introduced Queen Elizabeth 2, jet aircraft had already replaced ocean liners as a form of transportation. Nevertheless, Cunard has retained its tradition of making its famous New York to London itinerary the backbone of its sailing calendar. Cunard was purchased by Carnival Corporation in 1998. The Queen Mary 2 was christened in 2004, and at 150,000 tons is the largest cruise ship in the world (at least for now). Another new 85,000 ton vessel, Queen Victoria is currently under construction and is planned for release in 2005. Cunard is the only cruise line that has retained distinct "classes" of service with separate dining facilities based on the cabin category you occupy. If you are looking for a strong sense of British tradition and style with a high degree of luxury, Cunard is a cruise line to consider.

Our Experience (None)

Unfortunately, we have not had the opportunity to sail on Cunard as of the writing of this book.

Destinations sailed by Cunard ships:

Africa
Bermuda
Caribbean
Mediterranean
Scandinavia
South Pacific
Transatlantic

Asia/Far East
Canada
Europe
Panama Canal
South America
World Cruise

Cunard's 2004 Fleet				
Vessel Name	Inaugural	Tonnage	Length	Guest Capacity
Queen Elizabeth II	1969	70,327	963	1791
Queen Mary II	2003	150,000	1132	2620

Dining

Queen Mary 2

There are 10 restaurants in all run by a team of chefs that includes culinary advisor Daniel Boulud, one of the world's most famous chefs, and the celebrated Mediterranean and TV culinary luminary Todd English. Each QM2 stateroom is matched with a reserved table at a sea-view restaurant. You can always make reservations at one of the many optional dining alternatives. Room service is available 24 hours a day.

- **Britania Restaurant -** QM2's main dining room. 3-story Britannia Restaurant, reminiscent of the opulent dining salons of the past.
- **Princess & Queens Grill Restaurant** – Reserved for guests staying in one of the Q categories, savor the sublime creations of the Queens Grill, or the Princess Grill for P category guests. Cunard's Grill restaurants have been long acclaimed by food critics as the finest dining experience at sea.

The Perfect Cruise

- **Todd English** - Enjoy delectable Mediterranean cuisine -- al fresco if you choose. Todd English is one of America's leading chefs. He has been named both "Rising Star Chef" and "Best Chef: Northeast" by the James Beard Foundation. Chef English has appeared in numerous television shows including his own TV series *Cooking in with Todd English*. Reservations are required and a surcharge applies.
- **Kings Court** - You can enjoy a casual breakfast or lunch in Kings Court. At night it is transformed into four intimate dining venues: an **Asian** restaurant, an **Italian** trattoria, the **Carvery**, and the **Chef's Galley**, where guests experience one of the most unique epicurean adventures anywhere. Reservations are required and a surcharge applies.
- **Golden Lion Pub** - Fine lagers, ales and pub snacks are served in this British pub where you can enjoy a pint and watch televised sporting events.
- **Boardwalk Café** - Enjoy lunch at this casual eatery near the pool - in your bathing suit if you choose.
- **Winter Garden** - A proper British afternoon tea can be taken in the Winter Garden or Queens Grill Lounge complete with scones, clotted cream, fresh pastries, finger sandwiches and white glove service.

Queen Elizabeth 2

The restaurant where the passengers dine corresponds to their level of accommodation..

- **Queens Grill** –There is only one, unhurried sitting for 231 privileged passengers. Menus feature gourmet Continental cuisine, British signature dishes, American favorites and more eclectic offerings that combine seasonal and regional ingredients from different places where QE2 sails.
- **Princess Grill** – This intimate, single-seating restaurant can accommodate just 100 guests and features deep red fabrics combined with faux bronze statues.
- **Britannia Grill** – This Art Deco venue in hues of deep purple offers single seating and accommodates 108.

- **Caronia Restaurant** – Single-seating dining is offered for 554 passengers.
- **Mauretania Restaurant** – This dining room accommodates 530 passengers in two sittings. Its green and tan Art Deco décor is enhanced with strategically placed etched-glass partitions.
- **Lido Café** – Breakfast and lunch buffets are served in this casual restaurant. At lunch, there are carved meats and regional specialties. Guests have the option of sitting indoors or – weather permitting – dining al fresco overlooking the pool. Dinner is served on select nights.
- **Pavilion Café** – This small lunchtime venue, just off the pool, serves grilled items such as hotdogs, hamburgers, steak sandwiches and a daily specialty item, i.e. spareribs, German sausage, chicken, lamb chops, etc. There also is a mini-salad bar and homemade soups.
- **24 Hour Room Service**

Kid's Program

Cunard Line's Queen Mary 2 offers extensive children's facilities broken into three age groups: Nursery, 1-2, run by nannies, with cribs and beds in the facility; Play Zone, 3-5 and 6-8; and The Zone, 9-11. Children's Tea is served in the Kings Court, which is decorated with balloons, artwork place mats and crayons at each setting. The ship also has a Minnows Splash Pool for children only, Children's Disco, ball pool and Xboxes in the Zone and Play Zone.

Source: Cunard Line Public Relations Department

Delta Queen Steamboat Co. ★★★

Pros: Good food, great lectures, good entertainment, all-American atmosphere

Cons: Expensive, cramped cabins, limited facilities

Clientele: Mature adults

Profile

Delta Queen operates three stern-driven paddlewheel steamboats. The oldest of the three, Delta Queen, was built in 1927 (refurbished in 1998). The company refers to the river cruise experience as "Steamboatin'" and places a definite emphasis on American history, culture and literature, especially that of Mark Twain. A "Riverlorian" delivers lectures on 19th century river history. If you want to be immersed in Americana, Dixieland jazz, and good-ole friendly service, Delta Queen offers a unique alternative to ocean cruising.

Our Experience (1 cruise)

We sailed on Delta Queen's Mississippi Queen last year for a one-week cruise from Memphis to New Orleans. We really enjoyed the food and the service and were surprised by the quality of the entertainment. The cabin we were assigned, however, was extremely small and VERY noisy. So noisy that after two sleepless nights, we requested a new cabin (something we have never done before or since). We were assigned a new cabin which was much quieter, but even smaller than the first one. We had an opportunity to walk through the sister ship, American Queen, during this cruise and that vessel appeared to be much roomier. That being said, everyone we spoke with had a great time and many had sailed on several Delta Queen Cruises. This riverboat line definitely has a following.

Destinations sailed by Delta Queen:

United States

Delta Queen's 2004 Fleet				
Vessel Name	Inaugural	Tonnage	Length	Guest Capacity
American Queen	1995			
Mississippi Queen	1976			
Delta Queen	1947			

Dining

Delta Queen has a single assigned seating for dinner. Menus change each day and feature American and regional specialties. There is a breakfast buffet that changes daily and lunch is served in the dining room. Breakfast and lunch are open-seating. There are cookies and hot dogs available all day.

Kid's Program

The Kids Program on Delta Queen is really a Family Program that Delta Queen calls "Riverbonding" and features engaging onboard programs for young travelers, led by an enthusiastic Family Activity Coordinator. Kids can work on their Cub Pilot's Licenses, which means they'll learn how to tie knots, read a river map, and they'll attend a Riverwatch lecture under the stars. The Riverlorian will weave tales about life on a steamboat then and now. Other no-batteries-needed activities include kite flying off the back of the boat, an ice cream social, a scavenger hunt, a pool party and more. In port, you'll enjoy special family shore tours filled with American history, culture and lots of fun.

Disney Cruise Line ★★★★★

Pros: Disney theme, classy ships, great Disney shows, large staterooms, Castaway Cay, kids programs, family staterooms

Cons: Expensive, Disney theme and Mickey are everywhere

Clientele: Families, young adult couples

Profile

If you are familiar with Disney you already know that they don't do anything unless they can do it right. Disney Cruise Line began operations in 1998 with the introduction of Disney Magic. A year later, the company introduced her sister, Disney Wonder. Disney Cruise Line offers 3-night, 4-night and 7-night cruises to the Bahamas and Caribbean. 7-night combination Disney theme-park/cruise packages are also popular. An innovative dining concept has guests visiting a different restaurant on board each evening with a wait staff and dining companions that move with you. The kids programs are second to none, as you might expect. Disney has divided its ships into three sections with activities and venues: one for adults only, another for families; and a third for children only. If you are really into the Disney theme, or if you are looking for a great family cruise, Disney Cruise Line is a great choice.

Our Experience (1 cruise)

We sailed on Disney Wonder not long after her inaugural. Rickee and I were joined by my brother, John. We had a good time and could really appreciate the Disney theme integrated into the construction of the ship. Disney is definitely for families, or anyone that is really into anything Disney. Even though the evening entertainment consisted of Disney productions (Peter Pan, Beauty and the Beast, etc.), they were very well done. The food in the restaurants was good (not great), but we found the Animator's Palette restaurant to be very noisy. Palo, the adult-only restaurant, was exceptionally good. Castaway Cay sets new standards for private islands used by cruise lines. We cannot rate the cruise line because it has been too long since our last cruise, but Disney has an excellent reputation.

Destinations sailed by Disney ships:

Bahamas   Eastern Caribbean
Western Caribbean

Disney Cruise Lines' 2004 Fleet				
Vessel Name	Inaugural	Tonnage	Length	Guest Capacity
Disney Magic	1998	83,000	964	2400
Disney Wonder	1999	83,000	964	2400

Dining

There are three main dining areas on both Disney ships. There are two assigned seatings each evening for dinner.

Lumière's/Triton - Named for the elegant candelabra in "Beauty and the Beast", Lumière's is the main dining area on Disney Magic. Aboard the Disney Wonder, Triton's is a fine seafood restaurant named after The Little Mermaid's father.

Animator's Palette – This magical restaurant transforms itself from black and white to brilliant color as your meal progresses. Layer upon layer of color is added to the accompaniment of synchronized music, and classic scenes from Disney's animated films play during this unique dining experience.

Parrot Cay – Enjoy island-inspired cuisine to the beat of colorful Caribbean rhythms.

Palo – An intimate setting reserved exclusively for adults. Palo features Northern Italian cuisine and an exceptional wine cellar. Reservations are required. Service charge applies.

Kid's Program

With practically an entire deck devoted to kids, there's non-stop fun each day from 9 a.m. to midnight for five distinct age groups. Kids ages 3 to 7 make magic at Disney's Oceaneer Club. Kids 8 to 12 explore the universe at Disney's Oceaneer Lab. Teens enjoy their own private hangout at a New York-style coffeehouse called Common Grounds on Disney Wonder and the Stack on Disney Magic.

Oceaneer Club (ages 3-7) - Disney's Oceaneer Club offers age-specific activities guaranteed to transport young minds to the edge of their imagination. And, as an added convenience, parents are given pagers so families are always in touch.

Oceaneer Lab (ages 8-12) – Kids are divided into two age groups: 8 and 9, and 10-12. There are featured activities designed specifically for each group. And, of course, there are the Disney Counselors guiding them all the way.

The Stack and Common Grounds (ages 13-17) - The Stack brings wonder to the Disney Magic®, while Common Grounds creates magic on the Disney Wonder®. Both spots are dedicated to teens only and come complete with music, games and large-screen TV, even an Internet café. The Stack and Common Grounds are for teens ages 13 to 17 to meet on their own terms. Activities range from trivia to pool parties to all sorts of games and adventures.

Source: www.disneycruise.disney.go.com

Holland America ★★★★

Pros: Beautiful ships, 'no tipping required' policy, tradition, handicap facilities, friendly staff

Cons: Lackluster entertainment, language barrier with staff

Clientele: Mature adults, seniors, experienced travelers

Profile

Since 1871, Holland America Line has been sailing passenger ships around the world. In 1989, Holland America and its Westours Alaska tour operator were purchased by Carnival Corporation. Over the years, Holland America/Westours has established a solid reputation as a leading cruise/tour operator in Alaska. Even though Holland America offers itineraries to every part of the world, its Alaska cruises and cruise tours are legendary. Holland America's newest vessels, Zuiderdam, Oosterdam and Westerdam are all built on an ultra-modern design and incorporate every feature you could expect in a cruise ship.

Our Experience (1 cruise)

Our sailing aboard Holland America's Zuiderdam in 2002 showed us why this cruise line is so popular. The ship's décor was beautiful replete with expensive artwork. The mostly Indonesian staff was polished and friendly, although difficult to communicate with at times. The alternate restaurant, Odyssey, served excellent dishes that far surpassed the food served in the dining room. Holland America is seriously trying to re-invent itself into a cruise line that appeals to a younger clientele. The entertainment was abysmal on our sailing.

Destinations sailed by HAL ships:

Africa   Alaska

Antarctica	Asia
Australia/New Zealand	Bahamas
Canada/New England	Caribbean
Europe	Hawaii
India	Mediterranean
Mexico	Pacific Northwest
Panama Canal	Scandinavia
South America	South Pacific
U.S. East Coast	World Cruise

HAL's 2004 Fleet				
Vessel Name	Inaugural	Tonnage	Length	Guest Capacity
m/s Amsterdam	2000	61,000	780	1380
m/s Maasdam	1993	55,541	720	1266
m/s Noordam*	1984	33,930	704	1214
m/s Oosterdam	2002	85,000	951	1848
m/s Prinsendam	1988/2002	38,000	673	940
m/s Rotterdam	1997	62,000	780	1316
m/s Ryndam	1994	55,541	720	1266
m/s Statendam	1992	55,541	720	1266
m/s Veendam	1996	55,541	720	1266
m/s Volendam	1999	63,000	781	1440
m/s Westerdam	2004	85,000	951	1848
m/s Zaandam	2000	63,000	781	1440
m/s Zuiderdam	2002	85,000	951	1848

*Will leave the fleet in November 2004

Dining

Holland America Line offers three dining choices. The Main Dining Room has the traditional two assigned seatings; the Lido offers light and casual alternative dining; and the Pinnacle Grill offers an upscale, reservation-only dining experience.

- **Main Dining Room** – Full service breakfast and lunch with open-seating. Evening meals are offered with four assigned seatings.* Dinner times are 5:45 pm (First Upper), 6:15 pm (First Lower), 8:00 pm (Main Upper) and 8:30 pm (Main Lower). Five course menus change each evening. *Except the ms Noordam and ms Prinsendam, which have two seatings; 6:00 pm (First) and 8:15 pm (Main).
- **Lido Restaurant** – Relaxed, casual, buffet-style dining is offered here at breakfast, lunch and dinner. Choose from sizzling Asian stir-fry, popular pizza and pasta dishes, festive Mexican fare, fresh salads and gourmet sandwiches. Eat indoors in the air-conditioned restaurant or enjoy the fresh air on deck.
- **Pinnacle Grill** - Candlelight and fine décor create a romantic ambiance that sets the stage for fresh Northwest dishes and select wines. Reservations are required. Service charge applies.
- **24 Hour Room Service** – A limited menu is available all day. Restaurant menu is available during dinner hours.

Kid's Program - Club HAL for Kids

Holland America offers supervised fun for young cruisers. Club HAL® provides a wide variety of activities for kids ages 5 to 17. Participating youngsters receive an activity program delivered to their stateroom and a Club HAL t-shirt.

Club HAL activities are designed to be age appropriate. Examples include storytelling, arts and crafts, ice-cream sundae or pizza parties, ship tours and bingo for the little ones (ages 5 to 8). For 'tweens (ages 9 to 12) there's miniature golf, Ping-Pong, theme parties, on-deck sports events and scavenger hunts. Teens (ages 13 to 17) can enjoy a teen disco, dance lessons, arcade games, sports tournaments, card games, trivia contests, bingo, movies and videos.

Select itineraries even offer "kids-only" shore excursions to Half Moon Cay (HAL's private island in the Bahamas) and exploratory adventures in several Alaskan ports of call.

All activities are supervised by permanent, full-time Club HAL directors and assistants. Club HAL directors hold degrees in education, childhood development, recreation, leisure studies or related fields.

Holland America Line serves a wide variety of kid-pleasing food, including special sandwiches, tacos, hamburgers, hot dogs and pizza. Baby food, high chairs and booster seats may be requested in advance of boarding. Baby-sitting services are available for a small surcharge.

Source: www.hollandamerica.com

Norwegian Cruise Lines ★ ★ ★ ★

Pros: Lots of dining choices, great entertainment, Freestyle dining, activities

Cons: Service can be inconsistent

Clientele: Young couples, families, singles, first-time cruisers

CruiseReport.com Awards:

- Best at Sea – Entertainment (Norwegian Dawn)
- Best at Sea – Best Spa (Norwegian Dawn)
- Best at Sea - Best Pizza (La Trattoria/Dawn)

Profile

Freestyle Cruising is the hallmark of NCL and it flies directly in the face of cruise traditions. This cruise line has abandoned rigid dress codes, assigned seatings, and fixed dining times. NCL's newest ships have ten separate restaurants which include Asian, Italian, French, Continental and Mexican cuisines, just to name a few! Another feature of Freestyle Cruising is a more relaxed disembarkation process which allows you to remain in your stateroom until you are ready to leave the ship. All ships have Internet café's with Wi-Fi capability and 'hot-spots' throughout the ship. NCL is famous for its Chocoholic buffet which features a lavish display of the 'dark gold'.

Our Experience (2 cruises)

NCL exceeded our expectations in 2003. We were very impressed with the value and service aboard Norwegian Dawn. We think NCL is a great mass-market cruise line for young adults, families, singles and first-timers. When it comes to entertainment, no other cruise line can beat NCL (our pick for BEST Entertainment at Sea). We love the Freestyle Cruising concept, especially when it comes to dining. And talk about choice! With 10 restaurants to choose from, you can eat in a different one every night, and we did!

Destinations sailed by NCL ships:

Alaska
Bermuda
Caribbean
Hawaii
Mexico
Panama Canal
South America
U.S. Pacific Coast

Bahamas
Canada/New England
Europe
Mediterranean
Pacific Northwest
Scandinavia
U.S East Coast

NCL's 2004 Fleet				
Vessel Name	Inaugural	Tonnage	Length	Guest Capacity
Norwegian Crown	1988*	34,250	614	1026
Norwegian Dawn	2002	90,000	965	2240
Norwegian Dream	1992	50,764	754	1750
Norwegian Majesty	1992	40,876	680	1462
Norwegian Sea	1988	42,000	700	1518
Norwegian Star	2001	91,000	971	2240
Norwegian Sun	2001	77,104	853	2400
Norwegian Wind	1993	50,760	754	1748
Pride of Aloha	1999	77,104	853	2002
Pride of America	2003	NA	921	2146
Norwegian Spirit*	1999/2004	76,800	880	1996

*Formerly Super Star Leo.

Dining

Freestyle Dining - From elegant French bistros and Italian trattorias to Sushi and Tapas bars and more, there's a different dining option for almost every night of your cruise. NCL's newest ships offer up to 10 different restaurants, each featuring a diverse and ever-changing menu. 24-hour complimentary room service is also available. With Freestyle Dining you can dine whenever, wherever and with whomever you wish. There are no assigned seatings.

Kid's Program – Kid's Crew

NCL's complimentary Kid's Crew™ Program is designed for kids from 2 to 17.

Kid's Crew activities are carefully supervised by NCL's staff of youth counselors. There are circuses, crafts, parades, sports, games, stories and parties. They have campouts with flashlights and tents, and cooking classes where they can make pizza or pancakes with funny faces. There is T-shirt painting, face painting and poolside root beer floats, treasure hunts and sand castle competitions on NCL's private island. And NCL even offers shore excursions designed just for families.

Science Journeys - These six hands-on educational voyages into science and nature allow kids to discover insects, experiment with sea life or explore the world of pirates. Created for children between the ages of 3 to 12, Science Journeys are offered daily and last from 30 minutes to 1 hour.

Oceania Cruises ★★★★

Pros: Open-seating dining, great itineraries, excellent shore excursions, good value

Cons: Service can be inconsistent

Clientele: Adult couples and singles

CruiseReport.com Awards:

- Best at Sea – Best Shore Excursions

Profile

Oceania Cruises is one of the newest cruise lines which sprang up after the demise of Renaissance Cruises. Oceania's two former Renaissance "R" ships are large enough to deliver just about anything the bigger ships offer, yet small enough to feel intimate. Four separate dining venues with open-seating give guests plenty of choices when it comes to mealtime. The atmosphere is "country club casual" with no strict dress codes enforced and no formal nights.

Our Experience (1 cruise)

We were on the second scheduled sailing of this new cruise line. As you might expect with a brand new cruise line and new crew, there were a few rough spots when it came to service. However, overall Oceania did an exceptional job and promises to be one of the hottest new cruise lines in the industry. The ships are the perfect size and configuration for longer journeys and the company has excellent itineraries. A wide variety of dining options and excellent shore excursions make Oceania an excellent choice for a cruise vacation.

Destinations sailed by Oceania ships:

Europe
Mexico
Scandinavia
Caribbean

Mediterranean
Panama Canal
South America
Transatlantic

Oceania's 2004 Fleet				
Vessel Name	Inaugural	Tonnage	Length	Guest Capacity
Regatta	1998/2003	30,277	592	680
Insignia	1998/2003	30,277	592	680

Dining

All dining is open-seating. Oceania ships feature five dining venues:

- **The Grand Dining Room** features continental cuisine with menu choices that change every evening.
- **The Polo Grill** features prime beef, chops and fresh seafood.
- **The Toscana** features Italian cuisine with a touch of Tuscany.
- **Tapas on the Terrace** features flavors of the Mediterranean.
- **The Terrace Café** features café breakfast and lunch buffets.
- **24 Hour Room Service**

Kid's Program

Oceania does not have any structured programs for children.

Princess Cruises ★ ★ ★ ★

Pros: Personal Choice Dining, worldwide itineraries, beautiful ships, open-seating dining available

Cons: Lackluster entertainment, chaotic crowds in buffet

Clientele: Couples, families, first-time cruisers

Profile

Princess has so many ships going to so many destinations that is has something for everyone. The company is still trying to cast off the "Love Boat" image as it is anything but a cruise line for swinging singles. With over $3 billion in new ship builds since 1990, Princess has one of the most modern and impressive fleets in the industry. In 2003, Royal Caribbean and Carnival launched an all-out war to purchase Princess. After months of wrangling, Carnival finally outbid Royal Caribbean and took possession of Princess. Princess remains as its own brand with all of the qualities that have made it one of the most popular cruise lines in the world. Positioned somewhere at the high-end of the mass market cruise lines, Princess has an appeal that reaches a broad audience of cruise enthusiasts.

Our Experience (1 cruise)

We sailed on the fourth sailing of the Grand Princess in 1998 in the Mediterranean. The ship was beautiful. It was pretty hard to distinguish Princess from Holland America or Royal Caribbean. Food and service are comparable on all three lines. On the Grand Princess, we found the traffic patterns in the buffet lines to be chaotic and disorganized. Interestingly, on our voyage the bars and lounges all closed by midnight. Our mini-suite was very well-appointed and comfortable and the butler service was great. For such a large ship, tender operations went very smoothly, as did all of our tours.

www.PerfectCruiseBook.com

Destinations sailed by Princess:

Africa	Alaska
Asia	Australia/New Zealand
Bermuda	Canada
Caribbean	Europe
Hawaii	Mediterranean
Mexico	Pacific Northwest
Panama Canal	Scandinavia
South America	South Pacific
U.S. East Coast	U.S. Pacific Coast

Princess Cruises' 2004 Fleet

Vessel Name	Inaugural	Tonnage	Length	Guest Capacity
Caribbean Princess	2004			3100
Coral Princess	2002	88,000	964	1950
Dawn Princess	1997	77,000	856	1950
Diamond Princess	2002	113,000	952	2670
Golden Princess	2000	109,000	935	2600
Grand Princess	1998	109,000	935	2600
Island Princess	2002	88,000	964	1950
Pacific Princess	1999	30,200	594	684
Regal Princess	1991	70,000	811	1590
Royal Princess	1984	45,000	757	1200
Sapphire Princess	2004	113,000	952	2670
Sea Princess	1998	77,000	856	1950
Star Princess	2002	109,000	951	2600
Sun Princess	1995	77,000	856	1950
Tahitian Princess	1999	30,277	592	680

Dining

Personal Choice Dining – You can dine in the traditional two-seating system, or you can enjoy "Anytime Dining" open-seating dining. The choice is yours. Princess ships also have alternate dining venues where you can dine casually each evening.

- **Main Dining Room** – Princess offers traditional early seating and late seating dining as well as Personal Choice Dining in its main dining rooms. Full menu service is offered for breakfast, lunch and dinner. Menus change each day. Breakfast and lunch are open-seating.
- **Horizon Court/Lido Café** – Enjoy buffet-style breakfast and lunch at the Horizon Court or Lido Café. On most ships, the Horizon Court becomes a casual, bistro-style venue each evening after 10pm.
- **Sabatinis** (Offered on Grand, Golden, Star, Coral, Island, Tahitian, Pacific, Diamond, Sapphire, and Caribbean) – Upscale Italian cuisine is served here each evening. Reservations required. Service charge applies.
- **Sterling Steakhouse** (Sun, Dawn, Pacific, Tahitian Princess, Star, Golden, Royal, Caribbean) – Upscale steakhouse serving chicken and beef specialties. Reservations required. Service charge applies.
- **Painted Desert** (Grand) – Upscale Southwestern cuisine served in a casual atmosphere. Reservations required. Service charge applies.
- **Room service** – A limited menu is available 24 hours a day.

Kid's Program

Princess provides dedicated youth centers which are staffed by trained counselors for junior cruisers from ages 3 to 17.

Princess Fun Zone offers specific programs for kids ages 3 to 12. Their special Teen Center is dedicated to teen passengers.

On all vessels except Royal Princess, Tahitian Princess and Pacific Princess, you'll find completely equipped Youth Centers. There's everything from arts and crafts corners, games tables and movies to a splash pool area.

Princess operates youth programs on Royal, Tahitian or Pacific Princess when 20 or more children ages 3 to 17 are traveling on a given voyage. Children under the age of 3 are allowed to visit the Youth Center, if accompanied and supervised by a parent at all times.

The Sun, Dawn, Grand, Golden, Coral, Island, Diamond and Star Princess offer a toddlers' play area.

Radisson Seven Seas Cruises ★★★★★★

Pros: Polished service, beautiful ships, great dining, open-seating dining, complimentary soft drinks and bottled water, complimentary wine and spirits with dinner, gratuities included

Cons: Expensive (but worth it)

Clientele: Upscale, affluent adult couples and singles

CruiseReport.com Awards:

- Six-Star Award of Excellence 2002, 2003 and 2004.
- Best Cruise Line for 2002.
- Best at Sea – Accommodations
- Best at Sea – Internet Café
- Best at Sea – Butler Service

Profile

Radisson Seven Seas Cruises was born in 1995 from the marriage of Radisson Diamond Cruises and Seven Seas Cruise Line. Today, the company operates five luxury ships of varying sizes and configurations. The Radisson Diamond and Paul Gauguin carry 350 and 320 passengers respectively and deliver a high level of service for those who prefer a smaller, more intimate ship. On the other end of the spectrum, Seven Seas Mariner and sister ship, Voyager, deliver small ship luxury with big ship amenities to 700 guests. Somewhere in the middle, you find Seven Seas Navigator which services 490 guests. No matter which Radisson Seven Seas ship you choose, you are certain to be pampered in a style that very few cruise lines can claim.

Our Experience (3 cruises)

Seven Seas Voyager and Seven Seas Mariner offer big-ship entertainment and activities with a surprisingly intimate feel and exceptional service that rivals ships that only serve half as many guests. We love the spacious and tastefully decorated accommodations. The complimentary soft drinks, bottled water (anytime) and wine with dinner makes this cruise line a real value. World-cruise guests enjoy complimentary open-bar service throughout the ship!

Destinations sailed by Radisson Seven Seas' ships:

Africa
Antarctica
Australia/New Zealand
Bermuda
Caribbean
Hawaii
Mexico
Scandinavia
South Pacific
World Cruise

Alaska
Asia
Bahamas
Canada
Europe
Mediterranean
Panama Canal
South America
U.S. East Coast

Radisson Seven Seas' 2004 Fleet				
Vessel Name	Inaugural	Tonnage	Length	Guest Capacity
Diamond	1992	20,295	420	350
Paul Gauguin	1998	19,200	513	320
Seven Seas Mariner	2001	50,000	709	700
Seven Seas Navigator	1999	33,000	560	490
Seven Seas Voyager	2003	46,000	709	700

Dining

All dining is open-seating. Complimentary wine and spirits are served each evening.

- **Compass Rose Restaurant** serves full breakfast, lunch and dinner every day. A different menu is featured each evening with exceptional Continental cuisine.
- **La Veranda** serves buffet-style breakfast and lunch and transforms into a casual Italian bistro each evening. The menu here changes several times throughout each cruise.
- **Signatures Restaurant** (Seven Seas Voyager and Seven Seas Mariner) is a world-class French restaurant under the auspices of Le Cordon Bleu.
- **Latitudes** (Seven Seas Voyager and Seven Seas Mariner) is a casual venue serving Asian-inspired and regional cuisine.
- **Room Service** offers a full menu 24 hours a day. During evening restaurant hours, the Compass Rose menu is available for course-by-course dining in your suite.

Kid's Program – Club Mariner

Club Mariner is offered to families traveling with children during summer months from late June through late August. The program is available on Seven Seas Voyager, Seven Seas Mariner, Seven Seas Navigator and Radisson Diamond.

Club Mariner offers programs tailored to three different age groups:

- 5 to 9
- 10 to 13
- 14 to 17

The Club Mariner program is complimentary, and families register on board. The three age groups are supervised by trained youth counselors.

In Tahiti, RSSC offers special "Ambassadors of the Environment" program for kids aged 9 to 15. It is an educational (and fun) program run by staff from Jean-Michel Cousteau's Ocean Futures Society. It is the only sea-going version of his successful land program. Again, this is offered during the summer holiday period from late June to late August.

There is a $50 per child registration fee for this program as it involves many activities ashore on the islands.

Royal Caribbean International ★★★★

Pros: Innovative ships, endless activities, exceptional value, excellent entertainment, alternate restaurants, consistently good in all areas

Cons: Lots of announcements and solicitations

Clientele: Young couples, families, singles, first-time cruisers

CruiseReport.com Awards:

- Best Large Ship Cruise Line 2003
- Best at Sea – Loyalty Program (Crown & Anchor)
- Best at Sea – Alternate Dining 2003
- Best at Sea – Theatre (Serenade of the Seas)
- Best at Sea – Activities
- Best at Sea – Lido Buffet (Windjammer Café)

Profile

Royal Caribbean is a near-perfect "all-around" cruise line. Royal Caribbean's ships are unquestionably some of the most innovative and beautiful in the industry. The trend began in 1988 with the introduction of Sovereign of the Seas, the largest cruise ship ever built at that time. Two other Sovereign-class vessels were added to the fleet, Majesty of the Seas and Monarch of the Seas. In 1995, they upped the ante with the introduction of the first in a series of Vision-class ships, the Legend of the Seas. Vision-class ships were the first to offer 18-hole miniature golf courses. Not one to rest on its laurels, in 1999, Royal Caribbean blew the industry away with the first 142,000 ton ship afloat, Voyager of the Seas. There are now five Voyager-class vessels, each featuring rock-climbing walls, miniature golf, roller-blade tracks, an interior promenade and ice-skating rinks! All Royal Caribbean ships are now being retrofitted to include rock-climbing walls. In 2001, the company introduced yet another class of ships with the launching of Radiance of the

Seas at 90,500 tons. There are now four Radiance-class vessels in the fleet. In 2006, Royal Caribbean plans to introduce the Ultra-Voyager which will regain the title of the world's largest cruise ship.

Our Experience (7 cruises)

This is a great cruise line. We always look forward to a cruise on Royal Caribbean. We find that Royal Caribbean offers a lot more style than some of the other mass-market cruise lines. If you could get rid of the annoying announcements and persistent solicitations from photographers and waiters with trays of frozen drinks, you could easily mistake Royal Caribbean for a mid-level luxury cruise line. We think the quality of the food and service in their alternate dining venues, Chops Grill and Portofino, are the best in the industry. Royal Caribbean's entertainment is very close to the best in the industry, as well.

Destinations sailed by Royal Caribbean ships:

Alaska
Bermuda
Caribbean
Hawaii
Mexico
Panama Canal

Bahamas
Canada/New England
Europe
Mediterranean
Pacific Northwest
South America

Royal Caribbean's 2004 Fleet					
Vessel Name	Inaugural	Tonnage	Length	Guest Capacity
Adventure of the Seas	2000	138,000	1020	3114
Brilliance of the Seas	2002	90,090	962	2501
Empress of the Seas	1990/2004	48,563	692	2020
Enchantment of the Seas	1997	74,000	916	1950
Explorer of the Seas	2000	138,000	1020	3114
Grandeur of the Seas	1996	74,000	916	1950
Jewel of the Seas	2003	90,090	962	2501

Royal Caribbean's 2004 Fleet				
Legend of the Seas	1995	70,000	867	1808
Majesty of the Seas	1992	73,941	880	2356
Mariner of the Seas	2003	138,000	1012	3114
Monarch of the Seas	1991	73,941	880	2354
Navigator of the Seas	2002	138,000	1020	3114
Radiance of the Seas	2000	90,090	962	2501
Rhapsody of the Seas	1997	78,491	915	2435
Serenade of the Seas	2003	90,090	961	2501
Sovereign of the Seas	1988	73,192	880	2280
Splendour of the Seas	1996	70,000	867	2076
Vision of the Seas	1998	78,491	915	2435
Voyager of the Seas	1999	138,000	1012	3114

Dining

Royal Caribbean offers a variety of dining options on its fleet of ships.

- **Main Dining Room** – Full service breakfast and lunch menu each day. Main Seating and Late Seating dinner with assigned tables each evening. Menu choices change nightly.
- **Windjammer Café** – Buffet-style breakfast with omelet station. Buffet-style lunch with pasta[1] and carving stations. Casual alternative buffet-style dinner each evening.
- **Johnny Rockets** (Voyager Class Vessels) – 50's style diner serving hamburgers, hot dogs, fries, onion rings and milk shakes*.
- **Seaview Café** (Radiance Class vessels) – Casual dining available throughout the daytime offering burgers, chili, fish and chips and other light fare.

---

[1] Pasta stations available on some ships.

- **Portofino** (Radiance Class and Voyager Class vessels) – Upscale Italian-theme restaurant serving a variety of grilled specialty items and pastas. Reservations required. Service charge applies.
  CruiseReport.com Best at Sea Award for Alternate Dining.
- **Chops Grille** (Radiance Class vessels, Mariner of the Seas) – Upscale Prime steak and chop restaurant. Reservations required. Service charge applies.
  CruiseReport.com Best at Sea Award for Alternate Dining.
- **24 Hour Room Service** – Limited menu available 24-hours a day. Complimentary. Soft drinks extra. During main dining hours, select items from the evening menu are available from room service.
- **Pizzeria** – Fresh pizza served throughout the day. On Voyager-class vessels, pizza is available at Café Promenade. On Radiance-class vessels, it is available at the Solarium Café.

*There is a charge at Johnny Rockets for milk shakes.

Kid's Program - Adventure Ocean

This complimentary program is specially designed to blend educational activities with just plain fun. Activities are scheduled for five different age groups as follows:

- 3 to 5
- 6 to 8
- 9 to 11
- 12 to 14
- 15 to 17

Your child will get to learn about local customs, do cool science experiments, and make great new friends. To participate, your child must be three years of age and potty trained. Every member of Royal Caribbean's Adventure Ocean staff holds a college degree in education, recreation, or other related field, or has qualified-equivalent experience working with children ages 3-17. There are special kids-only meals, a TV station with programming just for kids, lots of great play areas, even a nightclub for teens.

Source: Royal Caribbean Corporate Communications Department and www.royalcaribbean.com

Seabourn ★★★★★

Pros: Intimate ships, great service, 5-star dining, complimentary champagne, wine and spirits, gratuities included in cruise fare, open-seating dining, and great lecture series, Wi-Fi Internet access

Cons: No balcony suites*, expensive (but worth it), minimal entertainment, few activities

Clientele: Affluent adult couples and singles

CruiseReport.com Awards:

- Six-Star Award of Excellence 2002
- Best at Sea – Caviar and Champagne
- Best at Sea – In-Suite Dining

Profile

Seabourn's clientele is made up of affluent, sophisticated travelers. Seabourn guests expect intimate surroundings and uncompromising service. The company's three "yachts" are actually small (10,000 ton) cruise ships that can accommodate 208 guests in pampered luxury. Seabourn's ships sail around the globe with some of the most exotic and interesting destinations of any cruise line. Exceptional service and style are apparent everywhere on these yachts. Even the embarkation process is effortless as you are greeted at the pier and escorted to your suite by a white-gloved attendant. Champagne and caviar are available 24 hours a day and will be delivered to you anywhere on the ship. Caribbean itineraries feature "Champagne and Caviar" in the surf.

Our Experience (1 cruise)

Our 7-night Canada/New England cruise aboard Seabourn Pride proved to us that this cruise line's reputation is well-deserved

The Perfect Cruise

having been long regarded as one of the best-of-the-best. A polished crew delivers a level of service that is exceptional. All soft drinks, liquor, wine and champagne are complimentary. Gratuities are also included in the cruise fare. The suites are roomy and have large walk-in closets and a large window. For sophistication, quality, and style, Seabourn is an excellent choice.

Destinations sailed by the Yachts of Seabourn:

Africa
Asia
Bahamas
Caribbean
Mediterranean
Panama Canal
South America
U.S. East Coast

Alaska
Australia/New Zealand
Canada
Europe
Middle East
Scandinavia
South Pacific

Seabourn's 2004 Fleet				
Vessel Name	Inaugural	Tonnage	Length	Guest Capacity
Seabourn Pride	1988/1997	10,000	440	204
Seabourn Legend	1992/1999	10,000	440	208
Seabourn Spirit	1989/1999	10,000	440	204

*Seabourn has refitted its vessels with what they refer to as "French Balconies" in select suites. However, these are not large enough to hold a chair or lounger. Basically, it is a sliding glass door with a platform for standing.

Dining

All dining is open-seating. Complimentary wine and spirits are served with lunch and dinner.

- **The Restaurant** serves breakfast, lunch and dinner. Evening menus have been designed by celebrity chef Charlie Palmer, whose style has been called 'Progressive

American', and whose flagship restaurant, Aureole, has won two James Beard awards. He has created over 300 recipes for Seabourn, allowing for a full 21-day menu cycle without repeats.
- **The Veranda Café** features casual breakfast and lunch buffets. In the evenings, the Veranda Café offers, in a more casual style, themed dinner menus which change each evening. Themes include Seabourn Steak Night, Ginger & Spice Asian night, From the Sea Seafood night, etc.
- **Room Service** is available 24 hours a day with the full Restaurant evening menu available for course-by-course in-suite dining during Restaurant hours.

Kid's Program

Seabourn does not offer any structured programs for children.

SeaDream Yacht Club ★★★★★★

Pros: Polished service, intimate yachts, exceptional cuisine, casual elegance, complimentary champagne, wine and spirits included, all gratuities included, open-seating dining

Cons: Expensive (but worth it), little or no entertainment, no balconies

Clientele: Affluent adult couples, corporate charter groups

CruiseReport.com Awards:

- Best Small Ship Cruise Line 2003
- 6-Star Award of Excellence 2003 & 2004
- Best at Sea – Food and Dining
- Best at Sea – Relaxation Cruise
- Best at Sea – Fitness Center

Profile

SeaDream Yacht Club was founded in September of 2001 by Norwegian entrepreneur Atle Brynestad, who founded Seabourn Cruise Line, and Larry Pimentel, who was President of Seabourn under Brynestad and later President and CEO of the merged companies Cunard-Seabourn. SeaDream emphasizes that it is not a "Cruise line", rather it is a yachting company. The difference is more than just terminology. Yachting is much more intimate and flexible than "cruising". A SeaDream yacht might adjust its sailing itinerary to allow for additional time in a particular port, something a cruise ship would never do. The two 108 passenger SeaDream vessels, SeaDream I and SeaDream II, are virtually identical and have been recently refurbished to evoke the yachting feel. Service levels are the highest in the industry with all cocktails, champagne and soft drinks complimentary. SeaDream has taken dining to a new level with excellent menus and dramatic presentation. Even though the service is uncompromising, the style is casual elegance.

Our Experience (2 cruises)

Cruising with SeaDream is the closest thing to having your own private, multi-million dollar yacht. The lack of balcony suites is offset by the size of the vessel. You are never more than a few steps from open deck space. When we disembark a SeaDream yacht, we always leave wanting more of the SeaDream experience. The highlight of our two sailings was the Champagne and Caviar Splash followed by an awesome beach Bar-BQ. Unique features offered by SeaDream include complimentary use of water sports equipment from the ship's marina, access to mountain bikes when in port, and use of Segway® Human Transporter (service charge applies). If relaxation and superb service are what you are seeking, SeaDream Yacht Club is as good as it gets.

Destinations sailed by SeaDream yachts:

Bahamas   Europe
Mediterranean   Southern Caribbean
Transatlantic

| SeaDream's 2004 Fleet |||||
Vessel Name	Inaugural	Tonnage	Length	Guest Capacity
SeaDream I	1984/2002	4,260	344	110
SeaDream II	1985/2002	4,260	344	110

Dining

All dining is open-seating. You can dine whenever and with whomever you wish. Complimentary wine and spirits are served with lunch and dinner.

- **The Restaurant** – Evening meals are served in the indoor Restaurant where the menu changes each day.
  CruiseReport.com Best at Sea Award for Food and Dining
- **Topside Restaurant** – Breakfast and lunch are served al fresco in this comfortable outdoor restaurant. When weather permits, evening meals here are served "under the stars".
- **24 Hour Room Service** – A limited menu is available 24-hours a day.

Kid's Program

SeaDream Yacht Club does not offer any structured programs for children.

Silversea Cruises ★★★★★★

Pros: Ultra-luxury, polished service, complimentary champagne, wine and spirits included, gratuities included, open-seating dining

Cons: Expensive (but worth it)

Clientele: Upscale adult couples

CruiseReport.com Awards:

- 6-Star Award of Excellence 2002 & 2004
- Best at Sea – Best Luxury Cruise
- Best at Sea – Best Maitre d'
- Best at Sea – Best Bar Service
- Best at Sea – Best Cruise Director (Ray Solaire)

Profile

Silversea is the consummate ultra-luxury small ship cruise line. With a diverse passenger list whose only commonality is their success in life and their demand for the very best, Silversea prides itself on setting the standards for luxury cruising. Silversea operates two 16,800 ton 296 passenger ships (Silver Wind and Silver Cloud), and two 28,258 ton 382 passenger ships (Silver Whisper and Silver Shadow). These four ships transport their guests to some of the most exotic locations on Earth. Every room on board Silversea is a suite, many with balconies. The atmosphere on Silversea is formal and stylish. Tuxedos and floor-length gowns are commonly seen on formal nights. All soft drinks, wine, beer and liquor, as well as all gratuities, are included in the cruise fare. Business-class air upgrades are also available on most sailings.

Our Experience (2 cruises)

On Silversea, you feel special from the moment you step onboard. The mood here is one of sophistication and style. The highly trained and skilled staff routinely goes out of their way to fulfill any request. We like to come up with crazy requests just to see how they will respond, and they have never disappointed us. We cannot seem to find anything they will not do for us. Your fellow Silversea guests will most likely be successful business people and retirees. We have never failed to make interesting friends aboard Silversea. If you can afford the very best in life, this is it.

Destinations sailed by Silversea ships:

Africa
Asia
Canada
Hawaii
Mediterranean
Middle East
Panama Canal
South America
Caribbean
U.S. Pacific Coast

Alaska
Australia/New Zealand
Europe
India
Mexico
Pacific Northwest
Scandinavia
South Pacific
U.S. East Coast

Silversea's 2004 Fleet				
Vessel Name	Inaugural	Tonnage	Length	Guest Capacity
Silver Cloud	1994/2003	16,800	514	296
Silver Shadow	2000	28,250	610	382
Silver Whisper	2001	25,000	610	382
Silver Wind	1994/2002	16,800	514	296

Dining

All dining is open-seating. Complimentary wine and spirits are served with lunch and dinner.

- **The Restaurant** - Full service breakfast, lunch and dinner served daily. The dishes created by Silversea's Master Chefs are complemented by those of La Collection du Monde, created by the world-class chefs of culinary partner Relais & Châteaux.
- **The Terrace Café** - An alternative to the more formal Restaurant, The Terrace Cafe offers the same culinary excellence but in a more casual setting. Evening menus accent regional Italian specialties, while lunch and breakfast offer sumptuous buffets and hearty grilled fare. And, as always, you have the option to dine when and where you prefer - including a table alfresco with the world and its bounty spread before you.
- **In-Suite Dining** - A regular room service menu is available 24 hours a day. During regular dining hours, however, you can order from the Restaurant menu, with your meal served course-by-course.

Kid's Program

Silversea does not offer structured programs for children.

Viking River Cruises ★ ★ ★

Pros: Relaxed environment, non-smoking, tours included

Cons: Scant onboard entertainment

Clientele: Mature adults

CruiseReport.com Awards:

- Best at Sea – River Cruise

Profile

Viking River Cruises is the largest operator of river cruises in the world. The fleet of 14 Viking River Cruises' ships sail the rivers of Europe, Russia and China. Viking River Cruises visits at least one port a day on virtually every itinerary and you can explore small villages off the beaten path that are inaccessible via an ocean cruise. Docking in the heart of town, you'll have more time to see the cities, not just travel to the cities. You'll experience ever-changing riverside scenery, as well as local nightlife, when your ship overnights in port.

Our Experience (2 cruises)

Our first Viking River Cruise was a 12-night European river cruise. Our second was a 7-night Yangtze River cruise in China. The pace is much slower and more relaxed than an ocean cruise. There is virtually no entertainment other than socializing with new friends in the evening. The emphasis is on the destination, not the ship. You can usually walk right off the boat and into town. Excursions are included in each city visited and the tours are very well conducted. This is a great value and a great way to see inland cities that are unreachable by ocean-going vessels. All guests are English-speaking, most from the U.S. and Canada. All tours are conducted in English.

Destinations sailed by Viking River Cruises' ships:

Europe River Cruise
Russia and the Ukraine
Yangtze River (China)

Viking River Cruises' 2004 Fleet				
Vessel Name	Inaugural	Tonnage	Length	Guest Capacity
Century Star	2003	NA	285	186
Viking Burgundy	2000	NA	365	154
Viking Danube	1999	NA	360	150
Viking Europe	2001	NA	375	150
Viking Kirov	1988/2001	NA	430	199
Viking Neptune	2001	NA	375	150
Viking Normandie	1989	NA	299	23
Viking Pakhomov	1988/2001	NA	430	199
Viking Pride	2001	NA	375	150
Viking Schumann	1994/2001	NA	311	124
Viking Spirit	2001	NA	375	150

Dining

A buffet breakfast is available each morning in the restaurant. Omelets and egg dishes are also available from the menu. A lunch menu that changes each day is served in the restaurant. There is a single dinner seating each evening. All meals feature open-seating, so you can dine with whomever you choose. Evening menus change each day.

Kid's Program

Viking River Cruises does not offer any programs for children.

Windstar Cruises ★★★★

Pros: Romantic sailing vessels, great service, open-seating dining

Cons: Minimal activities and entertainment

Clientele: Adult couples

CruiseReport.com Awards:

- Best at Sea – Best Romantic Cruise

Profile

Windstar introduced the romance of sailing ships to the cruise industry in 1985 when it launched its fleet of four-masted ships. The ships were revolutionary since they used their sails for up to 50% of their propulsion and relied on diesel-electric engines for backup power. The ships are a unique blend of cruise ship and sailing vessel. In 1988, Windstar became part of the Carnival family of cruise lines when it and its parent company, Holland America were purchased by Carnival. In 1997, Windstar purchased a larger five-masted sailing vessel and re-named her Wind Surf. The atmosphere on Windstar is casual with touches of elegance. Indonesian staff provides friendly service with lots of smiles. There are no formal nights and no neckties are required on Windstar. If you are looking for a romantic cruise with little to get in the way of your relaxation, Windstar is a great choice.

Our Experience (2 cruises)

Windstar offers an intimate cruise experience in a romantic setting. The friendly Indonesian staff is always smiling and ready to please. We loved the complimentary DVD's for in-room movies and the open-seating dining. Our Mediterranean cruise from Civitivecchia to Nice was unquestionably the most romantic cruise to date.

Destinations sailed by Windstar ships:

Costa Rica
Europe
Panama Canal
South Pacific

Caribbean
Mediterranean
Scandinavia
Transatlantic

Windstar Cruises' 2004 Fleet				
Vessel Name	Inaugural	Tonnage	Length	Guest Capacity
Wind Spirit	1988	5,350	440	148
Wind Star	1986	5,350	440	148
Wind Surf	1990/2000	14,745	535	308

Dining

All dining aboard Windstar is casual and open-seating. Windstar features menu items created by Celebrity Chef Joachim Splichal.

- **The Restaurant** – Evening meals are served with menu items changing daily.
- **The Bistro** – This alternative to the Restaurant offers menus which change periodically throughout the cruise. Reservations are recommended.
- **The Veranda** – This indoor/outdoor café serves up sumptuous breakfast and lunch buffets. Highlights include an outdoor BBQ with lobster, lamb chops and pork ribs.
- **24 Hour Room Complimentary Room Service**

Kid's Program

Windstar does not offer any programs for children.

Our Favorite Cruises

This section features seven of our favorite cruise ships. These reviews can also be seen on the CruiseReport.com web site.

Royal Caribbean
Our Favorite Large Ship Cruise

A Beautiful Serenade
Serenade of the Seas

Somewhere in the Atlantic Ocean sailing off the coast of Nova Scotia, Dan and Teresa from Atlanta, Georgia, are being served cocktails and hors d'oeuvres in the intimate Concierge Club, just one of the many amenities they enjoy from booking a suite aboard a brand new cruise ship. But this is not Crystal or Silversea, this is Royal Caribbean! As a friend of mine in Plano, Texas, would say "Who would have thunk it?"

Okay, maybe I am biased when it comes to Royal Caribbean. The first cruise that Rickee and I enjoyed together was on Grandeur of the Seas in '97. Since then, we have sailed together on dozens of ships from nearly as many cruise lines to all corners of the world. Yet, as we stepped aboard Royal Caribbean's new Serenade of the Seas, we were immediately reminded of why this cruise line continues to amaze cruise enthusiasts. With a gross tonnage of 90,500, Serenade of the Seas may not be one of Royal Caribbean's largest vessels (Voyager-class vessels are 138,000 tons). Nevertheless, this 'Radiance-class' vessel commands a distinctive presence wherever she sails.

The Ship

Royal Caribbean has a knack for designing and building impressive ships, and Serenade of the Seas is certainly no exception. Like her slightly older sisters, Radiance of the Seas and Brilliance of the Seas, Serenade's massive white hull is trimmed with blue-green glass lining the upper decks and topped off by the distinctive Viking Crown lounge (as are all Royal Caribbean vessels). With a gross tonnage of 90,500 and a beam of 105.6' (width), Serenade is able to squeeze through the Panama Canal, allowing her to service the east coast, Caribbean, Panama Canal, Hawaii and Alaska.

> **CruiseReport.com Tip** - Serenade of the Seas has two sister ships which are virtually identical in design and décor: Radiance of the Seas and Brilliance of the Seas. Jewel of the Seas, launched in March of 2004, is the last in the series of Radiance-class vessels.

Royal Caribbean's signature Centrum, located amidships, is nothing short of awe-inspiring. The open atrium extends from Deck 4 all the way to Deck 12 and sparkles with polished metal, a huge amount of tempered glass and low-voltage halogen lighting. There are six glass elevators in the Centrum, 2 of which offer a view of the Centrum as they raise and lower guests, while the other 4 are located on the outside offering breathtaking views of the ocean. There are 3 additional elevators located forward but none located aft on Radiance-class vessels. Speaking of glass, it is everywhere on Serenade of the Seas and it gives the interior a major "Wow!" factor.

In general, moving around this ship is surprisingly easy. The majority of public areas are located on decks 4, 5, 6, 11 and 12. There are staterooms on Decks 2, 3, 4, 7, 8, 9 and 10. The only thing impeding fore to aft movement is the Shops at Centrum which can become very jammed with shoppers at various times of the day.

Accommodations

The Junior Suite offers lots of space, comfortable seating and vast amounts of storage.

Guests aboard Serenade can relax in a variety of well-appointed staterooms and suites. Our Category JS (Junior Suite) was comfortable and spacious with a large walk-in closet better suited for a 14-day cruise than our 5-night Canada/New England cruise. The marble-clad bathroom features a granite vanity with sink, full-size bathtub/shower and two mirrored medicine cabinets flanking the large mirror. The queen-size bed is comfortable with the exception of its shape which is curved on the end. This is apparently done to allow more walking space around the bed in staterooms where the bed is located next to the balcony door. At 6' – 1" tall, I sometimes felt like my feet were hanging off the end of the bed. There are extra pillows stored in the closet and plenty of wooden hangers. The desk/entertainment unit has six storage drawers, a pull-out extension for a laptop computer and storage shelves everywhere. A full-size sofa (which makes into a full-size bed), a coffee table and a nice chair with ottoman make for a roomy sitting area. A nice feature is a privacy curtain which divides the living room from the bed. The 20" color television sits on a cabinet which houses the refrigerator/mini-bar. There are two bedside tables, each with its own drawer and an ingenious reading light. The balcony is large and is fitted with two chairs, a table and a lounge chair. Royal Caribbean's uses sliding glass doors instead of hinged doors to access the balcony. You can really appreciate the sliding glass doors after having been jolted out of bed on other cruise lines when a neighbor's hinged door slams shut at 6:00am. Notwithstanding the audible talking and television from the neighboring suite, the Category JS suite was extremely comfortable and probably well worth the cost to upgrade from a balcony stateroom.

All cabins are equipped with interactive television, telephone, computer jack, vanity tables with extendable work surface for laptop computers, refrigerator/mini-bar, hairdryer, 110/220 electrical outlets, convertible double/single hanging closet, and reading lights by the bed.

The interior staterooms on Serenade of the Seas seemed roomier than the one we occupied in 1997 on Grandeur of the Seas. Each contained a mini-sofa and had loads of storage space. For the budget-minded cruiser, these staterooms are quite comfortable. One step up from the interior stateroom is the standard ocean view stateroom which is basically the same size with the addition of a large picture window (a porthole on Deck 2). By far the most popular staterooms on Serenade of the Seas (and most newer ships) are the balcony staterooms. While there are a couple of variations of balcony staterooms, they are generally larger, and of course, feature a nice balcony. There are five categories of suite accommodations. The Junior Suite (Cat JS), the Grand Suite (Cat GS), the Family Suite (Cat FS), the Owner's Suite (Cat OS) and the Royal Suite (Cat RS).

> **Note from Rickee:** The mirrored medicine cabinet doors in the bathroom can be opened and positioned so that you can see your head from all angles, a great feature when it comes to styling your hair.

Dining

Virtually everyone agrees that food is an integral and important part of any cruise vacation. The one exception to this rule might be Rickee who often has to be reminded to eat. Remember Mikey from the old 60's cereal commercial who did not like anything? Well, that could easily be Rickee. So, if Rickee likes the food, it really means something. When it comes to food on Serenade of the Seas...Rickee likes.

When evaluating dining aboard a cruise ship, we take several things into consideration:

- Food quality & taste
- Preparation
- Presentation
- Variety
- Service

The evaluation has to be balanced against reasonable expectations. For example, a meal served in a dining room that serves 1,200 meals per seating/per night cannot be expected to deliver the same quality meal that you would expect from a 5-star restaurant with only 30 tables to serve. Therefore, we evaluate dining rooms based on how they compare to other dining rooms on other cruise lines. Given that disclaimer, we found the Reflections dining room to rate from very good to excellent for a ship this size. Breakfast served here was delivered fast and hot and everything was prepared to order. Unlike some other major cruise lines, Royal Caribbean still offers Eggs Benedict on the breakfast menu as well as made-to-order omelets, banana or blueberry pancakes and much, much more. Lunch in Reflections was good, but a couple of items delivered to the table were cool to lukewarm. Nevertheless, the wait staff was friendly and very efficient. We never spent more than 40 minutes in Reflections for lunch, another big plus. Evening meals in Reflections were no less efficient and the meals were more impressive. Royal Caribbean and sister cruise line, Celebrity Cruises, are two cruise lines that have maintained the traditional early and late seating in the dining room, fighting the temptation to move to a 'freestyle' type of dining. "We simply cannot deliver the quality and service that our guests have come to expect from Royal Caribbean with a freestyle system," says Persaud Latchman, Serenade's Food and Beverage Manager.

The Windjammer Cafe is Royal Caribbean's signature Lido Buffet. On Vision-class vessels, the Windjammer is located at the front of the ship while Voyager-class and Radiance-class vessels place Windjammer aft of the pool area. Royal Caribbean really got it right when designing Windjammer for the Radiance-class vessels. At first glance, the number of serving stations looks daunting and confusing. Your first reaction might be "where do I begin?" In spite of this, the layout works very well. There are multiple serving "kiosks" each serving its own courses. One kiosk serves salads and fruits, another serves hot entrees, yet another for desserts, and so on. The layout and design reduces long lines of people waiting for food. That's a good thing. Instead of serving trays, which can result in tipped over glasses of water or lemonade, Royal Caribbean has implemented platter-sized plates sure to please even the most aggressive buffet aficionado. For breakfast, there was the standard scrambled eggs, hash browns, bacon, ham, sausage, etc. The omelet station was making omelets or other egg dishes to order. If you position yourself just right at the omelet station you can even talk yourself into fresh-off-the-griddle pancakes! For lunch, Windjammer offers a wide selection of salads, hot entrees, vegetables and a fresh pasta station. In the evening, the Windjammer transforms into a very nice dining alternative. The lighting is lowered and there are plenty of open tables. The variety and quality of food served in the evenings is surprisingly good, especially the Sushi and Mongolian barbeque offerings.

For guests who want a truly unique dining experience, Serenade of the Seas offers two upscale restaurants which are open from 6:00pm until 10:00pm nightly. Chops Grille is the ship's resident steakhouse serving USDA Prime beef, veal and pork chops. Chops Grill is our new pick for Best Alternate Dining at Sea, nudging out Carnival Pride's Nouveau Supper Club (our previous pick for Best Alternate Dining). Chops Grill hits all the marks with great quality and near flawless service and presentation. The shrimp cocktail appetizer yielded 5 medium-size shrimp with a spicy sauce that had a hint of barbeque flavor. The salads were the least impressive part of the meal but were compensated for by the hearty bowls of cheese and onion soup and clam chowder. Meat is where Chops really shines. The veal chop has a tender smoky flavor that tastes like it was cooked over a hickory flame. The Prime Rib is a huge slab of tender beef cooked to perfection that can be cut with a fork, literally. I wish I could extol the virtues of Chops' desserts, but alas, there was no room left in the 36" waist pants to give it a try. There is a $20 per person service charge for dining in Chops

Grill, but it is one of the best bargains on the ship. Reservations are required.

Right next door to Chops Grill is Portofino, Serenade's Italian restaurant. Portofino is no less impressive in its own right than Chops. In fact, it was a real toss up as to which should be named 'Best at Sea'. Portofino's strength lies in its Antipasto, Zuppe (soups) and Insalate (salads), where Chops relies more on its main courses to impress. The Prawn Risotto is not to be missed. In fact, our waiter, Earnest, claimed that many guests order it as an entree. On our visit, the soup of the day was Cream of Asparagus and it was equally rich and creamy. The Caesar salad served in Portofino is made tableside and is better than the one served in Chops. The pasta dish was made fresh and had a delightfully rich red sauce, while the Veal Medallion and Prosciutto was fork tender and delicious. As with Chops, we were totally unable to force a dessert down, but we heard from many other passengers that the desserts were truly delicious bordering on decadent. There is a $20 per person service charge for dining in Portofino and reservations are required.

Cruisers who lament the notion of 'having' to pay for these alternate dining options should perhaps rethink their attitude.

1. These restaurants are optional. There are plenty of other places on the ship to enjoy a meal and not incur an additional service charge.

2. The value of these restaurants far exceeds the $20 per person service charge. The food quality, presentation, service and atmosphere are comparable to restaurants with meal prices in the $50 to $75 per person range.

3. Cruise fares are far lower today than 20 years. Even with dinner for two in both restaurants, the total cost of a cruise aboard Serenade of the Seas is likely to be hundreds less than it would have cost 25 years ago

The Solarium Cafe serves pizza and other snacks from 3pm to 7pm on most days and is located in the Solarium on Deck 11. The

Seaview Cafe on Deck 12 is a nice place for a quick lunch or a late night snack. This restaurant serves burgers and other sandwiches, soups, salads, chicken fingers and hot wings.

Guests who wish to enjoy a cup of Cappuccino or a Mocha Latte along with a sweeping view of the ocean will want to head to Latte-Tudes on Deck 5 Centrum. Even though there is a charge for the coffee drinks served here, the quality of the 'Seattle's Best™' coffee exceeds the complimentary coffee served in Windjammer, Reflections or other dining areas. Complimentary cookies, cakes and other sweet temptations are available here to enjoy with your coffee. Coffee bars have become a popular addition to most new ships in the past few years, but none have anything as nice as Latte-Tudes. The coffee drinks are competitively priced with your local Starbucks, and I personally prefer Seattle's Best to Starbucks. The four computer terminals with Internet access found in Latte-Tudes make this a perfect place to sip morning coffee and check email!

Of course, if all else fails, you can always pick up the phone in your stateroom and order from the complimentary room service menu! Full breakfast service is available each morning and sandwiches and snacks are available 24 hours a day. During dinner meal times, you can even select dishes from the evening's menu and have them delivered to your stateroom or suite.

Bars and Lounges

When the sun goes down, the lights come up on Serenade of the Seas to reveal a ship built for fun and nightlife as much as it was for daytime activities. Guests who enjoy good music accompanied by a well-made cocktail need look no further than the Lobby Bar on Deck 4 where there is a string quartet or Jazz trio playing nearby from 4:30pm until 1:00am. Intimacy and elegance is the order of the day as you sip the bubbly (or any other drink) in the Champagne Bar on Deck 6 Centrum. The signature bar on any Royal Caribbean ship has to be the Schooner Bar (Deck 6) just aft of the Centrum. The Schooner Bar is the perfect place to listen to pianist Denny Phelps or Latin Guitarist, Rico Duarte, and enjoy a cocktail before you have dinner at Portofino or Chops Grill.

> **CruiseReport.com Tip** - Mixed drinks at the Pool Bar and Sky bar are served in much smaller plastic glasses than in the other bars on the ship, yet they are the same price.

Sports enthusiasts have not been forgotten. The Pit Stop Sports Bar located aft of Casino Royale features walls lined with plasma televisions playing sports events from around the world. The de-facto late night haunt is the Vortex Disco Bar located on Deck 13 in the Viking Crown Lounge. Another section of the Viking Crown Lounge has been designated as Hollywood Odyssey, the ship's cigar bar. Of course you can also quench your thirst at the Pool Bar (Deck 11) or Sky Bar (Deck 12) on warm afternoons by the pool.

Activities

Royal Caribbean has designed the Voyager-class and Radiance-Class ships, as well as its advertising campaign, to appeal to young adults (at any age, married or single) who lead active, energetic lives. Those looking to stay in shape after a night of partying and dancing need look no further than Deck 12 on Serenade of the Seas. For true adventure seekers, there is the 33-foot rock climbing wall which doubles as the rear panel of the ship's exhaust stack. Wanna-be hoopsters will find a basketball court (that can also be converted to a volleyball court). The golf simulator ($25 per hour) lets you play a round of golf on your choice of famous golf courses from around the world while the slightly less-challenging miniature golf course offers 9 holes of putting fun. The ShipShape Fitness Center is on Deck 12 forward and is well-equipped for stretching and toning muscles you did not even know you had. The center has a full set of free weights, Life Fitness™ circuit trainers, LifeCycles™, LifeStride™ treadmills and LifeFitness™ elliptical trainers. Royal Caribbean has spared no expense by installing the highest quality, commercial grade equipment in this facility. There are a host of ShipShape classes throughout the day including stretching, aerobics, Pilates yoga, etc. A nice locker room for changing into workout gear is on Deck 12 in the spa area with lockers, showers, steam and sauna. Well done!

Serenade of the Seas does not abandon those who may have consumed mass quantities the night before and simply need something less aggressive to pass the time. The pool on Deck 11 is one of the largest we have seen on any cruise ship and has impressive waterfall jets shooting from one end of the pool. This will be a popular hangout when Serenade does its Southern Caribbean itinerary. Deck 11 aft in the Solarium is where you can lay around a quiet adults-only pool. The Solarium has a retractable glass roof which can be closed in cooler climates (e.g. Alaska). There are two hot tubs here, a Balinese theme pool area with lush plants, sculptures of wild animals and a Balinese carved teak gate by a waterfall. This area is very relaxing and a great place to take a swim followed by a nice nap. And did we mention, no unaccompanied kids allowed in this area?

Other daytime activities on board include the Fine Art Auctions which are held in the Centrum on Deck 4. The auctions are conducted by Park West Galleries and there are hundreds of works from which to choose. Park West claims that you can purchase art here and save 40% to 80% off the land gallery prices. For whatever reason, there were lots of people at the auctions doing lots of bidding. Unfortunately, the auctioneer's 'barking' can be heard on every deck of the ship in the Centrum area, which can be a little distracting for those who wish to read in the library, which is located on Deck 7 Centrum.

Pampered guests will certainly make their way to the Serenade Day Spa where they will find a variety of massage treatments, facials, hair and nail treatments. Bingo fanatics will love Royal Caribbean's Snowball Jackpot Bingo, offering unquestionably the most generous payout of any cruise line. Bingo cards are available for $10 to $35 and the big final jackpot is almost always several thousand dollars. Hardcore gamblers will be pleased to see that Casino Royale has everything a Vegas aficionado could want. There are 195 slot machines, including poker machines, ranging from quarter to $5. Table games include Craps, Roulette, Black Jack, and Caribbean Stud Poker. Casino Royale's slots accept real quarters, so there is no need to get tokens from the cashier. There is a Casino bar where you can take a break from the action and enjoy an exotic libation. Something you will only see on Royal Caribbean are self-leveling billiard tables. The tables are located between the Schooner Bar and the Safari Club on Deck 6.

If you think Royal Caribbean has forgotten about the younger cruisers, you would be wrong. The ship's Adventure Ocean program has a full-time staff of 10 that does nothing but keep the young ones occupied from sunrise to way past sunset. Activities are divided into four different age groups:

- Aquanauts 3 to 5
- Explorers 6 to 8
- Voyagers 9 to 11
- Navigators 12 to 14
- Guests 15 to 17

Each age group has its own daily schedule of activities which start at 9:00am and extend until 1:00am on some evenings. For teens, there is a fully-equipped video arcade and Fuel, a teen disco and soda bar. Very cool. For the younger kiddos, there is a fully-equipped daycare center with computers, games, big screen TV, and all kinds of other 'kid's stuff' to keep the little ones occupied. After hours babysitting is available for a small fee.

Entertainment

Serenade of the Seas' Tropical Theater represents the Royal Caribbean's ongoing commitment to providing guests with top-notch entertainment. "This ship has the latest in stage and sound technology, on land or sea," says Rennie Watt, Stage and Production Manager. The Tropical Theater features advanced computer-driven lighting, sound, and stage effects. But great entertainment relies on more than technology. Great talent must also be present to put on a memorable show. The Royal Caribbean Singers and Dancers, who put on two production shows during a 7-day cruise, consist of four vocalists and a troupe of 10 dancers. Before a show makes it to the ship, the entertainers are hired through the company's Miami entertainment office then are shipped off to Ft. Lauderdale to train and rehearse each show at the Royal Caribbean Productions studio.

Leading the entertainment effort on Serenade of the Seas is Allan Brooks, the ship's cruise director. Brooks has been a cruise director for only a year and a half, but you would never know it to watch him at work. Allan is as comfortable on stage as he is walking down the hall. Having served on the old Viking Sun, Majesty of the Seas and as Assistant Cruise Director on Monarch of the Seas, the young Canadian finds himself managing a staff of 80 on the cruise line's newest ship. Brooks' former life as an improvisational comedian is evident when you watch him work the room during any of the events he hosts.

The two production shows on Serenade of the Seas* are "Stage to Screen" and "Vibeology". As a "song and dance tribute to some of the most memorable stage and movie musicals," Stage to Screen fell short of providing a memorable show. Even though the vocals are good and the dance routines complex and well-executed, the musical numbers were hardly recognizable. Vibeology is, hands-down, the better show of the two. This high-energy production allows the vocalists to show off their range and ability to harmonize better than in Stage to Screen. The dancers excelled in both shows, as did the Serenade of the Seas Orchestra. Both shows featured impressive costumes, stage and lighting effects and even a few surprises.

The real star of both shows is the Tropical Theater itself, unquestionably the best theater design on any cruise ship we have seen to date. A great ship theater begins with good, comfortable seating and great sightlines. There is nothing worse than showing up at the theater and not being able to find a seat without a support structure (pole) blocking your view of the stage. The Tropical Theater has very few obstructed views and the seating is not only comfortable, but functional. One great design feature was the cup holder located in the arm of each chair which has been ingeniously designed to hold a flat bottomed glass or a stemmed wine glass. No more red wine tipping over and ruining the expensive evening gown!

The Tropical Theater is also host to Celebrity Showtime which features a variety of guest performers. It is safe to say that there is something going on in the Tropical Theater each evening to entertain and delight guests. The theater is also used during days at sea for other entertainment like the popular Love and Marriage Game Show.

*It should be noted that production shows do change over time. The life of a show varies from 12 to 18 months.

Summary

To say that we were impressed with Serenade of the Seas would be an understatement. The ship and her staff deliver everything, and more, that anyone can reasonably expect from a value-driven, mass-market cruise line. Royal Caribbean is the only cruise line that is using its loyalty program, Crown & Anchor Society, to give guests significant incentives to book future cruises with Royal Caribbean. Having access to the Concierge Club is reason enough for someone like me to qualify as a Diamond member (10 or more cruises). There really is no reason not to book a cruise on this ship.

Norwegian Cruise Line
Our Favorite Entertainment Cruise

The Dawn of Freestyle Cruising
Norwegian Dawn

Mega cruise ships dot the landscape, or seascape, at the Port of Miami on a Saturday morning. A line of floating resorts extends for more than a mile waiting for anxious cruisers to board. In the middle of the line is a brand new ship that, at first glance, looks festive in comparison to all the rest. NCL's Norwegian Dawn is a stark white 91,700 ton ship that is covered in what looks like, well…graffiti! There are colorful signatures of the famous French impressionists Renoir, Van Gogh and Matisse. A rendition of the Statue of Liberty sprinkled among a few brightly colored ribbons of blue, pink and green graces the port side of the ship. If nothing else, it is different. The exterior of the ship is not the only thing different about Norwegian Dawn. She is NCL's newest ship, designed and built to fulfill the company's commitment to 'Freestyle Cruising', a concept aimed at offering guests a choice of dining, entertainment and activities.

"We quickly became big fans of NCL's Freestyle Cruising."

The foundation for Freestyle Cruising was laid when NCL pioneered the concept of 'alternative' dining with the introduction of the 'Le Bistro' restaurant several years ago. Before long, every major cruise line had copied the concept so that, now, just about every ship afloat offers some form of alternative dining. Most cruise lines offer a single alternative dining venue, the idea being that guests will try the alternative restaurant one evening and stick to the early or late seating arrangement for the remainder of the cruise. Freestyle Cruising goes much further; there is no assigned early or late seating. Guests can enjoy dinner in any of the 10 restaurants whenever they like and sit with whomever they wish. Even though some cruisers with whom we spoke expressed a preference for the traditional early/late assigned dining on other cruise lines, we quickly became big fans of Freestyle Cruising.

The Freestyle Cruising theme carries through to the ship's dress code. The standard evening dress code is 'Resort Casual' with the one exception being an 'optional formal' night. As long as you are out of your shorts, t-shirts and jeans by 5:00pm, just about anything else goes. If you forget to bring a tie, no problem! You can leave the tux and evening gown at home. After all, you are on a Freestyle vacation!

> **CruiseReport.com Tip** - If you are thinking about bringing your own bottle of liquor to enjoy in your stateroom, forget it! We saw a security person hand check a carry-on bag after it had passed through the X-Ray machine and confiscate a bottle of Scotch from one guest trying to 'smuggle' one aboard. NCL will hold the contraband for you and return it to you upon disembarkation.

The ship's interior décor can best be described as 'festive'. NCL has used just about every color in the spectrum to give the Dawn a bright, happy mood. Bright blue carpeting with splashes of orange, red and yellow can be found throughout the ship. There are seahorses, starfish and shells woven into the carpeting of the hallways and staterooms. Furnishings are no less lively, complete with colorful seating. The Spinnaker Lounge features a selection of odd-shaped chairs that look like they belong in a circus instead of on a cruise ship. This ship does not take itself too seriously; it is all about fun and frivolity.

Measuring 166 square feet, our balcony stateroom (Cat BB) is one of the smallest balcony cabins we have occupied. The small size is underscored by poor design of interior space and furnishings. For example:

- A large square table in the corner holds an ice bucket and glasses but also blocks access to the sliding door to the balcony.
- A smaller coffee table sits in front of a 4-foot wide sofa (which converted to a bed). The result is that there is very

little room between the coffee table and the corner table which also hampers access to the balcony.
- There are only three drawers, which we quickly filled. The closet space is adequate for 7-day cruises.
- There is a small vanity with a narrow mirror, but very little light. The vanity can quickly fill up with cosmetics, creams, lotions and well, whatever.
- The ship's designers chose to put the one and only 110 AC outlet at the back of the vanity table, so to recharge a computer or digital camera, you may find yourself knocking items off the vanity when plugging in the transformer. Unless the vanity table is kept clear, you will be forced to set your laptop or camera on the small round stool underneath the vanity.
- There is a small refrigerator which, as on most cruise ships, keeps water and soft drinks only moderately cool.
- There is only room for one bedside table and it contains no drawers.
- The bathroom is short on storage with only one narrow shelf above the sink.
- The shower stall is very large and comfortable and has a full-size sliding glass door.
- The separate water closet for the toilet is nice, but takes up available space from the bathroom that could be put to better use.

In spite of these shortcomings, the category BB stateroom is livable. The queen-sized bed is comfortable and the linens and bedding are nice. There are liquid soap and shampoo dispensers in the shower and near the sink, but no hair conditioner is provided. A shoe shine cloth, hand lotion and shower cap are provided. There is a powerful hair dryer located on the vanity.

Best Spa at Sea

No matter what your lifestyle, you are likely to find something to interest you on Norwegian Dawn. For the active and athletic crowd, Dawn features a sports deck with basketball, jogging track and golf driving net. The El Dorado Fitness Center has a large workout room with four elliptical machines, eight treadmills, recumbent bicycles, a rowing machine and circuit machines. There is also a separate spin room with several bikes. A gym area with mats is available for stretching and is the venue where many of Dawn's organized classes, ranging from kick boxing to yoga and stretching, are held. There are separate men's and ladies' locker rooms (with decent-sized lockers) each with a steam room, sauna and showers. There is no charge for using the exercise equipment, steam, or sauna on the Dawn and the exercise room is open 24 hours a day (lockers are available from 8:00am until 8:00pm). A coed spa area features a 37-foot lap pool, a Jacuzzi and a Hydro bath. El Dorado Fitness Center is arguably the nicest one we have seen on any ship to date. The El Dorado Spa and Beauty Salon is managed by the reputable Steiner group.

A Great Casino

A slot players club plus plenty of table games and a spacious casino make the Dawn Club Casino our pick for Best at Sea!

Gamblers will love the Dawn Club Casino, one of the largest afloat (and our pick for Best Casino). There are 207 slot machines ranging from nickel slots to $25 slots, with the majority of machines being quarter and dollar slots. There are 10 Black Jack tables, Let It Ride, Caribbean Stud Poker, 2 full-sized Craps tables and 2 Roulette tables. Here's a cruise ship first: NCL's Reel Players Club lets slot players accumulate points for slot play and redeem points for gifts. Another smart move on NCL's part: they keep the slots open all night long while the ship is at sea. Obviously someone at NCL understands the gambler mentality. If they offered free drinks during play, you would swear you were in a Vegas casino.

NCL has not forgotten families. The Dawn features a well-equipped kids' center complete with a kids' cinema, a game room, computer center and bunk beds for afternoon naps. There is a large video arcade for teens, organized activities for various age groups, and a separate T-Rex kids' pool complete with water slides, waterfalls, water cannons and more.

Of course, there are those who just want to lie around in the sun, read a book and relax. You are in luck, too. Dawn has expansive deck space with plenty of lounge chairs. The main pool, located on Deck 12, is large and surrounded by four hot tubs. You can sit poolside and sip on the drink of the day, or sit in the hot tub and share a "Helmet of Beer" with friends (NCL's beer bucket shaped like a football helmet). If you are seeking refuge from the crowd, there are lots of little nooks and crannies forward on Deck 13 where you can place a lounge chair and relax in relative peace and quiet. A well-equipped library on Deck 12 offers plenty of current-release books that you can check out and right across the hall is a spacious, well-lit and quiet reading room. Shuffles card room is equipped with card tables and board games.

My typical morning aboard the Dawn begins with a trip to the Java Café for a cup of decaf as I work on this review. To my taste, the free coffee served in Blue Lagoon is too strong and somewhat bitter. The coffee served in the Venetian restaurant is better, but I prefer a more peaceful place to work, and Java café fits that bill. Even though I am more than willing to pay the $1.50 per cup for the coffee at Java, I find the policy of charging full price for a coffee refill to border on price gouging. This exceeds Starbucks' refill price of 50 cents. Also, the $1.50 per cup is really $1.74 once the "autogratuity" of 15% is added. That makes Java Café's 8 oz. cup of coffee roughly the same price as Starbucks' 20 oz. Venti cup!

> **CruiseReport.com Tip** - Find an Internet Café in port. The Internet Café on the Dawn is too slow and too expensive to use except in case of emergency. I found an Internet Café in downtown St. Thomas that charged only 15 cents per minute with a lightning fast connection. There is another one at Havensight mall (where the ship docks) that charges $3 for 15 minutes. The ship charges 75 cents per minute. You do the math!

After my coffee, I am off to the Internet Café on Deck 9 to check email. As with many major cruise lines, NCL has partnered with Digital Seas to provide Internet access on board its ships. Basically, Digital Seas rents space onboard each ship for its Internet operation and they, not NCL, set the pricing and policies. I should point out that the Dawn offers wireless Internet access of which I took full advantage. This service allows laptop users to access the Internet from various locations around the ship. If your laptop has WiFi 802.11b compatibility, there is no additional charge for wireless access. If your laptop does NOT have this capability, the Internet Café will rent you a wireless card for $10 per day. This is a great idea; unfortunately the reality is not so great. First of all, the wireless reception only works in certain public areas such as the lobby, the Internet Café and the pool area. So you can forget working wirelessly from your stateroom. The next problem is power. You will not find any 110 volt AC outlets anywhere on the ship (except for your cabin where wireless does not reach.) Therefore, you will be limited to working within the life of your laptop's battery. If your laptop is like mine, the battery is rated for 4 hours of life and in reality, gives you about 45 minutes before the screen goes black. Whether you work wireless on your laptop, or use one of the 23 computers in the Internet Café, you will still have to pay for Internet time, and time does not come cheap. The basic charge is 75 cents per minute. There are two packages available where you can purchase a block of 100 minutes for $55 (55 cents per minute) or 250 minutes for $100 (40 cents per minute). I chose the 100 minute plan since all I was going to do was check email each day. What I did not know at the time was that the Internet connection was comparable to a 14,400 modem (I actually did an online test to check the speed.) As a result, I ran through my 115 minutes in 5 days and found myself having to shell out another $25 for 33 more minutes (75 cents per minute). I should point out that the slow speeds were not the fault of the wireless connection. I observed others using the computers in the Internet Café and their speeds were slow as well. All in all, I spent $80 on Internet and spent very little time on the Internet. Compare that to the $99 I pay for a full year of unlimited Internet access with NetZero®!

Cruisereport.com Tip - If you are using a laptop computer and have a power transformer capable of running on 220 current, invest in a 220 (male) to 110 (female) plug adapter. This is a 2 round pin plug adapter that should fit any cruise ship outlets. I bought one at Boolchands Cameras in St. Thomas for $3. You should be able to get one at any Radio Shack before your cruise.

Unlike the Internet service, feeding people is one thing that the Dawn does very well. On most days, the Dawn features a poolside barbeque that is too tempting for me to pass up. This is as close to a real cookout as you can get on a ship. There are charcoal grills set up by the pool where slabs of charred ribs, steaks, burgers, hot dogs, sausage and chicken breasts are cooked. I am a rib man, so they pile my plate full of meaty ribs slathered in sauce. I think it is about the sixth rib when all of the frustration of the Internet café becomes a distant memory. After rib number eight, I feel myself slipping into a pork coma. I think need a nap. It is all I can do to get through the steak! Groggy from my ribfest, I stumble onto a deck chair in a shady spot next to Rickee, close my eyes and let the fat and cholesterol work their magic.

The poolside barbeque is not the only option for lunch. There is a nice lunch buffet served in the Garden Café (Deck 12) or you can have a course-by-course luncheon in the Venetian restaurant. The Bimini Bar and Grill on Deck 14 forward, overlooking the pool area, offers Caribbean snacks, hot dogs, hamburgers and cocktails in a colorful Bahamian beach atmosphere.

Afternoons aboard the Dawn are filled with the activities that have become the trademarks of the cruise industry. There's bingo, trivia, music by the pool, various games and contests, dance classes, exercise classes, etcetera, etcetera. It is impossible to be bored on the Dawn, unless you choose to. The Oasis Pool on Deck 12 is the hot spot with Latin music, frozen drink specials, hot tubs and sun-baked bodies everywhere. It is here you will find Sprinkles Ice Cream Bar, albeit hidden in the middle of the pool bar. But be prepared to pay for your ice cream here to the tune of $2 for soft serve and up to $3.95 for hand-dipped HagenDaz.

After 5:00pm, Norwegian Dawn transforms into a lively entertainment and dining resort like no other ship afloat. The multiple themed restaurant concept is unique to NCL's new Freestyle Cruising ships (Dawn, Star and Sky) and really sets NCL apart from the rest of the industry. There are several lounges and bars where pre dinner or after dinner drinks and entertainment can be enjoyed; in fact, there are 12 in all. If you are looking for a quiet and classy place for drinks, check out the Star Bar on Deck 13. The leather seating, low lighting and piano music make this a romantic spot for drinks before dining at Cagney's Steakhouse. For a high-tech, funky lounge and nightclub with live music and dancing, visit Dazzles on Deck 7. Dazzles is also host to what might be the most professional Karaoke setup at sea. Gatsby's is Dawn's champagne bar featuring nightly piano entertainment and is conveniently located outside both Le Bistro and Impressions restaurants on Deck 6. Pearly King's Pub is an English pub/sports bar located on the port side of the ship just behind the Reception desk on Deck 7. Here you can get a variety of beers served in pint and 1/2 pints, and complimentary fish and chips, potato chips, salsa and popcorn from 5:00pm until 9:00pm each night. The Dawn Club Casino Bar can keep you well-oiled while you play video poker. Dawn's panorama lounge is The Spinnaker Lounge, located on Deck 12 forward. Spinnaker holds more than 500 people and is a venue used for dance music, comedy shows, bingo, etc. Cigar aficionados will certainly want to visit Havana Club on Deck 6 where you can get hand-rolled premium cigars, ports, cognacs and malt whiskeys. For a late night espresso, cappuccino, or frozen coffee drink, there's always the Java Cafe on Deck 7. On some evenings, there is music and dancing poolside where you can enjoy a drink from Topsiders Bar before dinner.

Dining

Bamboo is Dawn's Asian Fusion restaurant and this one was right on the mark. The cover charge was only $10 per person and even that was discounted before 6:30pm to $5 per person. I had the Three Flavors Pork and Rickee ordered the Beef with Rice. Both dishes were very good as was the Tempura Soba. I ordered a Spicy Tuna Roll ($2) from the Sushi bar and it was excellent. If you choose to eat Sushi, you can order ala carte from a menu, or have 'all you can eat' Sushi for $10. That is a bargain for Sushi lovers. There is a Teppanyaki room where you can enjoy Japanese Hibachi for an additional charge (in addition to the cover charge.)

For a taste of Tex-Mex, we headed to Salsa one evening. Rickee's quesadillas and my beef fajitas were tasty. Another plus, there is no cover charge for Salsa, but reservations are required. The food here is comparable to what you might expect to get at your local Chilis or TGI Fridays. The food may not knock your socks off, but who doesn't like to go to Fridays or Chilis every now and then just to change things up?

> **CruiseReport.com Tip!** - Make reservations to dine in Le Bistro at least one evening during your cruise aboard Norwegian Dawn. It is well worth the $12.50 for the experience.

The crown jewel in Dawn's restaurant lineup would have to be Le Bistro, an upscale French restaurant with a decor featuring original works of art by Van Gogh, Matisse, Monet and Renoir. The standard cover charge for Le Bistro is $12.50 but there are some optional specialty menu items that require an additional charge ranging from $18.00 to $20.00. A Surf & Turf combination rounds out the menu at $20. The Caesar salad was near perfect and the mushroom soup served in a sourdough bread bowl was hot and delicious. The Surf & Turf combined two medium size tails with a huge filet mignon that must have been two inches thick. The lobster was firm but not overcooked or chewy. The steak was cooked perfectly to order and was above average for a cruise ship steak. My special request for creamed spinach in place of rice was fulfilled. The bananas foster flambé dessert was served hot and fresh with a large scoop of vanilla ice cream.

> *"We twice opted for lunch in Venetian and really liked the 16th century Italian grand villa style décor and the polished service."*

There are three 'traditional' multi-course style restaurants on Dawn where the menu changes every evening. These dining rooms each have a different theme and décor. The Venetian is the largest and is located on Deck 6 aft. Impressions and Aqua are mid ship on Deck 6. We twice opted for lunch in Venetian and really liked the 16th century Italian grand villa style décor and the polished service. In Aqua, where the trendy decor was created by the famous English designer Conrad, we were served by a female waiter and her female assistant. This was perhaps the best service we received in any of the restaurants. Impressions is decorated in the style of a 1900s grand French dining room with representations of famous art from French Impressionist painters. On our visit, the service seemed a little hurried. I was not offered mint jelly with my rack of lamb. I am sure I could have asked and it would have been delivered, but it is fairly common for a waiter to offer this accompaniment with lamb.

Cagney's Steak House is Dawn's resident steak house serving Certified Angus Beef. Even though it had the highest base cover charge of $17.50, Cagney's was somewhat of a disappointment. The service during our visit was extremely slow, not the fault of the wait staff, but the kitchen. We waited for close to an hour between our soup dish and entrée and when the food finally arrived, it was only lukewarm. Rickee ordered the T-bone and I had the lamb chops. In spite of the claims that only Certified Angus Beef is served, I could not ascertain a significant difference in flavor or quality over what was served in the regular dining rooms. The portions, however, were much larger. The Caesar salad dressing had a sweet taste that was anything but Caesar. All in all, we did not feel that Cagney's was worth the $17.50 per person cover charge.

Each evening, one corner of the Garden Cafe is converted into La Trattoria, an intimate Italian bistro. Reservations are required at La Trattoria but there is no cover charge. It is worth a trip to La Trattoria just for the pizza. The pies here are hand made fresh to order and they are delicious (the only other pizza we could find was served at the Garden Cafe and was not nearly as good). A large Chicken Parmagiana is thick, juicy and covered in melted Mozzarella and Marinara sauce. The service here was crisp and efficient, but not as polished as we found in some of the other dining venues.

The Garden Café is Dawn's Lido Deck buffet located aft of the pool on Deck 12. As cruise ship buffets go, Garden Café is pretty good. Where Garden Café does its best work is at breakfast. There are multiple serving lines with bacon, sausage, scrambled eggs, pancakes, pastries, etc. There is an omelet station where you can get an omelet made fresh to order. From noon until 2pm each day, the Garden Café becomes a lunch venue serving a variety of meats, vegetables, salads and desserts. Although the selection of dishes was not vast, the choices changed every day. For me, it is pretty hard to pass up the poolside barbeque for Garden Café. Each evening, the Garden Café is open for casual dining from 5:30pm until 10:00pm. We did not have an opportunity to try dinner here, so we cannot comment. One thing worth noting about the Garden Cafe is its Kid's Cafe. Here is a place for the kids to eat complete with kid's size buffet and small tables and seats.

Best Entertainment at Sea

After dinner, most guests will head to the Stardust Theatre (Deck 6 & 7 forward) for one of three Jean Ann Ryan production shows, a magic show, or a comedy/juggler show. The shows offered by Jean Ann Ryan Productions are not to be missed. They feature incredible vocals combined with high-energy dance choreography and superb lighting and stage effects. These are some of the best shows at sea. The Stardust Theater can hold 1,037 people and has the best sightlines of any theatre at sea. There are almost no obstructed views and the slope of the theatre prevents the person sitting in front of you from blocking your view. The only negative is the seating itself. There is simply not enough legroom between rows of seats. My knees were literally pressed against the seat in front of me (I am 6' 1"). Another oversight is the lack of tables or glass holders. There is nowhere to set a drink other than on the floor between your legs. Consequently, there were a lot of spilled drinks and glasses lying around after the show, a potential hazard for people exiting a crowded theatre.

Some evenings feature a comedy show in The Spinnaker Lounge followed by an energetic live band. You can dance the night away in Dazzles, or enjoy late-night Karaoke. Needless to say, there is always something going on after dark all over the ship.

All in all, NCL has a definite winner with Norwegian Dawn. It is nice to see a cruise line/ship that distinguishes itself from 'the pack' of other contemporary cruise lines and ship designs. Freestyle Cruising is a winning concept and we can only hope that other cruise lines catch on and take NCL's lead.

Silversea Cruises
Our Favorite Luxury Cruise Line

Sterling Silver Whisper
Silver Whisper

Michael and Pat M., a couple from England, look far too young to have already accumulated 100 sailing days with Silversea. Yet, after they complete their next Silversea cruise of 34 days from Auckland to Acapulco, they will have accomplished that milestone. Jean and Peter A., also from England, are longtime Seabourn patrons enjoying their first Silversea cruise. Werner and Wilma S. are cruising with their daughter and son-in-law. The four of them flew from their home in Switzerland to join the Silver Whisper for the 14-day Caribbean cruise after which they will return home. In March 2003, Werner and Wilma fly from Switzerland to meet Silver Whisper in Acapulco for a Panama Canal cruise. What could possibly be so special about the Silversea experience to attract so many people from around the world? "The staff is always smiling and happy and each time we return we get to see the same folks we became friends with from our previous Silversea cruises," says Pat M.

"A happy crew makes for happy passengers," says Cruise Director Ray Solaire. Ray, a 30-year cruise line veteran, spent 20 years with Cunard Line and has been with Silversea from its beginning. He demonstrates the energy of a man half his age and this energy seems to carry over to the entire crew of the Silver Whisper. This sort of attitude cannot help but contribute to a memorable cruise experience, as we were about to find out during our first Silversea experience.

Exceeding expectations becomes increasingly difficult when so much is expected to begin with. Like Rolls Royce in the auto industry, Silversea has established a brand synonymous in the cruise industry with the ultimate in luxury and is not bashful about charging the highest per diems for its product. Cruise fares on

Silversea can range from $350 to over $1000 per day, per person (depending upon such factors as suite selection, cruise itinerary, early booking discounts, Venetian Society discounts, and seasonal rates.) Make no mistake, the Silversea Experience is designed from the ground up for those who expect the very best and are willing to pay to get it. But, is it really worth the high price? "Absolutely," says Peter A., a first-time Silversea guest. "The level of service, the luxury of a smaller ship experience and the flexible dining options are well worth the price." This sentiment is shared among many Silversea guests who return to this premium cruise line time and time again.

One thing you notice immediately when you book a Silversea cruise is the incredible attention to detail. Virtually nothing has been overlooked in the quest to provide the best of everything for the Silversea guest. This is evident as soon as your silver foil-stamped cruise documents arrive wrapped inside a real calfskin ticket jacket embossed with the distinctive Silversea "S" logo. That same attention to detail carries through to the onboard experience. Each suite is fully-stocked with quality Italian Bvlgari-brand bath products. Bathroom floors, walls and vanities are drenched in rich Italian marble, and beds are wrapped in the finest linens and topped with fluffy down pillows.

At 25,000 tons, the Silver Whisper is more than twice the size of the Seabourn Pride and carries as many as 388 guests with a crew complement of 300. This results in the highest space-to-guest-ratio in the industry. Launched in 2001, Silver Whisper is the newest of Silversea's four ships. Her identical twin sister, Silver Shadow, was launched in 2000. Two smaller sister ships, the Silver Wind and Silver Cloud, each with a tonnage of just under 17,000, provide accommodations for 296 passengers. "We like the intimacy of the Silver Cloud," says James M., a Venetian Society Member with over 115 days aboard Silversea, "but we prefer the roomier suites and the public space of the Silver Whisper and Silver Shadow."

All-Out Luxury

When it comes to pure pampering and a feeling of luxury, no other cruise line has quite what Silversea does. First-class, all the way.

After checking in at Pier 29 in Ft. Lauderdale, a white-gloved Silversea staff member escorted us on board where we were immediately greeted by Cruise Director Ray Solaire. A welcoming line of sharply dressed, smiling staff members offered crystal flutes filled with chilled Moet & Chandon Brut Champagne[1] which we graciously accepted. Another white-gloved stewardess then walked us to our suite where we were to see our home for the next 2 weeks. Our Verandah Suite (suite 502) is the forward-most suite on Deck 5. About 80% of the accommodations onboard Silver Whisper (and her sister Silver Shadow) are Verandah Suites. There are a few Vista Suites available which are the same size, but have a large picture window instead of a balcony.

The well-designed Verandah Suites measure 345 square feet, are nicely appointed and tastefully decorated. The interior of the suites reflects the same understated elegance that is found throughout Silver Whisper. The emphasis here is on quality materials, workmanship, and creature comfort, not colorful, overwhelming decoration. Bathrooms are large by cruise ship standards and feature separate tub and shower stall and two sinks. The walk-in closet is large enough to hold plenty of clothes for any length voyage and still have room for an adult to get dressed with the door closed. This is a nice feature for early-risers who do not want to wake their traveling companion in the morning. The closet has intelligently been placed between the bathroom and the bedroom, serving as an effective sound barrier. The bedroom area consists of a queen-sized bed, 2 end tables and a small vanity at the foot of the bed with a well-lighted mirror. Finally, the living/dining room area features a large wall unit which has a desk, refrigerator, bar and

---

[1] Since the date of this review cruise, Silversea has changed its champagne to Phillipponat, a Premium French champagne.

entertainment center (Television/VCR combo). Opposite from the wall unit is a comfortable sofa, a chair, and a coffee table that can be converted to a dining room table for room service. The back wall of the living room is actually a floor-to-ceiling sliding glass door leading out to a teak balcony where you'll find two lounge chairs with ottomans, and a small table just the right size to hold morning coffee and croissants.

Every suite has a beautiful fresh flower arrangement, fresh fruit is replenished daily or upon request, and a bottle of chilled Moet & Chandon champagne is waiting for you when you arrive. In fact, Moet & Chandon[1] Champagne is poured throughout the ship and is included in your cruise fare, as are a nice selection of wines, all mixed drinks, soft drinks and bottled water, making the Silversea Experience an all-inclusive experience. Our suite was kept immaculate throughout the cruise by our Austrian stewardess, Martina.

> **CruiseReport.com Tip** - Is there something you want that's not on the menu? Ask your waiter. I requested a Caesar salad, creamed spinach and/or green beans every evening.

The ship itself is very well laid out with a reception area mid-ship on Deck 5 with the purser's desk, tour desk, and the offices of the cruise consultant and hotel manager. Most of the public rooms aboard Silver Whisper are located aft on Decks 5, 6, 7 and 8 with the exception of the Mandara Spa and the Observation Lounge found on Deck 10 forward. The Casino and boutiques are located mid-ship on Deck 5. This layout makes traversing the ship very quick and easy. Moving vertically is made possible by four stairways and four elevators located aft from Deck 3 thru Deck 8 and one staircase and elevator forward. The elevators are small and slow, but they get the job done. The stairs are so well-designed and easy to negotiate, we rarely saw anyone using the elevators unless

---

[1] Since this review was conducted, Silversea has replaced Moet & Chandon with Philipponnat champagne.

required to do so because of a wheelchair. The ship is also very accommodating to wheelchairs with several ramps in front of doorways. There are even wheelchair-designated public restrooms in many areas of the ship.

The décor of the ship is understated almost to the point of sterility. There is a contemporary monochromatic feel to the interior spaces with walls virtually void of colorful artwork with the exception of The Bar and The Restaurant which do have a few splashes of red and orange. The furnishings throughout the public rooms are constructed of rich woods and fabrics and are very comfortable. In spite of this lack of color and panache, the ship radiates a beautiful elegance.

> **CruiseReport.com Tip** - Enjoy dinner in the Terrace Cafe for an intimate candlelit dinner. Reservations are limited to 50 people per evening.

When the ship is in port, guests can walk leisurely off the ship without the hassle of long lines. Even tender operations are very efficient and smooth. Of course, you can also enjoy an organized excursion arranged through the ship's tour desk. Shore excursions are competitively priced with other cruise lines and we noticed at least one Silversea crew member accompanying every tour.

Sea days aboard Silver Whisper can be enjoyed at the ship's pool on Deck 8 where attendants will spoil you. On hot afternoons, you will be offered chilled face towels, and fresh watermelon and pineapple. A cool drink is always available from the pool bar to be delivered to your lounge chair. And you can forget about having to dry your hands to sign for your drink because all of your drinks are complimentary on Silversea. If the pool is not your thing, you can relax in one of the many lounges on board to read a good book, converse with friends, or partake in one of the many activities offered by the Silver Whisper staff ranging from cooking demonstrations to trivia contests.

Silver Whisper guests who wish to connect to the Internet during their cruise may do so at the ship's Internet Café on Deck 8. Guests who have attempted to access the Internet from other cruise ships will immediately appreciate the way Silversea charges for access. Guests are charged $.75 cents per minute, but the charges are only accrued as files are being uploaded or downloaded from the net. The result is an affordable and fair way of paying for the service. "We view our Internet café as an extension of the service we offer to our guests," says Communications and I.T. Officer Vassant Ramakrishna.

A cruise aboard a luxury ship like Silver Whisper would not be complete without a relaxing trip to the spa. All Silversea ships feature spas operated by Mandara Spa which originated in Bali. Mandara Spa offers a variety of salon treatments including facials, waxing, hair styling, and nail care. But what we were looking for was a relaxing massage, and we found it. While I was enjoying 80 minutes of "Balinese Bliss", Rickee submitted herself to the "Massage Around the World". Both treatments were as good, if not better, than any we have received at sea or on land. At $160 each for 80 minutes, the treatments are a bargain. When you sail on Silver Whisper, you simply owe it to yourself to indulge.

Dining aboard Silver Whisper is what you would expect from a 6-star luxury ship. Breakfast and lunch are delivered to your table in the Restaurant, while a beautiful buffet is served in the less formal Terrace Café on Deck 7. Evening meals can be enjoyed in the more formal atmosphere of the Restaurant on Deck 3, or the more casual and intimate Terrace Café which is transformed into a candlelit bistro-style restaurant on most evenings. With virtually no exceptions, everything that was delivered from the galley was prepared to order and of exceptional quality and presentation. For those times when you don't feel like getting out, you can have room service in your suite. The living room table is converted into a dining table complete with linen tablecloth, china, and silver service for a memorable "en suite" dining experience. The complete Restaurant menu is available for room service during normal dining hours and there is a 24-hour menu available for the non-dining hours.

Where Silver Whisper really shines is her staff and service. It would seem that everyone working on Silver Whisper enjoys their work and truly loves their job. We did not encounter a single employee during the 14 days who was anything less than accommodating, friendly and sincere. You cannot walk down any hallway on Silver Whisper without receiving one or more greetings from staff members. All, of course, delivered with a smile.

As we prepared to disembark Silver Whisper, we suddenly realized why so many people return time and time again. While we are sad to leave our new friends behind, we are excited at the prospect of returning in the near future. For as we leave Silver Whisper, we see a new group of passengers waiting to board. We envy them because we know they will enjoy, in the words of Ray Solaire, many "Glorious Days" aboard Silver Whisper.

Radisson Seven Seas Cruises
Our Favorite Luxury Value Cruise

Even Better the Second Time
Radisson Seven Seas Mariner

It is 7:00 am on a December morning at sea, somewhere between Port Everglades and Grand Cayman, and the sun is rising from the water on the horizon. There is no sight quite like it, and perhaps that is why Radisson Seven Seas Cruises (RSSC) calls this beautiful room the 'Horizon Lounge'. There are only two other guests enjoying the 'Early Riser' coffee and this incredible view of nature beginning a new day. A beautiful ship, calm seas, an amazing sunrise and a good cup of coffee. Can life get any better than this?

Having been privileged to sail aboard Radisson Seven Seas Mariner on her maiden voyage through the Panama Canal in 2001, I suspected that gaining the 6-star rating would be a "gimme" for this beautiful ship. After all, it was Mariner that earned Radisson Seven Seas Cruises CruiseReport.com's "BEST Cruise Line Award" for 2001. So when we began working on the Luxury at Sea article for CruiseReport.com (a comparative review of 6-star luxury cruise lines), it was only fitting that we include Radisson Seven Seas Mariner in our review process.

A casual observer looking at the Radisson Seven Seas fleet might come to the conclusion that the company has been experimenting with a variety of ship designs. No two ships are alike.

- The Song of Flower is a small vessel that carries only 180 passengers.
- The Radisson Diamond is the only twin hull cruise ship and carries 350 passengers.
- The Paul Gauguin is a ship designed specifically to sail French Polynesia year round and carries 320 passengers.
- The Seven Seas Navigator is a 490-passenger cruise ship.

Even though Radisson Seven Seas has built a superb reputation over the years for service and quality, until the release of the 50,000 ton, 700-passenger Seven Seas Mariner, there was really nothing about their fleet to distinguish them from other 6-star cruise lines. The Mariner set new standards for luxury ships by becoming the first all balcony/all suite cruise liner afloat, a distinction it continues to enjoy until April of 2003, when her sister ship, Seven Seas Voyager, is officially launched. With Mariner (and Voyager) in the fleet, RSSC can now appeal to a consumer market previously dominated by Crystal Cruises: upscale travelers who desire luxury, but also want the facilities and amenities offered by a larger vessel.

In some ways, Mariner feels almost too big for its passenger capacity of 700. Don't get me wrong, that's a good thing. Even when the ship is filled to capacity, you feel like you are on a big cruise ship that is only half full. In fact, there are major cruise lines that pack 1,500 passengers on ships the size of Mariner. But on Mariner, there are no long lines, no crowds, no shoving. There are always plenty of deck chairs at the pool and they are intelligently spaced, each with its own small table. There's plenty of room to spread out, room to relax, room to enjoy. Hallways and public spaces are wide and uncluttered.

Accommodations aboard Mariner are roomy, comfortable and quiet. Our 452 sq. ft. Category B Penthouse Suite on Deck 10 was downright decadent. Deluxe Suites (301 sq. ft.) dominate the ship, but are still huge by cruise ship standards. But for those who can afford it, the Category A, B and C Penthouse suites offer a level of space and comfort that put them in a class by themselves. The marble bathroom is large with plenty of storage and a beautiful single sink vanity. If you exceed 6' in height, as I do, you will have to duck to shower in the combination shower/tub. Older or less mobile guests may find stepping up into the tub difficult. This problem has been addressed in the soon-to-be-released Seven Seas Voyager which will feature separate shower stalls in each suite. The walk-in closet has plenty of space for enough clothes for a world cruise. The bedroom features a plush queen-sized bed with fluffy down pillows and a European-style duvet. At the foot of the bed is a full-size lighted makeup vanity with stool, floor-to-ceiling mirror, and an occasional chair and ottoman. The living room is quite simply huge and is furnished with an L-shaped sofa big enough to seat 4 adults comfortably, a coffee table which converts to a dining table for 'en-suite' dining, and a massive wall unit with desk, TV/VCR, refrigerator fully stocked with soft drinks and bottled water, bar setup and tons of storage space. The back wall is solid glass with a very wide sliding glass door that leads out to an expansive teak verandah large enough for two chairs, a table and a chaise lounge.

Those who find it difficult to sleep past 6 AM, no matter how comfortable the bed, will enjoy the Early-Riser coffee and continental breakfast served in the Horizon Lounge and at the Pool Grill. The coffee served aboard Mariner is excellent throughout the ship. As you would expect from a 6-star cruise ship, coffee is always served in a porcelain cup and saucer. Orange juice tasted as though it was fresh-squeezed. The pastries were fresh and delicious.

For those who enjoy a 'proper' breakfast, the Compass Rose Restaurant offers a full menu including, of all things, baby lamb chops. A morning trip to the Compass Rose would not be complete without trying the Eggs Benedict and banana pancakes. A less formal breakfast buffet is served in La Veranda on Deck 11 (Pool Deck) aft and features two omelet stations concocting mixtures of eggs, vegetables, meats and cheeses. Or, you could enjoy your banana pancakes, omelet, coffee, and hot chocolate on your verandah as you watch the warm Caribbean Sea float by.

Butler Service - From delivering complimentary canapés to your suite each evening to course-by-course room service, these butlers do it all.

Those accustomed to luxury cruising have been willing to trade the activities and entertainment of larger ships for the intimacy, peace and relaxation of smaller ships. On Seven Seas Mariner, one is not required to make that choice. A quick glance at the ship's daily newspaper, "Passages," reveals a full list of activities hosted by cruise director Barry Hopkins and his staff. On our cruise, we enjoyed cooking demonstrations, wine-tasting, enrichment lectures, trivia contests, dance lessons, and much more. Needless to say, you will not be bored on Mariner unless you choose to be bored.

When stomachs begin to growl around noon time, hungry passengers can enjoy a course-by-course luncheon in the Compass Rose restaurant, or, a less formal buffet lunch at La Veranda. On our cruise, we noticed mountains of fresh boiled shrimp and crab featured every day at La Veranda, reason enough for us to opt for this venue each day. La Veranda's buffet luncheon items change daily and include a carving station and a pasta station. La Veranda offers the option of inside or al fresco dining; in either case, meals are enjoyed on tables draped with white linens and set with china and silver flatware. Those with an incurable sweet tooth will find refuge here. La Veranda delivers enough temptation in the form of cakes, pies, ice cream and other delicacies to make your dentist smile. The Pool Grill, a new addition since our maiden voyage in 2001, offers freshly cooked to order burgers with all the trimmings, all-beef hot dogs, chicken breasts, minute steaks, and a salad bar. Additionally, on certain days, a theme lunch buffet is set up in the Pool Grill area. During our voyage, a Mexican taco bar and an Oriental Wok Buffet were offered.

Seven Seas Mariner Daily Activities

- Wake up and Walk with fitness instructor
- Silent Art Auction
- Aerobic Intervals with fitness instructor
- Daily Quiz
- Lower Body Toning with fitness instructor
- Coffee Chat and IQ Challenge
- Paddle Tennis

- Beatles Mania Trivia
- Lunchtime Melodies
- Popcorn Movie
- Informal Bridge Play
- Golf Chipping
- Game Time: Checkers
- Ping Pong
- Tea Time
- Tea Time Trivia
- Circuit Training with fitness instructor
- Bingo
- Stretch and Relax with fitness instructor

Those who like to fight off the extra pounds that typically come from a week or more of indulgence will undoubtedly find themselves in the ship's adequately-equipped fitness center. There are eight health club-quality treadmills, a stair step machine and a couple of massive, awkward elliptical trainers. Free weights and a weight machine should sustain weight lifters while an ample workout floor is available for stretching and serves as the area where yoga and aerobics classes are conducted by the ship's fitness staff.

Evenings aboard Mariner typically begin with pre-dinner cocktails in one of the ship's three lounges. The Horizon Lounge is located aft on Deck 6 and is the largest of the three; the Mariner Lounge is on Deck 5 and just steps from the Compass Rose and Latitudes restaurants. My favorite was the Observation Lounge on Deck 12 forward. The Observation Lounge was never crowded and has more personality than the other lounges. Soft drinks and bottled water are complimentary throughout the ship on all RSSC cruises, as is wine with dinner, but you must pay for alcoholic beverages. While this prevents RSSC from being considered an "all-inclusive" cruise vacation, it is not a big deal, especially for moderate to light drinkers. Drinks are competitively priced, served in large heavy glassware, and contain a very generous portion of liquor. A Glenlivet Single Malt Scotch on the rocks was only $4.25, gratuity included. All lounges feature self-serve canapés and hot hors d'oeuvres before dinner. We found the bar staff throughout the ship to be very attentive and friendly.

Evening meals aboard Mariner reveal another of the ship's distinctions…choice. There are four dining venues to choose from on Mariner, each with its own character and unique menu. The Compass Rose is the ship's main restaurant and takes the form of a more traditional cruise ship restaurant. The menu at Compass Rose changes each evening, offering a selection of soups, salads, entrées and desserts. As you would expect, the food and service in Compass Rose is superb. What makes Compass Rose special, and helps to elevate Seven Seas Mariner to 6-star status, is the single open seating arrangement that allows you to dine whenever and with whomever you wish. The more we cruise, the more we come to appreciate the single seating concept, to the point that we have made it a requirement in order for a cruise line to receive our 6-star rating. Mariner's dinner hours are from 7:00pm until 9:30pm, giving guests a wide choice in when they wish to dine. La Veranda transforms from a morning and lunchtime buffet into a respectable, albeit informal, Italian-style bistro in the evenings. The menu at La Veranda changes daily, but always includes a trip to the restaurant's incredible antipasto cart loaded with marinated delicacies, and Bananas Foster prepared nightly as a dessert selection. No reservations are required for La Veranda. Exotic flavors can be found at Latitudes, the ship's Asian fusion restaurant. In this quiet, intimate restaurant, guests are able to enjoy a sampling of everything on the menu. Reservations are required for Latitudes. At the top of the list is Signatures, Mariner's French restaurant, operated under the auspices of Le Cordon Bleu of Paris. We were pleased to find that Signatures was just as good, if not better, than we remembered (which was excellent). Reservations are required at Signatures, as are jackets for gentlemen. The Cappuccino-style chicken soup was outstanding; the Halibut had a buttery crisp searing to its flaky and delicious meat. The warm chocolate tart with caramel ice cream is beyond description. A cruise aboard Mariner is not complete without an evening at Signatures. And of course, if you just don't feel like getting out, you can enjoy any items from the Compass Rose menu in your suite, served course-by-course.

After dinner, it's show time! The Constellation Theatre is a great venue with comfortable seating and excellent sight lines. The latest sound and lighting technology has been added to give the performers every advantage. The group of eight Peter Grey Terhune Singers and Dancers deliver vocals and dance numbers backed up by the Seven Seas Mariner Quintet.

Those who wish to travel in style and elegance, but also want to include their children are often at a loss when it comes to 6-Star cruise ships. Most luxury liners simply do not have the staff and facilities to offer children's programs. RSSC, on the other hand, does offer a selection of sailings specifically for families. Note: These sailings are indicated with a special notation on the CruiseReport.com web site.

Our second voyage aboard Mariner confirms what we found on our maiden voyage. This is a first rate, 6-Star ship with a great crew and excellent service. Anyone considering booking a suite on one of the mass market cruise lines should seriously consider Radisson Seven Seas Mariner (or the soon-to-be-released Voyager) as an alternative. Those who do will receive a much higher level of service, a nearly all-inclusive value and most of the facilities offered by the larger ships. What you won't get aboard the Mariner is the frustration of long lines, crowds, forced dining hours, and annoying solicitations for onboard purchases. Radisson Seven Seas definitely qualifies for our 2002 6-Star Award of Excellence rating!

SeaDream Yacht Club
Our Favorite Small Ship Cruise Line

Sea Dreams Do Come True
SeaDream II

Did you ever dream of being rich? Perhaps your dot.com company went public and overnight you became a multi-millionaire? Instead of standing in line with thousands of passengers waiting to board the latest mega-cruise ship, you leisurely sail the Caribbean on your own private yacht. A yacht fully staffed with a crew focused on serving your every desire. Your private onboard chef prepares culinary works of art that are befitting of any 5-star restaurant. If you want champagne and caviar at 3am, no problem. After all, it is your yacht, right?

> **Did you know?** - SeaDream Yacht Club is the recipient of three Editor's Best at Sea Awards for Food and Dining, Relaxation and Fitness Center!

Wake up! You are not dreaming, you're sailing on SeaDream Yacht Club, perhaps the next best thing to owning your own private yacht. Best of all, you don't have to be a multi-millionaire to enjoy all the benefits of your dream vacation aboard a SeaDream yacht.

Even though SeaDream is a relative newcomer to the burgeoning cruise landscape, the cruise line is owned and managed by people who really understand luxury sailing. Unlike mainstream cruise lines that are embattled in a race to see who can build the biggest ship and pack the most buffet-hungry passengers onto their ships at a time, SeaDream has a different approach. SeaDream ships are actually large "yachts", each serving as home to 108 guests and 89 crew members. Do the math and you will see that, unless the yacht is completely full, there is close to one crew member for every passenger!

The Yachts

SeaDream operates two identical yachts, SeaDream I and SeaDream II. The ships were originally the Sea Goddess I and II. Even though the yachts were built in 1984/1985, they underwent a major redesign and refit in 2002. The décor is understated and elegant throughout the public spaces. At 4260 tons, these "ships" are fully stabilized, and offer most of the amenities you would find on much larger vessels.

SeaDream yachts look like small cruise ships, but feel like large yachts. As a result, guests feel like privileged, affluent yachters instead of mass-market cruise ship passengers. The Top of the Yacht Bar on Deck 6 epitomizes the yacht feel with its gleaming varnished teak bar and stools.

Accommodations

There are three categories of staterooms/suites on a SeaDream yacht. The Yacht Club Stateroom is 195 sq. ft. and includes a queen-size bed, sofa, large picture window, marble-lined bathroom, flat-screen LCD television with DVD player, a CD player/stereo, mini-bar/refrigerator, desk/vanity, and closet. On our first cruise with SeaDream (January 2003), we were in a Yacht Club Stateroom (412) and found it to be very comfortable. On this journey, we enjoyed the expanded Commodore Club Stateroom, which is actually two adjoining Yacht Club staterooms. One side of the Commodore Club Stateroom serves as a living room and the other as a bedroom. The best part of the Commodore Club Stateroom is dual closets and two separate bathrooms! At 390 sq. ft., we would highly recommend the upgrade to the Commodore, especially when sailing on back-to-back cruises of 14 days or longer.

SeaDream staterooms are decorated with blue and beige carpeting and fabrics and we saw no signs of wear and tear since our first visit a year earlier. Staterooms offer a lot of storage space, with a nice desk/vanity area which also serves as the entertainment center. The sofa is large enough to comfortably seat 3 adults, and, of course, there is an upholstered chair. There are small touches of elegance and quality everywhere you look. The entertainment center can be concealed behind etched glass doors; a set of crystal glassware is provided in each stateroom; there is a flat-panel LCD television; plenty of wooden hangers in the closet; and Bvlgari amenities in the bathroom. The bathrooms are small, but elegantly trimmed in marble. Even though there is no bathtub, there is a large walk-in shower stall with a multi-jet shower.

The bedding and linens contribute to the relaxation and rejuvenation one experiences aboard a SeaDream yacht. The comfortable mattress is covered with a warm, "tropical weight" European-style down comforter and topped with the most comfortable down pillows in my recent memory. The Turkish towels are soft and extra "thirsty". Each stateroom includes complimentary use of a bathrobe and slippers.

Activities & Entertainment

The activities aboard SeaDream revolve around the destinations (ports-of-call) and water. The activities director will offer you a variety of shore excursions when the ship is in port. If the ship is docked, you may want to try out one of the yacht's Segway Human Transporters. For $49 you can spend 45 minutes defying gravity on this two-wheeled contraption, amazing all who pass by you. Or, perhaps you would like to make use of one of the yacht's 10 mountain bikes? A crew member will happily deliver one, complete with helmet, to the dock for you. When the ship is anchored in a small cove or bay and local officials and the weather permit, the marina is put out and guests have complimentary use of the yacht's kayaks, water skis, wave runner, snorkeling gear, sail boats, etc. Of course, the best activity may be none at all.

In the evenings, you can enjoy an after dinner drink in the Main Salon as you listen to Bobby play the piano and sing. There is a "big screen" movie shown in the Main Salon at 10:00pm each evening. Perhaps the best entertainment is simply sitting under the stars at the Top of the Yacht Bar engaged in conversation with one of the many interesting people you meet on a SeaDream yacht vacation.

Certainly the highlight of any SeaDream Caribbean cruise is the beach party and barbeque. Guests are ferried to a private beach using the ship's Zodiac (a small dinghy boat) beginning at 10:30 am. At high noon, the yacht's horn blasts loudly in the distance signaling the call for caviar and champagne to be served "a la surf". Chef Robert floats a surfboard out into the ocean, waist high in water, and serves wading guests caviar while waiters, also waist high in the water, serve chilled champagne. This exercise in decadence continues for at least 15 minutes until everyone has had an opportunity to indulge. Afterwards, guests wade ashore for an impressive luncheon of barbeque spare ribs, prime rib, hamburgers, hot dogs, fried chicken, salads, and desserts. Troubles seem to just melt away in the warm Caribbean sun, on a deserted beach, with great food, good friends and of course, plenty of champagne!

Dining

SeaDream has taken dining at sea to a whole new level. There is simply no finer dining experience at sea, and few on land, than the one offered by SeaDream Yacht Club. That's why we awarded SeaDream our Best at Sea award for Food Quality in 2003 and again for 2004. The yacht's galley, under the expert direction of head chef Robert van Rijsbergen has improved on what was an already exceptional menu. Evening menus presented in the Dining Salon have been extended to include an Oriental Wellness cuisine, an alternative menu popular with those of us who love Chinese and Thai dishes.

Early risers can enjoy a cup of coffee and Danish at the Top of the Yacht Bar on Deck 6 at 7:00am. Full breakfast service begins at 8:00am at the Topside Restaurant on Deck 5. There is a small buffet of fresh fruit and pastries with cooked items being offered on the breakfast menu. All breakfast menu items are prepared fresh to order, not scooped from a pan of pre-cooked items like on some ships. Omelets were made perfectly and to order. A request for a side order of baby lamb chops will produce three double chops of lightly seasoned and grilled lamb. Enough for a lunch portion! There are also pancakes, French toast (or is it now called Freedom Toast?), bacon, ham, sausages, and much more.

All breakfast and lunch meals are served outdoors at the Topside Restaurant. Dining al fresco really adds to the yacht-like feel of the vessel and is a major plus in our opinion. Lunch service begins at the Topside at 12:30 with a menu that changes daily. There is a salad buffet which regularly features specialty items like large cocktail shrimp and crab claws. There are too many standout items on the lunch menu to mention here.

Dinnertime is something very special on a SeaDream yacht. On most evenings, dinner is served in the Dining Salon located on Deck 2. However, when the weather permits, the yacht features "Dining Under the Stars" at the Topside Restaurant. The dining room feels more like a 5-star restaurant than a typical ship's dining hall. The décor is tasteful with understated tones and light woods and features dramatic glass works of art lining the walls. The dining room is quiet, serene, and a perfect setting for the creations that come from the galley. There are plenty of tables for two, four, six and a couple of tables that can accommodate up to eight guests. Of course, the tables can be re-arranged by dining room staff to fit special requests. The evening menus are extensive and cover a wide range of tastes. In addition to the ever-changing selection of soups, salads, main courses and desserts, there is a selection of 'always available' alternatives. This selection includes such items as lamb chops, sirloin steak, Caesar salad, steamed vegetables, and pasta.

We are pleased to report that the problems we noted last year with the yacht's water have been resolved! The strong chlorine taste has been removed thanks to a new filtration system.

Bars & Lounges

You are never more than 50 feet from a glass of champagne or complimentary cocktail on SeaDream! And, if you are out on deck, all you need to do is raise your hand and an attentive waiter will deliver your favorite beverage post-haste. There is the Pool Bar located, as you might have guessed, poolside on Deck 3. The Main Salon, also located on Deck 3 is inside and is used for evening gatherings, entertainment and cocktails. The most popular lounge is the Top of the Yacht Bar on Deck 6 where the drinks flow freely from 5:00pm until everyone goes to bed.

SeaDream's open bar policy means that all of your champagne, wine and spirits are complimentary. There is an additional charge for some premium brands, of course. However, Glenfiddich single malt scotch is poured complimentary, as is Dewars White Label and many other popular brands. The "house" champagne is Heidsieck. If you want a bottle of Cristal, it is available for $140 per bottle. Compare that to the $600 per bottle price charged at some Las Vegas nightclubs!

There are two complimentary wines served with dinner each evening, one red and one white. Ferenc, the wine steward, will present the wines before dinner with a brief explanation of each wines origin, taste and nose. Wine glasses at dinner never go empty before being refilled. There are complimentary wines offered at lunchtime, as well.

The SeaDream Experience

A "yacht" vacation is unlike a typical cruise. The pace is much slower and more emphasis is placed on relaxation and personal service. The atmosphere is casual, yet elegant. This is reflected in the yacht's dress code which is referred to as "yacht casual". While some gentlemen will wear a jacket to dinner in the evenings, others will wear a nice sport shirt and slacks.

While many cruise line brochures boast about having staff members who remember your name and your favorite drink, SeaDream actually delivers on this claim. This may be due, in part, to the fact that the vessel only serves 108 guests making it easier to remember names, and partially due to excellent training. The service levels aboard SeaDream have become the standard to which we compare all other cruise lines.

SeaDream places considerable emphasis on the outdoors. Breakfast and lunch are served al fresco at the open air Topside Restaurant. Weather permitting, cocktail hours are held at the Top of the Yacht

Bar or poolside. And then there are those water toys! The Balinese sun beds are a SeaDream trademark and take lying in the sun to a whole new level of comfort. In case you did not notice, there are reading lights strategically placed on many of the deck loungers and sun beds, perfect for reading outside under the stars on warm Caribbean nights.

One final note, SeaDream is designed for adults. While children are welcome, there are really no facilities for them. We recommend that you take the kids on Disney or Royal Caribbean. SeaDream should be your dream vacation away from the kids!

Full-Yacht Charter

"Our members expect an upscale experience with uncompromising service. A SeaDream charter fits our needs perfectly..."

Susan L. Sheets
President
National Aircraft Resale Association

It is no surprise that SeaDream yachts are popular choices for corporate meeting and sales incentive charters. With a capacity of 108 guests each, the yachts are the perfectly suited to this task. Corporations and associations routinely charter these vessels individually or in tandem. In addition, many private families, some with their own yachts, charter the SeaDream twins for family reunions and various celebrations like anniversaries, birthdays, etc.

"When compared to a 5-star hotel or resort, our all-inclusive yacht charters are very competitive and offer a truly customizable experience," says Jennie Foster, Director of Business Development for SeaDream Yacht Club.

Since Our Last Cruise

This was our second sailing aboard SeaDream II in the past 12 months. Since our last review cruise, a few changes have been made:

- A new restroom has been added on Deck 6.
- New toilets have been installed in all staterooms and public restrooms.
- Formal afternoon tea service has been suspended.
- Heidsieck has replaced Pomeroy as the complimentary champagne.
- Protective shades have been added to the Topside Restaurant.
- New water filtration system removed the chlorine taste from water.

With the exception of the lack of a formal afternoon tea service, the experience in 2004 is virtually identical to 2003. We noticed on our last cruise on SeaDream that we were the only ones who showed up for the tea service anyway. Of course, tea and cookies are available by request 24 hours a day, so a formal service is really not missed. Cookies and sandwiches are offered at the Topside Restaurant buffet in the afternoon in lieu of tea.

The yacht has been meticulously maintained during the last 12 months. She looks as fresh and new as she did in 2003. Service levels have been maintained to keep SeaDream at the top of our list of cruise vacations.

Conclusion

The challenge for SeaDream will be to maintain the already high standard of quality and service they have established. Even when 'nit-picking', it is difficult to find fault with this product. There are, of course, a few things we would like to see added or changed:

- The ability to purchase the same brand of incredible linens, robes, towels and pillows used by SeaDream would be a great addition.
- Increase the DVD movie selection.
- Allow passengers the ability to get cash ($US) on their shipboard account.

These vessels have a loyal following dating back to their days as Seabourn Sea Goddess yachts. Repeat passengers are the rule more often than the exception. This is a vacation for sophisticated adults who want to get away from it all and spend a week or two of relaxation with unobtrusive pampering.

Viking River Cruises
Our Favorite River Cruise Line

Rhine & Moselle Exploration
Viking Danube

A cruise enthusiast might be tempted to compare a river cruise to an ocean cruise. Of course, this is like trying to compare the experience of driving a Corvette to that of a Ferrari. While both are sports cars and both are very fast, the experiences are quite different. One thing is obvious: there are places that a river can take you that the ocean simply cannot. Rivers were the super highways of Europe (and most other countries) until the 1900's. Trade and commerce were only possible because of barges that moved massive amounts of goods along the river. Towns and cities sprang up all along the rivers of the world because access to water meant access to fishing, import and export. Some of the most charming destinations in Europe are accessible by river.

One company that has seized an opportunity to transport interested travelers to these gems of the river is Viking River Cruises. The company operates 25 river cruise vessels making it the largest river cruise operator in Europe. Our cruise aboard Viking Danube was to begin in Basel, Switzerland and take us up the Rhine River to Amsterdam with a brief side trip up the Moselle River in Germany.

Our journey begins as many others with the dreaded flight from Dallas-Fort Worth to Basel, Switzerland. Two Viking River Cruises representatives met us at the Basel airport as soon as we cleared Swiss customs, which was an incredibly easy process. Miraculously, all checked luggage arrived in spite of enduring four separate flights on three different airlines. Within minutes, we were being whisked away to meet the ship on Viking River Cruises's chartered bus.

Approaching the Viking Danube docked at Basel is anything but awe-inspiring. Looking sort of like a 'real' cruise ship that someone stepped on and flattened, the ship is 360 feet long and only 54 feet wide (beam). Embarkation is simply walking on board and showing the receptionists your ticket and passport. There are no lines to stand in and before you know it, you have your room key. The process could not be more efficient.

There are three passenger decks serving a total of 150 guests. You board the ship on Deck 2 forward in the reception area. Go forward from reception and you are in the Viking Lounge. A stairway in reception leads down to the dining room on Deck 1. Traversing aft from reception you will find a hallway with Category B staterooms and a staircase leading up to Deck 3 where Category A staterooms are lined up. At the end of Deck 3, there is a small library and a fitness room with a sauna, whirlpool and even a tanning bed. There is a single elevator which runs from Deck 1 through Deck 3. There are a few Category C staterooms located on Deck 1. All staterooms are 'river view', or outside cabins. Category A and B cabins are identical in size and configuration (A are located on Deck 3 while B are located on Deck 2) and have large windows while Category C cabins have much smaller windows.

> **CruiseReport.com Tip** - Dress onboard these ships is casual. Even the formal nights will find many wearing nothing more than dress shirts and slacks.

Accommodations are admittedly small, but efficient, for a 12-night journey on the Rhine. The ship builder has done a relatively good job of utilizing 154 sq. ft. of space with maximum efficiency. The window is at least 6 feet wide and 4 feet tall (Cat A & B) and offers you dramatic vistas of German landscape even while you are stretched out on your bed. The bed is a king which can be separated into 2 twins on request. Pillows and bedding are very comfortable. In fact, the mattress is as comfortable as any you will find anywhere. You might be surprised to find individual duvets. Pillows are filled with soft down but firmer pillows are available with a call to the front desk. The room has a deep window ledge which we quickly filled with items that won't fit in the small closet. Closet space can be tight if you bring clothes for 12 days, so pack light or plan to leave some items folded in your suitcase and stowed under the bed. The bathroom is a decent size with a shower stall, large sink and glass shelves to use for your personal toiletries. Viking River Cruises provides complimentary shampoo, soap and body lotion.

The main public areas of the Viking Danube where everyone congregates are the Viking Lounge on Deck 2 and the Sun Deck on Deck 4 (topside). The Viking Lounge is large enough to hold every guest on the ship. There is a full service bar serving beer, wine and mixed drinks. Drink prices are comparable with other cruise lines and hotel bars. You will pay € 4.00[1] for a beer or a Scotch and water. A Coca-Cola, however, will set you back a whopping € 2.40 ($2.75 US) so you may want to pick up a few cans in ports along the way to keep in your cabin. Even at peak periods, the bar service provided on Viking Danube was efficient. Even though it is not mentioned anywhere on the bar menu, a special request for cheese and crackers was met with a nice platter of Brie, Pepper and Goat cheeses with crackers. No charge.

> **CruiseReport.com Tip** - If you plan to exchange US currency for Euros or Swiss Francs, you should shop around to get the best exchange and commission rates. Viking River Cruises will exchange money onboard, but you will pay a 10% commission. On our trip, US $200 would only get you € 165 and change. You may want to ask your travel agent if they offer currency exchange before you leave. Local ATM's in Europe offer the best exchange rates using your bank ATM card since they don't charge a commission.

The Sun Deck is basically the roof of the boat. The Wheelhouse (Bridge) is located forward behind which you will find a covered seating area about 30 feet long. Behind the covered area is the rest of the boat's roof area which is wide open and full of tables with chairs and also lounge chairs. This area never feels crowded and makes a great place to watch the castles and vineyards of Europe float by. On days when the wind is not blowing, this is a perfect place to sit and relax, read a good book, or even take a brief nap.

---

[1] € is the symbol for the Euro

There is no bar service on the Sun Deck but occasionally you will see a bar waiter cleaning up and if you request a drink, it will be delivered with a smile. Viking River Cruises seems to be fairly liberal in their liquor policy so you can probably get away with bringing aboard that bottle of German or French wine you purchased in town and enjoying it with friends.

The smoking policy on board is very friendly to non-smokers. There is no smoking allowed in any rooms. Smoking is permitted in a small area on the starboard side of the vessel outside the lobby doors. There are no ashtrays anywhere on the ship, even in the Viking Lounge!

Smooth Sailing – There is no need to worry about sea sickness on a river cruise. These ships offer a rock-solid ride with almost no detectable motion. Engine and mechanical noise is also minimal.

Viking River Cruises has divided its market into English and non-English speaking cruises. Therefore, everyone on board your cruise will speak English and most likely be American or Canadian. Other Viking River Cruises ships that serve the European and Asian populations are not sold in the U.S. What this policy lacks in providing ethnic diversity, it makes up for in ease of communication. Guests are, therefore, not required to sit through endless announcements in multiple languages. Even though the crew is primarily European, they all speak impeccable English.

The 'typical' guest on our sailing was American, married and probably had grandchildren. At 47, I felt like one of the youngest aboard. There were a handful of "30 somethings" aboard and even one couple celebrating their honeymoon! River cruises tend to attract a more mature clientele due to the lack of glitzy entertainment, casino and rigorous activities.

River cruising is all about the destinations, not the ship itself. These vessels are designed to move you down (or up) a river from one historic location to another efficiently and comfortably. The ship does not 'get in the way' of the destination. This type of cruise offers the opportunity to visit quaint villages located way off the beaten tourist track, something not possible for a large cruise ship.

Viking Danube offers guests an Early Riser coffee and Danish in the Viking Lounge between 6:00am and 6:30am each morning (times vary from day to day). The coffee here is from one of those instant injection machines. It is drinkable, but not as good as the coffee in the dining room. A breakfast buffet is served in the dining room from 7:00am until 9:00am. Eggs cooked to order (omelets, poached, over easy, etc.) are available upon request. Lunch is typically served from noon until 2:00pm in the dining room and each day the menu will feature a salad bar, a choice of 2 soups, 2 entrees and 2 desserts. An abbreviated lunch buffet is also served in the Viking Lounge. Dinner is served between 7:00pm and 7:30pm each evening. The dinner menu features a choice of 2 salads/appetizers, 2 soups, 2 entrees (one of which is always fish) and 2 desserts. The overall quality of the food served onboard ranges from average to good with no real standouts other than some of the dessert offerings. The pastries were excellent. Even though you won't go hungry on a Viking River Cruise, you will probably welcome the opportunity to sample regional cuisine at one of the local restaurants when in port.

> **CruiseReport.com Tip** - Pack umbrellas! You never know when it will rain in Europe in the summer. We ended up having to buy 3 umbrellas in port to get 2 that worked. Viking River Cruises does not have umbrellas available so remember to bring your own!

One of the best features of a Viking River Cruise is that excursions are included in the cruise fare. Virtually every port visited featured a bus tour, a walking tour, or both. In some cities, there are additional excursion offerings which are optional and do cost extra. All of the tours we attended were very well-conducted by knowledgeable local guides. The inclusion of excursions dramatically increases the value of a Viking River Cruise experience. Getting on and off of the ship is extremely easy. Just drop your room key off at the reception desk on your way out (so they know that you are off the vessel) and walk off. There are no long lines and no crowds. Since the ship usually docks right in town, you may be only minutes from local restaurants, bars, museums, parks, shops and other points of interest.

After a busy day of touring quaint villages, castles, and walking through cobblestone streets, guests are welcomed back aboard Viking Danube to enjoy dinner served in the main dining room. There is a single seating at 7:00pm (7:30pm on some days) but guests can sit wherever they wish and dine with whomever they wish. The dining room has tables set for 6 or 8 guests. There are no tables for 2 or 4. Service in the dining room is efficient and friendly. After dinner, guests may choose to enjoy a drink in the Viking Lounge and dance to the music of Gitomir, the ship's sole entertainer.

Everyone will appreciate the level of service and friendliness of the staff and crew. Even though there are only 38 crew to serve 150 guests, the quality of service is extremely good. As with most small vessels, a smaller crew seems to exude the feeling of an extended family. Everyone is smiling and seems to really enjoy their job. That can only result in a good cruising experience for Viking River Cruises guests.

What Do Others Say?

Virtually every passenger we spoke with during our 12-day cruise gave a thumbs-up to the Viking River experience. Many of our new friends have been on several Viking River cruises in the past and plan to do more in the future. The typical guests were married retired couples and have cruised on both ocean and river cruises. One guest we spoke with had been on 55 cruises, 14 of which were river cruises.

> **Important Notice.** While other cruise ships, which are typically larger, offer a variety of entertainment and activity options, a Viking River Cruise focuses more on excursions than on onboard activities and entertainment.

Windstar Cruises
Our Favorite Romantic Cruise Line

Windstar Redux
Wind Surf

The romance of the sea has been captured in a sleek 5-masted vessel quietly slicing through the deep blue Caribbean Sea, her sails billowing in a steady warm wind on a sunny day. Her crew, dressed in white shorts, white socks and white deck shoes, scurry around the ship tending to guests' needs, carrying out a myriad of tasks. The privileged few who sail as guests enjoy a tranquility that can only be found aboard a sailing vessel. The definition of a "cruise vacation" has been redefined. This is no ordinary cruise; it is, in fact, "180 degrees from ordinary".

Windstar Cruises' Wind Surf is the largest ship in the 3 ship fleet at 14,745 tons. In fact, she is the largest sailing ship in the world. If the 26,881 sq. feet of Dacron sails is not enough to propel the ship to its destination, she has 4 diesel-electric engines which can move the ship at speeds up to 14 knots. There is no mistaking Wind Surf when she pulls into port with her 5 masts, each rising 221 feet above sea level. To smooth out the ride for her 308 guests (maximum capacity), Wind Surf is fully stabilized.

Windstar Cruises was acquired by Holland America Line in 1988 and both lines became part of the Carnival Cruise Line family in 1989. However, both Windstar and HAL have retained their own unique identity, management and clientele demographic. Like Holland America, Windstar staffs its vessels with friendly, smiling Indonesians who are more than willing to attend to each and every guest's needs.

We were anxious to see how Wind Surf, having just undergone extensive refurbishment, looked now compared to our 2001 Mediterranean cruise aboard her. Some areas were beginning to look pretty worn at that time. For one week in November, 250

Italian craftsmen descended upon Wind Surf to work their magic. We are pleased to report that the public areas of the ship look brand new with fresh carpet and fabrics, wood flooring, and wood wall paneling. While the staterooms have retained their efficient design, they have been upgraded with new carpet, fabrics, mattresses and flat-screen LCD televisions. The VCR's have been replaced with DVD/CD players. A cigar bar has been added to the Terrace Bar and is open until midnight each night. The Compass Rose lounge has also undergone a facelift with new seating, drapery, carpeting and additional outdoor shade provided by a new canopy.

While not as intimate as her sister ships, Wind Spirit and Wind Star (each carry 148 passengers), Wind Surf offers guests a mix of large cruise ship amenities in a smaller, more intimate setting. In fact, once aboard you feel like you are on a small cruise ship instead of a sailing vessel. However, once you step outside and look up at her massive sails unfurled in the wind, there is no mistaking Wind Surf for any other cruise ship.

Embarkation procedures take place in the Main Lounge on Deck 4. After passing through security, you proceed to the Main Lounge where you surrender your passport, receive your room key and on board charge cards, then have an opportunity to enjoy complimentary cocktails and hors d'oeuvres. All in all, the process is very efficient and relatively painless. Once you have received your key you are escorted to your stateroom by one of Wind Surf's stewards (which, by the way, are all male).

Accommodations

There are two basic designs of accommodations aboard Wind Surf: the Stateroom, which is 188 sq. ft., and the Suite, which is 376 sq. ft. All staterooms and suites are ocean view with portholes. There are no balcony staterooms on Wind Surf; this is, after all, a sailing ship. Staterooms are located on Deck One, Two and Three with all suites located on Deck Three. There is also one Owner's Suite (501) located on the Bridge Deck.

At 188 sq. ft., Wind Surf's staterooms are models of efficiency. There is plenty of storage via 6 drawers and lots of shelves and compartments. The closet is adequate and is stocked with wooden hangers. A small wooden built-in desk is large enough to hold your laptop computer and there is a 110 volt outlet hidden underneath the desk (contrary to what Windstar's literature says). The desk also serves as home to a bowl of fresh fruit and a basket of mini-bar munchies for purchase. The bathroom is much larger than it looks. The shower and toilet are each enclosed in separate circular encasements with the vanity/sink in between. There are two large mirrored medicine cabinets with lots of storage and a shelf connecting the two. The new flat screen LCD television is mounted across from the bed above the storage drawers. The screen is large and bright and provides a good viewing angle from the bed. Even though the television is mounted on a swivel bracket, it does not swivel enough so that you can watch it while seated at the desk. The DVD/CD player is located above the mini-bar/refrigerator next to the bed. Ours did not include a remote control, so starting and stopping the DVD/CD could not be done from bed. The refrigerator is stocked with typical mini-bar items for purchase like Coke, tonic water, fruit juices, beer, bottled water, etc.

With the exception of some annoying banging noises which appeared to be coming from the outside of the ship (not from the hallway or another stateroom), our stateroom was very quiet. The thermostat worked flawlessly, as did the hot water in the shower. We did hear some complaints from other guests who were unable to get hot water in their staterooms, but we did not experience this. Our stateroom attendant, Hadian, was near perfect. Our stateroom was kept spotless, we always had fresh towels and the bed was turned down when we returned from dinner each evening. We did notice unsightly brownish water coming out of the sink faucet on more than one occasion and we heard rumors that there were problems with the ship's desalinization unit. To the credit of the Wind Surf staff, complimentary liters of bottled drinking water were left in our stateroom to compensate. We found the new mattress to be a little too firm for our liking, but we were unable to find other guests who agreed with us. All in all, Wind Surf's staterooms continue to be some of the most comfortable (and quiet) 'non-balcony' staterooms at sea.

The Windstar Experience

In a word, the Windstar experience is about romance. In fact, the editors of CruiseReport.com have chosen Windstar as the "Best Romantic Cruise". Cruising on Windstar is very laid back and casual. However, that should not be confused with 'tacky'. There are no formal nights, no need to pack a tuxedo, or even a tie for that matter! Evening attire is 'country club casual' throughout the ship. As long as you don't wear shorts, blue jeans and t-shirts after 6:00pm, everything else is pretty much fair game. Most gentlemen guests will wear dress slacks and sport shirts in the evening with ladies wearing dresses or dressy pant suits.

The clientele tends to be mature with only a few guests dipping into the 20-something range. On our two cruises, we would guess the average age to be in the 40 to 55 range. There were no children on this cruise and we only noticed two children on our 2001 Mediterranean cruise.

The staff is friendly and very service-oriented without being pushy. There are no trays of frozen drinks being solicited poolside. In fact, there are very few overt sales attempts of any kind. Even gratuities are not solicited onboard Windstar.

Public address announcements are only made at port arrivals and departures, or if there is necessary information from the bridge. The general atmosphere onboard is very peaceful and quiet.

The Wind Surf and Wind Spirit (her smaller sister ship) spend winter months in the Caribbean and summer months in the Mediterranean. We have been fortunate enough to have sailed both itineraries, and both are wonderful.

Dining aboard Wind Surf is quite different than aboard larger cruise ships. For one thing, there is no 'formal' breakfast or lunch service in the ship's main restaurant. The ship's Lido restaurant,

Veranda, is the venue for both breakfast and lunch service. Breakfast is served here at 7:30am (8:00 am on sea days) and consists of a large buffet of fruits, pastries, bacon, sausages, cheeses and cereals. An omelet station located just outside on the deck can create fresh egg dishes to order or, you may order other items from the menu such as Eggs Benedict, waffles, pancakes, etc. There is also a continental breakfast served in the Compass Rose lounge from 6:00am until 11:00am.

Lunch service begins at 12:30pm in Veranda, a little later than we are used to. Each day's lunch buffet follows a different 'theme' with Mexican one day, Italian another and so on. There are plenty of salad choices, fruits, vegetables and meat dishes. The outdoor grill always offers hamburgers, hot dogs, sausages and chicken sandwiches.

At 4:00pm each day there is a very informal Afternoon Tea service in the Compass Rose lounge (located aft on the Bridge Deck) with small sandwiches, cookies, pastries and, of course…tea.

Dinner is served from 7:30pm until 9:30pm and is available in the Restaurant or the Bistro. The Restaurant is the larger of the two and is the main dining venue aboard the ship. Both venues offer open seating with no set dining times. Guests are free to dine whenever and with whomever they choose. Both venues offer plenty of tables for two and wait times are minimal. Reservations are recommended for the Bistro, as it is a smaller, more intimate setting with fewer tables.

Each evening a different menu is available with a selection of salads, appetizers, soups, main courses and desserts. A 'light' menu is available for those who may be counting calories, and there is always a vegetarian menu available. Food quality and preparation are befitting of a premium cruise line. But what really makes dining aboard Windstar a treat is the polished and friendly service. The Indonesian and Filipino wait staff are energetic and always smiling. One reason for the efficient service is simply one of staffing. Wind Surf has enough staff to take care of the guests, unlike some ships we have sailed recently that appear grossly understaffed. On Wind Surf, we never had to wait to have water or tea glasses refilled.

Orders were taken quickly and each course was served soon after the previous course was finished, yet we never felt like we were being rushed.

The food itself ranges from average to good with a few standouts. The Tournedos of Beef served one evening at dinner was exceptional as was the chocolate soufflé topped with ice cream. The signature Lobster BBQ luncheon was also a big hit. Chef Mark loads the outdoor grill with lobster tails and it is all–you-can-eat. There are also BBQ ribs, lamb chops, salmon and grilled steak. Definitely a low-carb dieter's dream!

Each evening you will find guests congregating in one of Wind Surf's lounges. The Lounge located on the Main Deck (4) is the largest and is adjacent to the ship's small casino. There is a dance floor and bandstand and plenty of comfortable seating. Live music is available here before and after dinner and sound levels are low enough to allow conversation.

The Compass Rose is the ship's indoor/outdoor lounge located aft on the Bridge Deck (5). The Compass Rose actually offers a choice of three seating areas: indoor, outdoor covered (under a canopy), and outdoor uncovered. This is the perfect place to enjoy a Caribbean or Mediterranean (depending on your itinerary) sunset.

The Terrace Bar on Deck 6 is located just above the Compass Rose and has been retrofitted to include a new cigar smoking room. The Terrace Bar is open from 9:00pm until Midnight.

The Lounge and Compass Rose offer complimentary hors d'oeuvres from 6:30pm until 7:15 or so. The bar service staff is very friendly and efficient. Prices are also extremely competitive. A scotch and water is only $4.50 and a glass of champagne only $3.50. Unlike most other cruise lines, gratuities are NOT automatically added to your bar tab.

Remember, this is a small ship by cruise ship standards. So, there are no glitzy Vegas-style shows; no big name entertainers. This ship is about romance, relaxation and intimacy. The Wind Surf does offer live dance music in the Lounge each evening before dinner from 6:30pm to 8:00pm and again after dinner from 9:15pm till closing. (There is also live music in the Compass Rose at similar times during the evening. One evening's entertainment featured a crew talent show.)

In-room entertainment is available via the DVD/CD player and flat-screen LCD television. Complimentary DVD's and CD's are available 24 hours a day from the ship's library. There is a good selection of recent releases as well as some classics. There are four movies running on the ship's closed-circuit television. The movie choices change each day. There is also 24-hour CNN World News. At times, much to our dismay, the ship's programming would cut out momentarily to a blue screen, as if a signal had been lost. This is understandable with CNN which requires a satellite, but we were puzzled as to why it also occurred with the ship's movie channels.

The majority of daytime activities on Wind Surf revolve around the water and the ship's water sports platform (located aft on Deck 2). When the ship is anchored, the marina can be lowered to provide a platform from which a variety of water sport activities can be enjoyed. The ship offers scuba, water skiing, kayaking, sailing and wind surfing. Of course, these activities are subject to weather and sea conditions and swimming is not allowed off of the platform. Unfortunately, the marina was not working during our cruise due to a problem with the hydraulics necessary to raise and lower the platform. To its credit, the crew compensated for this by moving many of the marina activities to an alternate tendering platform on the side of the ship. There are two swimming pools on Wind Surf, one located on the Star Deck mid ship, and the other aft on the Main Deck. There are also two whirlpools next to the Main Deck pool. Plastic loungers with green padded cushions are plentiful around both pools and along the outer decks.

When the ship is in port, there are a variety of shore excursions available. One advantage to booking shore excursions on board is priority access to tenders going ashore. Tour guests are escorted past any lines waiting for a tender. And while on the subject of tenders, this was our only major disappointment with Wind Surf. The tenders were small, overcrowded on occasion, hot and stuffy.

A solution would be to operate three tender boats simultaneously between ship and shore instead of just two.

An Internet café is located on the Bridge Deck forward next to the conference room. The Internet connections were 'up' throughout the cruise and access speeds were acceptable for a satellite system, about like a good 56k dial-up system. Prices for Internet access are a little on the high side at 75 cents per minute. Packages are available for $55/100 minutes (55 cents per minute) and $100/250 minutes (40 cents per minute). 250 minutes may sound like a lot, but when you figure that you are paying for the time to read and compose email messages, time (and money) tends to fly by quickly. If you do not have your own email account, the ship can assign you a temporary one so that you can send and receive email.

Perhaps the best activity aboard Wind Surf is no activity at all. There is a lot to be said for spending a lazy day around the pool with a good book, enjoying the sun and the Caribbean breeze while sipping on a banana daiquiri. We never had a problem finding a quiet, secluded spot on deck to relax. This activity can easily extend into the evening as well, with cool breezes and cocktails under the stars.

Wind Spa

Wind Surf has a full-featured spa offering massage, aroma therapy, facials, hydrotherapy, stress management, hairstyling, manicures, aerobics and fitness programs and a sauna (co-ed).

My Wind Spa Experience – by Rickee Richardson

The Wind Surf is the only Windstar ship large enough to offer the luxury of a full-service spa, the Wind Spa®. Naomi, Manager of Wind Spa, and her highly-trained and competent staff of eight, stand ready to pamper Wind Surf guests from head to toe.

Salon services such as haircuts, styling, hair coloring and highlights are available. Of course, a full range of body treatments, facials and massages are offered, as well as manicures and acrylic nail application. Even though Naomi and her staff will recommend products to "remedy what ails you", there is no high-pressure sales pitch commonly found at many cruise ship spas.

Each day the Wind Spa offers a "Spa Special" featuring different services at discounted prices. I decided to try one of the specials called "Pick and Mix". I was able to choose from a list of available services from which I could select three. My "Special" began with something called the Alpha Capsule, where spending 25 minutes is supposed to offer a level of relaxation equal to 4 hours of uninterrupted sleep. While it was a peaceful, comfortable 25 minutes, I did not get the effect of 4 hours of sleep. My second experience was a wonderful neck, shoulder and scalp massage followed by my final treatment…a manicure. All this "pampering" for only $69! On another day I treated myself to a pedicure ($55), which was enhanced by a foot and ankle massage. Overall, my experience with Wind Spa was relaxing and enjoyable and a considerable bargain to boot.

The Best Cruise Lines in the World

At CruiseReport.com, we are continually evaluating and comparing cruise lines in a variety of service areas. Unlike popular magazines that have Reader Survey awards, our awards are strictly based on our personal inspections of the cruise lines during a typical 7-day or longer cruise. Reader Survey awards are great, but they are not objective and cannot be relied upon for comparison purposes. Many readers may vote for a particular cruise line as their favorite, yet they may have never sailed another cruise line and, therefore, have little or no basis for comparison. By contrast, when we choose a cruise line for an award, it is based on our comparative analysis of a wide variety of cruise lines and ships.

CruiseReport.com awards are given each year based on the previous year's reviews. Here are the 2003 CruiseReport.com award results:

The Best Cruise Lines in the World for 2003

Best Large Ship Cruise Line 2003 - Royal Caribbean International

Best Small Ship Cruise Line 2003 - SeaDream Yacht Club

Previous Award Winners

Best Cruise Line 2002 – Silversea Cruises

Best Cruise Line 2001 – Radisson Seven Seas Cruises

Best at Sea Awards

Best Luxury Cruise	Silversea Cruises
Best Romantic Cruise	Windstar Cruises
Best Entertainment	Norwegian Cruise Line
Best Food	SeaDream Yacht Club
Best Fun Cruise	Carnival Cruise Line
Best Loyalty Program	Royal Caribbean International Crown & Anchor Society
Best Shore Excursions	Oceania Cruises
Best Internet Café	Radisson Seven Seas Cruises
Best Bar Service	Silversea Cruises
Best In-Suite Dining	The Yachts of Seabourn
Best Lido Buffet	Royal Caribbean International Windjammer Café
Best Caviar and Champagne	The Yachts of Seabourn
Best Spa	Norwegian Cruise Line Norwegian Dawn
Best Relaxation Cruise	SeaDream Yacht Club
Best Activities	Royal Caribbean International
Best Theater	Royal Caribbean International Serenade of the Seas
Best Butler Service	Radisson Seven Seas Cruises
Best Accommodations	Radisson Seven Seas Cruises
Best Interior Décor	Celebrity Cruises Celebrity Summit
Best Fitness Center	SeaDream Yacht Club
Best Alternate Dining	Royal Caribbean International Chops Grill
Best Pizza	Norwegian Cruise Line
Best Value	Carnival Cruise Line

These awards are based on our *personal* experiences. These awards are subject to change based on future experiences. You can get detailed information on these awards and more at www.cruisereport.com.

Extras

You can use this bonus section to help with the preparation of your cruise vacation. Make sure to take the book with you on your cruise so you can keep valuable notes and have access to important information.

Pre-cruise Checklist

___Travel Insurance

___Mail on hold

___Bills paid

___Itinerary contact information left with family/friends

___Photocopies of passport(s)

___Photocopies of credit cards

___Prescriptions up to date (plenty to last through end of cruise)

___Someone to care for pet(s)

Important Information

Travel Agent Information

Travel Agency Name	
Agent Name	
Address	
Office Phone	
Cell Phone/Pager	
Email Address	

Travel Insurance Company

Insurance Company Name	
Policy Number	
Address	
U.S. Phone Number	
International Phone	
Email Address	

Friends and Family

Enter the names and addresses of those whom you would like to send a postcard from your cruise.

Name

Address

Email Address

Name

Address

Email Address

Name

Address

Email Address

Name

Address

Email Address

Name

Address

Email Address

Packing Checklist

	Airline tickets		Sunglasses
	Cruise Tickets		Sunscreen
	Passports(or state issued birth certificate)		Video Camera
	Camera & Film		Recharge transformer(s)
	Power Strip		Travel Alarm Clock
	Traveler's Checks		Travel Insurance Papers
	Walkie-Talkies		The Perfect Cruise (This Book!)
	Comfortable walking shoes		Photocopies of passports
	Photocopies of credit cards		Swimwear

Cruise Speak

We don't want you to look puzzled when some other passenger tries to impress you with some 'cruise speak', so we have included this handy list of words and phrases.

Amidships	The middle of the ship	**Astern**	Behind the ship.
Berth	A bed or bunk for sleeping.	**Bow**	The most forward part of the ship (the pointy end).
Bridge	The navigational center of the vessel, generally located at the forward end of the ship.	**Bulkhead**	A wall separating a ship's compartments.
Disembark	Leave the ship.	**Draft**	The depth from the bottom of the keel to the waterline.
Embark	Get on board the ship.	**Funnel**	The smokestack of the ship.
Galley	The ship's kitchen.	**Keel**	The lowest longitudinal center line of the vessel.
Knot	One nautical mile per hour. A nautical mile is approximately 6080 feet, compared to a land mile which is 5280 feet.	**Latitude**	The distance north or south of the Equator.
Leeward	The direction away from the wind.	**Longitude**	Distance east or west of the Meridian of Greenwich.
Pilot	A person who navigates ships into or out of a harbor, or through difficult waters.	**Port**	The left side of the vessel looking forward.
Windward	In the direction of or toward the wind.	**Starboard**	The right side of a ship.
Tender	A small vessel, usually one of the ship's lifeboats, used to take people ashore when the ship is anchored.	**Pitch**	Rocking (forward-aft) motion of the ship that may be felt in heavy seas.

Index

9

9/11 .... 54, 85

A

activities 42
advance reservations 99
Adventure Ocean 208, 233
advocate 72
afternoon tea 103
airfare 29, 56, 68, 72
airlines 63
Alaska 31, 32, 91, 93
alcoholic beverages 29
all-inclusive 24, 29, 250, 258
alternate dining 99
amenities 92
American Express 55, 59
anniversary 30
art auction 119, 136
ATV tour 120

B

back-to-back 39
baggage claim 74, 95, 96
balcony 49
ballroom dancing 116
Barcelona 35
Big Band 116
bike riding 120
bingo 30, 258
Bingo 129
birth certificate 83, 84
Black Jack 128
boarding card 98

C

book online 69
booking a cruise online 69
booking direct 72
Boolchands Cameras 241
bottled water 29
breakfast 101
breakfast in bed 40
Brilliance of the Seas 224
budget 26
buffet 110, 245
butler service 256

C

cabin steward 29
Cagney's Steak House 245
California Wine Country 173
Camp Carnival 165
Cappuccino 230, 259
Captain A. Corsario 151
Captain's Welcome Reception 114
Caribbean 23, 28, 31, 32, 33, 93
Caribbean Stud Poker 116, 128, 232
Carnival 27
carving station 102, 110
casino 30, 54, 116, 128
Casino Royale 128, 231
CDC 87
Celebrity Cruises 27, 44
cell phone 127
Centrum 224
champagne 40
Charlie Palmer 211
children 43
Chops Grille 228
cigar lounge 116
Cirque du Soleil 168
civic groups 60
Civitavecchia 35

www.PerfectCruiseBook.com   293

CLIA 55, 65
Club HAL 190
Coast Guard 85, 86
commission 62, 64, 69
Compass Rose 203, 259, 281
complimentary cocktails 132
concierge 30
Concierge Club 223
consortium 56
Control Classic 8
Cozumel 122
Craps 128, 232
credit card 59
cruise consultant 64
cruise specialist 21
cruise tickets 94
Cruise West 27
cruise-only agencies 65
cruising with friends 150
Crystal Cruises 27
CSA Insurance 81
Cunard 27, 32

D

dance lessons 119
Denali National Park 35
deposit 55, 56
Digital Seas 240
dining 44, 46, 99, 252, 264
disco 51, 116
discount 56
disembarkation 97, 141
Disney Cruise Line 27, 43, 185
doctor .... *See* Medical
documentation 94
dolphins 120
dress codes 84
dry cleaning 136
Dubrovnik, Croatia 36
duty-free shopping 122
DVD 50, 268

E

early booking 55
Eggs Benedict 110, 227, 256
El Dorado Fitness Center 239

embarkation 97, 271, 277
enrichment lectures 118, 137
entertainment 42, 54, 115
etiquette 134
Europe 31
Expedia 69, 70

F

family reunions 60
Fanning Island 37
fine jewelry 135
fire 130
first-time cruisers 163
fitness center ... 29, 114, 118, 231, 258
formal 90
free cruise 60
Freestyle Cruising 236
Ft. Lauderdale 33

G

Galveston 33
glacier tour 120
Golf 258
Grand Cayman 33, 122
Grandeur of the Seas 11
gratuities 30, 139
group leader 61
group space 60, 68
Guarantee Fare 58

H

Half Moon Cay 190
Hawaii 32, 37
helicopter tour 120
hiking 120
Holland America 27
home-based 66
hors d'oeuvres 115
horseback riding 120
hot tub 117
Hotels.com 82
hurricane 34

294   The Perfect Cruise

I

ice cream 29, 165
identification............................83, 86
incidentals......................................29
informal 90
Inside Passage................................34
Internet 30, 62
Internet café 118, 126, 240

J

Jean Ann Ryan Productions...........246
Jewel of the Seas 224
jewelry..121
Johnny Rocket's 102

K

Karaoke 117
kayaking 35
kick-boxing..................................118
kids 43, 44
Kid's Crew .... *See* NCL Kid's Crew

L

La Trattoria..................................245
La Veranda 203
large ships......................................42
last minute 57
Late Seating 44, 45
Latitudes 203
launderettes.................................135
laundry............................29, 135, 136
Le Bistro 243
Le Cordon Bleu 259
library..119
Lido 91, 101, 102, 103, 109, 110, 165, 189, 205, 227
Lido Restaurant 165
lifeboat...................................51, 100
lifeboats 120
liquor 131
local cuisine 122
Logo shirts 135

London 82
low-carb 109
luggage 143
luggage tags 95
luxury 249

M

MacUser Magazine 8
magicians 115
Main Seating 44, 45
Maitre d' 99
Mandara Spa 252
medical..29
medical emergency 75
medications 92
Mediterranean 31, 35
Mexican Riviera..............................32
Miami..33
Michael's Club..............................116
midnight buffet.............................108
motion 42
motion sickness..............................88
movie theater...............................130
movies 30
muster...100

N

NCL 10, 27, 194, 237
New Orleans...................................33
Norwalk virus...........................85, 87
Norwegian Dawn 103, 236
Nouveau Supper Club 107

O

obstructed views............................51
ocean view 51
Oceania Cruises 27, 103
online travel agency 65
OnlineAgency 8
open-seating 46, 99, 196
Orbitz 69

P

Pacific Princess 199
packing 90
Panama Canal 31, 132
Park West Galleries 232
passport 83, 92, 97, 121
pasta stations 102
patches 88
Paul Gauguin 255
personal attention. 42
Personal Choice Dining 198
Phillipsburg 122
photographer 98, 115
photos 30
Pilates 118
Pinnacle Grill 189
PITA 8, 65
pizzeria 29, 165
Poker machines 128
Polo Grill 196
pool 29
Port Canaveral 33
port charges 29, 68
port lecture 118
portholes 49
Portofino 36, 229
post-cruise 81, 94
pre-cruise 81, 94
prescription 92
Pride of Aloha 38
Pride of America 38
Princess Cruises 27
Princess Fun Zone 199
Promenade Deck 117
proof of citizenship 83
Purser's office 140

Q

Queen Mary 2 42

R

Radiance of the Seas 224
Radisson Diamond 255
Radisson Seven Seas Cruises . 27, 101, 129, 132, 254

Ray Solaire 247
rebate 68
Reel Players Club 239
religious groups 60
re-positioning 32
restaurants 42
reverse gratuity 139
romance 276
room service 108, 194, 203, 212
Roulette 116, 128, 232
Royal Caribbean 27, 223
Royal Caribbean Singers and Dancers
 233
Royal Princess 199

S

safety 85
sanitation 87
scones 103
Sea Goddess 269
Seabourn 27
Seabourn Pride 155
SeaDream II 148
SeaDream Yacht Club 27, 91, 261
Seattle 34
security 85
Serenade of the Seas 223
Seven Seas Navigator 255
shipboard account 135
shipboard credit 59
ship-to-shore 126
shopping 120
shore excursion 118, 120
shore excursions 99
shorts 91
Signatures 203, 259
Silver Whisper 247
Silversea Cruises 103, 128, 247
slot machines 116, 128, 239
small ships 42
smoking 130
Snowball Jackpot Bingo 232
soft drinks 29, 30
solarium 232
Song of Flower 255
South America 31
South Beach Diet® 108
souvenirs 135
Sovereign of the Seas 41

spa 29, 40, 54, 118
special needs 52
special occasion 40
special requests 111
specialty restaurants 29
SS Norway 10, 41, 54
SS Victoria 11
St. Thomas 122, 241
stabilizers 42, 88
Star Clippers 27
stateroom 49
stingrays 120
suites 50
sun block 91, 132
sun tan 132
sundries 135
Sushi 103, 165, 228
swimsuit 91, 92

T

Tahitian Princess 199
Tampa 33
Tapas 196
team trivia 119
tender 120
Terrace Café 218
The Restaurant 211, 218
tipping 138
Titanic 41
Topside Restaurant 264
Total Choice Dining 165
tour desk 99
tour guide 139
transfer vouchers 94
transfers 29, 68, 95
travel agent 21, 57, 62, 64, 71, 82
Travel Guard 79
travel insurance 22, 56, 59, 74, 94
Travel Insured 81
Travelocity 69

tuxedo 91

U

U.S. Customs 97, 142
U.S. Embassy 86
U.S. Immigration 143
upgrades 58

V

Vancouver 34
Venice 35
veranda .... *See* balcony
Viking River Cruises 159, 270
Voyager of the Seas 39
VSP 88

W

weddings 30, 41
Welcome Aboard Dinner 115
whale watching 35
Wi-Fi 127
Wind Surf 153, 276
Windjammer Cafe 227
Windstar Cruises 27, 152, 276
wine tasting 118
wrist bands 88

Y

Yangtze River Cruise 147
yoga 118

Find Your Perfect Cruise

CRUISE REPORT .COM

See why CruiseReport.com is one of the most popular cruise web sites on the Internet.

- In-depth ship information, deck plans, ship images for 26 different cruise lines and 223 ships
- Consumer reviews and ratings
- Exclusive editorial reviews and ratings
- Thousands of itineraries with map images
- Search engine to find cruises based on destination, month, cruise line or port of embarkation
- Port information for thousands of ports around the world
- Personal "Hot List" of your favorite cruises
- Cruise review submission form

CruiseReport.com is a *free* web site, visit as often as you like!

www.CruiseReport.com

www.PerfectCruiseBook.com

Visit our web site today:

- Give us feedback about this book.
- Locate a 'Perfect Cruise Specialist'.
- Learn about our latest cruise adventures.
- Tell us about your cruise experiences.
- Register to receive emails on cruise discounts and other special offers.

Watch for details about upcoming books in the Perfect Cruise series…